Nationalism after Communism
Lessons Learned

CPS BOOKS

Andrea Krizsán (ed.) (2001)
Ethnic Monitoring and Data Protection. The European Context.
Published jointly with the
Human Rights Information and Documentation Center (INDOK)

Miklós Sükösd and Péter Bajomi-Lázár (eds.) (2003)
Reinventing Media. Media Policy Reform in East-Central Europe

Andrea Krizsán and Violetta Zentai (eds.) (2003)
Reshaping Globalization. Multilateral Dialogues and New Policy Initiatives

Judit Sándor (ed.) (2003)
Society and Genetic Information. Codes and Laws in the Genetic Era

forthcoming

Daniel Smilov (ed.)
Party Funding, Campaign Finance and Corruption in Eastern Europe

Nationalism after Communism

Lessons Learned

Edited by

ALINA MUNGIU-PIPPIDI

and

IVAN KRASTEV

CENTRAL EUROPEAN UNIVERSITY PRESS

BUDAPEST – NEW YORK

The publication of this volume was made possible by a grant from the United Nations Development Programme (UNDP) and its Regional Bureau for Europe and the Commonwealth of Independent States (RBEC) and by the support of the Central European University

Gerald Knaus, Kristof Bender and Marcus Cox,
"The Political Economy of Interethnic Relations:Ahmeti's Village or the Macedonian Case"
© European Stability Initiative. Reprinted with the permission of the European Stability Initiative

King, Charles. "The Benefits of Ethnic War: Understanding Eurasia's Unrecognized States."
World Politics 53:4 (2001), 524-552 © The Johns Hopkins University Press.
Reprinted with permission of The Johns Hopkins University Press.

Copyeditor: *Alison Rose*
Design and typesetting: *Judit Kovács/Createch*
Production: *Kinga Szántó*
Printed in Hungary by *Createch Ltd.*

English edition published in 2004 by
Central European University Press
An imprint of the Central European University Share Company
Nádor utca 11, H–1051 Budapest, Hungary
Telephone: (+36-1) 327-3138 or 327-3000
Fax: (+36-1) 327-3183
E-mail: ceupress@ceu.hu
Website: www.ceupress.com

400 West 59th Street, New York NY 10019, USA
Telephone: (+1-212) 547-6932
Fax: (+1-212) 548-4607
E-mail: mgreenwald@sorosny.org

Library of Congress Cataloging-in-Publication Data

Nationalism after communism : lessons learned / edited by Alina Mungiu-Pippidi and Ivan Krastev.
p. cm. — (CPS Books ISSN 1587 6942)
Includes bibliographical references and index.
ISBN 963 9241 76 8 (pbk.)
1. Europe, Eastern—Ethnic relations—Political aspects. 2. Former Soviet republics—Ethnic relations—Political aspects. 3. Nationalism—Europe, Eastern. 4. Nationalism—Former Soviet republics. 5. Post-communism—Europe, Eastern. 6. Post-communism—Former Soviet republics.
I. Mungiu, Alina. II. Krastev, Ivan. III. Series.
DJK51 .N359 2004 305.8'09171'709049—dc22
2003025321

Contents

5

Acknowledgements

This book is a product of the 'Bluebird: Agenda for Civil Society in South-Eastern Europe' research project's work on the 'Future of Nation-States'. This research group was sponsored by the Netherlands Ministry of Foreign Affairs—MATRA Programme and the Regional Center for Europe and the CIS of the United Nations Development Programme (UNDP). The conference 'Nation-Building versus State-Building— Lessons Learned,' where papers in this book were first presented, also benefitted from the generous support of NATO and the Central European University. Ben Slay, Director of UNDP's Regional Center, Lisa Smirl and Tomasz Anusiewicz, UNDP regional advisors for democratic governance, provided constant support and useful advice. Participants in the group's events at the Central European University and the European University Institute in 2002–2003 offered insightful comments. The editors wish to express their gratitude to everyone of them, and, last but not least, to Alison Rose, who carried out the language editing work with infinite patience.

The views expressed in this book belong to the authors only and do not engage in any form the sponsors of this publication.

About the Authors

KRISTOF BENDER, MARCUS COX and GERALD KNAUS Analysts, *European Stability Initiative*, an international think tank based in Berlin, Germany

FLORIAN BIEBER Senior Non-Resident Research Associate, *European Centre for Minority Issues*, Belgrade, Serbia and Montenegro

MATTHIJS BOGAARDS Lecturer, Politics Department, *University of Southampton*, United Kingdom

VALERIE BUNCE the Aaron Binenkorb Professor of International Studies and Chair of the Government Department, *Cornell University*, United States

VLADIMIR GLIGOROV Staff Economist, *Vienna Institute for International Economic Studies*, Austria

CHARLES KING Associate Professor, School of Foreign Service and Department of Government, *Georgetown University*, United States

IVAN KRASTEV Chairman, *Center for Liberal Strategies*, a think tank in Bulgaria; Research Coordinator of the Blue Bird Project

ALINA MUNGIU-PIPPIDI UNDP Consultant for Early Warning Systems in the Balkans, Director, Romanian Academic Society

PHILIP G. ROEDER Associate Professor, *University of California, San Diego*, United States

I.

Introduction

Sense and Prejudice in the Study of Ethnic Conflict: Beyond System Paradigms in Research and Theory

Alina Mungiu-Pippidi

The Challenge

What if a policymaker, charged with crafting a peace arrangement for an ethnic-conflict situation, asked an academic what practical wisdom the theories of ethnic conflict and nationalism could offer to help draft such a plan? One could hardly wish to be the academic in this unenviable position. Even assuming that the answer would not fall within the usual lines of normative theory, applicable to a world where both justice and the capacity to do what is right are universally and evenly distributed, it is doubtful that useful advice could be summoned. If the academic is a constructivist, the answer might be that the groups involved should be taught a completely new version of their ethnogenesis and history of conflict, one showing that they belong to group a or group b merely by chance, and their ancestors killed each other because they had been taught an inaccurate history. If the academic is a primordialist, the answer might be that groups inherit a culture as a given and that solidarity within one's cultural kin is so strong that ethnic groups are essentially unable to understand and show any sensitivity toward the needs of other groups. If the academic is an instrumentalist, the answer might be that because ethnic enrollment is the shortest way to profit, maximizing groups are bound to mobilize sooner or later and try to get the spoils from other groups.

Advice falling into one or another of these categories has indeed been given, and an entire cottage industry of history textbooks, written with the sole task of deconstructing other history textbooks, has emerged. From the Republika Srspka to the Dnestr Republic, however, ethnic warriors know precisely the small amount of history they want to know and refuse to learn a new one. The international community accepted ethnic cleansing when drawing new—even if initially internal—borders on the grounds that coerced cohabitation cannot be enforced by democratic means. All the while coerced separation, a preferred policy of nondemocrats, is often a fact of life. The international community also pushed equal economic opportunities, in the hope that such reform would bring ethnic peace, even when different groups had made it clear that they do not seek fairness but only their own advantage. On top of it all, in the early nineties, as nobody seemed willing to step between the ethnic groups, who had a history of conflict, the soundest advice seemed to be containment, not the resolution of such conflicts.

Resolving ethnic conflict seems to be a lost cause for both policy makers and academics. But does it need to be? Can there be a bridge between the world of academia—suffocated by political correctness and ambition driven system paradigms[1]—and the world of those who craft policies to promote interethnic peace and cooperation, with little knowledge of theory, scarce time to do proper research, and limited financial resources? This is the challenge this book tries to address. It is a book by academics with experience as policy advisors, from the Balkans to Chechnya, and, while not theoretically blind altogether, it is strictly grounded in empirical research. Beyond theoretical postulates and normative ideals, considerable experience has been accumulated in the postcommunist world on ethnic conflict and nation and state building. This experience needs to be revised, now more than a decade after the fall of the Berlin Wall. What does the postcommunist experience of ethnic conflict share with other nationalisms and ethnic conflicts, and what, if anything, is special about the postcommunist experience? What is the best way to manage ethnic conflicts within a state or between neighboring states? What institutions work and under what circumstances?

Being so policy oriented, some chapters of this book include little theoretical discussion; some actually draw on what were originally policy reports. This introductory chapter will therefore sketch briefly the essential debates of nationalism and ethnic-conflict theory with relevance for policymaking. Nationalism and ethnic-conflict theory are two partly overlapping, partly distinct bodies of knowledge. Nationalism is an umbrella term, covering elements such as national awareness and mobilization, the expression of national identity, and loyalty to the nation, labeled by some authors as patriotism. The exercise of nationalism is a community's assertion of sovereignty in the form of a nation-state. Nationalism as an ideology "(...) calls on its supporters to subordinate the common interests (based on class, religion or party, for example) that they share with their fellow citizens to those that they share with other members of the national group" (Barry, 1987: 353). Nationalism as an expression of identity defines the nature of an individual's relationship to a collectivity. Much has been written on what turns an ethnie into a nation. There is enough evidence that every ethnie has the potential to become a nation, given the proper circumstances, and some academics have gone so far as to claim that every ethnie is a nation without a territory of its own (Oomen, 1997).

Ethnonationalism, the political principle postulating that every ethnic group which considers itself a nation has a legitimate claim to sovereignty, should be dis-

---

1. The term was coined by Janos Kornai.

tinguished from patriotism, which is individual loyalty toward one's country or state, manifested in the respect for a national contract (such as the willingness to answer positively when drafted for military service). Contemporary states are communities of redistribution, regardless of the ethnicity of their inhabitants and the fairness underlying the redistribution process. Ethnonationalim only occurs when ethnic groups regard the state as their own—not of the entire body of citizens—and try to use the state for their sole purpose and in virtue of some ethnic attribute, not of individual citizenship. In practice, it is not so simple to distinguish between the two. This is due to the long practice of states of being ethnically biased toward the majority group. But as long as the official state position is one of impartiality, meaning that citizenship is ethnically blind and rights are individual, ethnonationalism designs precisely the opposite situation.

The body of contemporary research on these topics is so complex and vast it resists easy classification along the three directions sketched above. Nor can the three arguments summon consistent research endorsing one position, as no empirical research can fairly support explain-all theories. Therefore system paradigms should be approached with extreme caution, as wars among their adepts seem more often then not, as Ludwig Wittgenstein would have put it, wars over vocabulary, not facts. Rather than embarking on the usual exercise of attributing labels to literature and scholars that never fit well, this introductory chapter attempts to illustrate that enough knowledge exists to articulate a *middle-ground* theory of ethnic conflict, one to cover both contemporary and historical cases, and provide the basis for fair predictions and sound policies. In this approach, we follow Donald Horowitz in his plea for an intermediate stand and agree to his "radical claim—that the attraction of analysts to seemingly irreconcilable hard and soft positions on all these issues are themselves a manifestation of the same underlying propensities to cleavage, comparison, and self-definition by opposition" which inform the conflicts they are trying to explain (Horowitz, 1988: 35). Therefore, this introduction examines the most popular false dichotomies in theories of ethnic conflict and nationalism to illustrate that, in recent years, considerable grounds were gained by an intermediate approach that is able to inform policy. A classification of ethnic conflicts, drawing on both psychological and development models, is then proposed at the end of this introduction.

The Given, the Natural, and the Learnt

The core of the main theoretical debate in ethnic-conflict studies focuses on the given or acquired character of ethnic identity and bonds. Positions vary from a so-called hard primordialist view, claiming that cultural identity is a given, to a soft one, claiming it is socially constructed by manipulative elites. Horowitz is correct to stress that few take the extreme hard or soft views; most positions are, in fact, centrist, but, then, Horowitz himself is labeled a "primordialist" by Htun and Singh (2000). Both Horowitz and Walker Connor have avoided being classified a primordialists, and Daniele Conversi, editing his book on Connor's heritage, endorses the view that Connor was, in fact, an enemy of all the isms. This is perhaps his most important legacy, but it still remains disputed.

As these opposing views inspired very different sets of policies, each grounded in rather fundamentalist illusions and delusions, a descent into the body of research providing the basis for an in-between approach is necessary. Clifford Geertz, usually quoted with Edward Shils as the standard bearer of primordialism, stressed the importance of one's bond with one's culture. Individual thought is shaped by the culture one shares—notably by language, and everything entailed by it. A country's politics, Geertz stated, "reflect the design of its culture," which "is not cults and customs, but the structure of meaning through which men give shape to their experience, and politics is not coups and constitutions, but one of the principal arenas in which such structures publicly unfold" (Geertz, 1973: 311–12). Furthermore, beyond acculturation, Geertz sees "an unaccountable" and "absolute import" deriving from the bond itself, which is then regarded as primordial:

> By a primordial attachment is meant one that stems from the 'givens'—or, more precisely, as culture is inevitably involved in such matters, the assumed 'givens'—of social existence: immediate contiguity and kin connection mainly, but beyond them the givenness that stems from being born into a particular religious community, speaking a particular language, and even a dialect of a language, and following particular social practices. These congruities of blood, speech, custom and so on, are seen to have an ineffable, and at times overpowering, coerciveness in and of themselves. One is bound to one's kinsman, one's neighbor, one's fellow believer, ipso facto; as the result not merely of personal affection, practical necessity, common interest, or incurred obligation, but at least in great part by virtue of some unaccountable absolute import attributed to the very tie itself. The general strength of such primordial bonds, and the types of them that are important, differ from person to person, from society to society, and from time to time. But for virtually every person, in every society, at almost all times, some attachments seem to flow more from a sense of natural—some would say spiritual—affinity than from social interaction (Geertz, 1963: 1089–110).

Does this imply that cultural identity does not have a sociogenesis but is truly primordial, or inborn, as the critics of Geertz allege (Eller and Coughlan, 1993)? Empirical evidence illustrates that a change of identity is, in fact, possible at times. People do switch from one group to another, although this does not happen frequently. More frequent, however, is the situation when individuals brought up in different cultures from that of their parents and socialized to become members of their host culture acquire, through acculturation, a new identity which can, at times, act quite powerfully on their behavior. This seems strongly related to the individual's ability to speak the language of his or her new culture, though evidence is rather mixed (Lanca and Alskins, 1994). The fact that identities are learned through social experience does not diminish their importance for the individual or groups. It also does not mean that, within the normal set of one culture in its own so-called cradle, thus ruling out cases of migration, forced acculturation, or catastrophic events which may uproot a community, the bonds of culture do not tie individuals strongly, though the strength of these bonds may vary. The conclusion is that it is reasonable *to expect people to think, feel, and behave from within a certain cultural framework.* This framework is created through years of history and common experience and is as expressed in the social representations[2] of this history and experience. It is not only ethnic bias which we often encounter in practice, understood as ancient prejudice or hatred, but frequently a genuine cognitive bias arising from being socialized in a particular culture. An individual has to be well educated and well traveled to look on the world from a truly individual and cosmopolitan perspective, emancipated from one's culture. It is better not to expect this from ordinary people.

What remains of the givens, if sociogenesis is thus admitted? The best answer is provided by theories of psychology, which also underpins Horowitz's ethnic-conflict theory. Social-identity theory, as developed by Henri Tajfel and his many followers, derived on the basis of laboratory experiments and considerable fieldwork as well, stipulates that groups have a drive to acquire a positive social identity. This is usually obtained by maximizing differentiation and competition among groups (Tajfel, 1974). Social comparison feeds identity, and, in order to have a high self-esteem, a group tends to compare itself positively against others, thus seeking positive differentiation. Even when assigned randomly to different groups in experiments, members tend to form in-groups, invent some features of their separate identity,

2.   The term was coined initially by French social psychologist Serge Moscovici and is widely used in European social psychology. Social representations are widespread individual representations with a social construction, providing a certain interpretation of a fact or event whose experience is shared by a community. See Doise (1990) for more clarifications on this concept.

and favor the in-groups and prejudice the out-groups. This discriminative behavior is little influenced by the presence of a unique reward, so it cannot be explained by a scarcity-of-resources hypothesis. In one of these experiments, for instance, the possible rewards are distributed between groups as follows: (1) in-group and out-group profit combined is maximal; (2) the in-group's profits are maximal; (3) differences between in-group profit and out-group profit is maximal. Subjects tend to choose the third variant, thus prefering that their group have more superiority than what they earn in absolute terms. To illustrate his point, Tajfel quotes a Russian proverb that also circulates in many variants among other peasant cultures, from the Balkans to Mexico. God offers Ivan a wish. However, there is a catch: "Your neighbor will get twice what you get," God tells Ivan. The small catch makes Ivan uneasy, as he cannot settle with the idea that whatever he gets will only be half of what his neighbor will have. What does he choose? He finally asks God to blind him in one eye.

Tajfel also noticed that social categories come with important affective meanings, and he spoke of the "great heights of intensity that social identification may involve" (Tajfel, 1982). He thought affect operated primarily through self-esteem. Groups need to have a high self-esteem, and members must develop various strategies to cope with its possible scarcity, including group desertion when possible. Social identification is thus desirable because it is seen as a source of self-esteem (Tajfel and Turner, 1979). In every cultural group, one can find strong evidence of in-group favoritism, although less so in groups with a historical experience of being seen as occupying the bottom rung of society (Pratto and Sidanius, 1998). National favoritism may be only one particular case of more general in-group favoritism, and favoritism of one's national group may only be a special case of the general rule of attitude theory, according to which people tend to prefer the familiar to the unfamiliar.

In another widely quoted Tajfel experiment, European children showed marked ethnic favoritism, ranking photographs of representatives of their own national group as the best liked or attributing best liked photographs to their own national group. This national favoritism decreased with age in the Tajfel experiments. The children who showed such preferences were well below the age when they become able to grasp more abstract notions such as country and nation (Tajfel et al., 1970: 245–53).

The tendency to cleavage is therefore well documented by evidence. Ethnicity is just one source of cleavage and bias, but the most frequent one, as it provides automatic and permanent membership, positive bias toward one's group, and often recognizable markers and boundaries. It is, in other words, economically convenient as a source of identity. Religious identity comes next, but even on isolated islands where inhabitants apparently share common traits, various cleavages are invented (Firth, 1957). Individuals categorize people into classes and exaggerate similarities among themselves and differences from others, a phenomenon known in social-judgment theory as assimilation and contrast effects. They seem to derive value from the groups to which they belong (Brewer, 1997: 205; 1991: 476), not the other way around. Indeed, they derive satisfaction from the group's success, even when their own contribution to that success is palpably absent (Brewer, 1979: 322). A willingness to sacrifice for group interests and participate in collective action is predicted more by a sense of collective deprivation than it is by individual deprivation (Brewer, 1991: 478–79).

What appears then to be given, or natural, is the tendency to cleavage and build a positive social identity by comparison, the act of social classification, not the cultural bond itself, be it religious or ethnic, which emerges out of a specific historical context (see also Comaroff and Comaroff, 1992: 64). But this acknowledgement also renders the debate less relevant for the policy world. If cleavages and discrimination are to be assumed, ethnicity, more than anything else, is likely to provide a basis for them. Shaking discrimination off would not be easy, despite being able to deconstruct its contextual character.

Symbols in a World of Bounded Rationality

Among the false dichotomies in ethnic-conflict theory, the alleged tension between the affective and rational uses of ethnicity is our next concern. Does Walker Connor's formula that "man is a national animal" imply that ethnic allegiance is just a matter of sentiment? Do people lose reason when strongly attaching to an ethnic identity, answering to appeals from nationalist leaders, or endangering one's life when fighting for one's country? Or does evidence support those who see ethnic groups as social-capital groups, providers of goods for members? The best example to illustrate the claim that this dichotomy is exaggerated is language, the main instrument of self-ascription.

Language is the chief vehicle connecting personal and collective identity and the main discriminant between the in-group and the out-group. It acquires significance as the main medium of socialization, articulating the social representations that constitute the tissue of a culture and is also the most salient ethnic marker. "One's behavior, and in particular one's language behavior, is the best reflection of one's ethnic allegiance" (Giles, 1977: 326). Furthermore, there is evidence that exposure to another language strengthens feelings of identity and loyalty toward one's ethnic group or language. Social psychologists have increasingly accepted that it is in the situation of language contact that people most readily become aware of the peculiarities of their language vis à vis others. In addition, the purity of standardized language most easily becomes the symbol of group integrity. Language loyalty breeds in contact just as nationalism breeds on ethnic borders (Weinrich, 1974). Language is thus an essential provider of national identity.

On the basis of such empirical observations, the state has traditionally forced its linguistic policies on linguistic minorities to create good subjects or good citizens. Knowing the official language becomes a sort of guarantee of good citizenship. In addition, using a language other than the official one may encourage large linguistic groups to lay a claim to self-determination. These linguistic battles are sometimes reduced to minor squabbles, seemingly symbolic and trivial, but, in fact, are not so. Resources tend to be distributed according to linguistic lines. Fighting for an equal status for two languages, for official bilingualim, as the Canadian Parti Quebecois did in the 1970s, was not only symbolic, but also had practical value. The stake of such battles is in the reorganization of the state along linguistic lines. This type of policy can be noticed in Belgium and Quebec and implies the demand for the political system's reform and a decisive change of the rules of the game (Melluci, 1989). Language also matters for both public and private employment, and groups assume it matters even more than it does. Linguistic loyalty is guaranteed by the simple fact that most people are unable to become fully proficient in more than one language, so, for example, they feel threatened if job interviews are conducted in a language other than their own. Therefore, the answer to Elie Kedourie's influential question of why groups based on linguistic difference are entitled to states of their own is simply that a state of one's own is the most convenient for groups, so a justification must and will be found. Humans seek convenience and demanding a state for a linguistic group is tended to be viewed as rational behavior. Convenience may not provide *legitimacy*, but one should not disregard the salience of behavior based merely on seeking convenience, which always becomes more important than simply a battle for such. Psychologists often portray humans as cognitive misers (Fiske and Taylor, 1994). But humans are convenience-seekers, which is not the same as profit-maximizers because it suggests that they tend to strike a balance between the effort invested and the profit gained—even if this stops short of the greatest profit. This is the world of bounded rationality.

So are the language wars, which play a role in many ethnic conflicts, waged for interest or pride, or for convenience or symbolic use? The answer is for both. Fighting for the use of one's language in the state administration, for instance, explained by Walker Connor (1972) as the need for self-identification and political affirmation, cannot be grounded solely in the affect or the reason. The revival of small languages has become fashionable in our times, just as assimilation was fashionable a century ago. John Stuart Mill and other nineteenth-century thinkers considered assimilation a positive phenomenon. Mill thought that it was to the advantage of the Bretons and the Navarrese to be assimilated into the French culture (Mill, 1977: 549–51). Historically, assimilation is the process by which individuals belonging to culturally distinct groups come to have complementary habits of communication (for example, a common language) because of contact with each other and the ensuing social learning. When the ability to communicate grows faster than the need to do so, good prospects arise for creating a common identity. However, when assertiveness outruns assimilation, separatist movements and national mobilization are likely to result (Deutsch, 1966). Controlling these processes is, therefore, of crucial practical importance for both states and the international community.

States have often resorted to fighting dissident groups by linguistic means. Communist Albania repressed the Albanian Gegs, imposing a standardized language based heavily on the Albanian Tosk dialect (Biberaj, 1999: 16). Some successor states of the former Soviet Union, such as those in the Baltics, which are insecure because of the large numbers of Russian-speaking minorities on their territory, pursued aggressive policies of nation building, making use of the local language the *prima facie* condition for citizenship. In states where the majority did not consist of a group that was seen to enjoy a positive social identity, such as in Moldova, the move to use language as a condition for citizenship was resisted, and the Russian speaking minority won the battle. In states where the right incentives existed to prompt assimilation of Russian speakers into the new community, minorities accepted the trade-off and learned the local language, as in the Baltics (Laitin, 1998). Language plays therefore both a symbolic role, indicating the group's status, and an instrumental one, providing access to resources controlled by a group or state. There is no conflict among the two. The former predicts and accompanies the latter.

Explanations, such as the one put forth by Kaufman, that the symbolic-politics approach is useful because it offers "not only a way to take attitudes and myths seriously, but also a way of thinking about the interaction between elites and masses" explain, in fact, nothing at all. The fact that leaders both manipulate and respond to symbols is merely a banal observation" (Kaufman, 2000: 203). Symbols cannot be found in isolation from more practical issues, such as the division of power and resources, and individuals must always look to their history to see where they come from. Do symbols have their own existence, or are they merely tokens of a group's social identity? They are tokens, and more: *the instrumental and the symbolic cannot be separated.* People may be moved by symbols, but symbols always stand for something, be it a group's self esteem or more conspicuous advantages. In one way or another, *symbols are indicators of the group's position in social comparison, which constitutes the main stake in ethnic relations.* Symbols should be seen therefore both as *permanent* indicators of group status, and as indicators of the group's *current* position. Not even the slightest concession can be made over them because it would signal that a group is at disadvantage or on the defensive, thus affecting its positive social identity, with all the ensuing practical consequences.

To conclude, ethnicity is salient "because it can combine an interest with an affective tie," as Bell has already put it perfectly (Bell, 1975: 169). Neither the views stressing the extreme importance of affect, as Walker Connor's, nor those of rational-choice theorists that purport an individual always gains from ethnic affiliation, can become explain-all theories. As Horowitz (1998) observed, just as the family is simultaneously an emotional and an economic unit, so the ethnic group takes on instrumental tasks. But an ethnic group cannot be described solely in terms of, or be reduced to, the performance of those tasks. Ethnic violence is a mix of both spontaneous and organized activity, of grassroots frustration and cool-headed organization: "Passion might come first; organization could not succeed without it; but passion would attract organization. Interest can mobilize people along the lines of their passion, but only if there is passion to mobilize around" (Horowitz, 1998: 15). Here, again, social-identity theory chartered useful territory when depicting individual strategies to bolster self-esteem (Tajfel, 1978), including behaviors as varied as altruistic sacrifice (which can provide invaluable rewards in terms of self-esteem; we have the unfortunate example of suicide bombers) and identity switching (Christian renegades in the Balkans, for instance, became part of the Ottoman ruling class). There is a delicate balance to strike between an interest that can be identified as such by an external observer and the interest to remain high on the social-identity scale, even if a sacrifice may be required. More than anything else, ethnic related behavior is a matter of bounded, not pure, rationality.

Who Leads and Who Follows?

Primordialists are said to promote the idea that the masses are the source of evil. If ethnicity has a thick substance and is a given, perception of threat makes groups aggressive. Groups then seek leaders to mobilize and defend them. On the other hand, instrumentalists and constructivists tend to blame manipulative elites and ethnic entrepreneurs for ethnic conflict, which may arise even when feelings of antipathy among groups are not present. (Fearon and Laitin, 1996; Hardin, 1995: 147–50). The best-known work in this line is Paul Brass on India, who alleged that elites manipulated ethnic identities in their quest for power (Brass, 1997). Breuilly (1982) and even Hobsbawm (1990) go even further, assuming that elites and leaders construct ethnic identities and conflict by manipulating history, myths, and symbols, as well as actual needs. Without such engineering, the argument goes, there would be no conflict. An in-between vision, offered most notably by Connor (1994) and Horowitz (1995), alleges that elites and masses operate under the same intellectual and affective constraints. Engineering is necessary, but engineers emerge out of a social need for them. Remove one engineer, and another would replace him.

To be certain, modern ethnic conflict is often associated with leaders, as it seldom comes in a totally nonpolitical form. Both ethnic parties and rebel armies need politicians and generals. Slobodan Milosevic provides the textbook case of this dilemma. Was Milosevic solely responsible for the Yugoslav conflict? He certainly manipulated it to the best of his ability. His regime organized rock shows to boost national feelings and rally supporters, where the famed singer and wife of his paramilitary deputy, Arkan, featured prominently. But he was an elected politician who fell only when the majority no longer voted for him, and he had to cheat elections to remain in office. On the other extreme, the ethnic rioters who clashed in Brooklyn or Los Angeles at the end of the twentieth century did not have leaders. Osama bin Laden is an idol—more than a leader—for Arab nationalism.

Leaders are very visible, but ethnic groups seem to use them at least to the extent that they are used in turn. Furthermore, leaders are made of the same material as followers, holding the same or more hostile attitudes than their followers (Horowitz, 1997: 439, 457, n. 31). Leaders who try to ignore the politics of ethnicity in ethnically divided societies often find themselves outbid on the extremist flanks by leaders more in tune with mass hostility toward other groups (Rabushka and Shepsle, 1972: 80–86; Milne, 1980). Not surprisingly, the elite-competition view has been criticized for creating an inaccurate image "of evil politicians and innocent masses" (Kakar, 1996: 150–51) and for leaving too little room for individual acts by ordinary people who engage in conflict behavior (Pandey, 1992: 41). Good models should try to "respect the interests and intelligence of elites and masses" both (O'Leary, 1998 in Chirot, 2001: 41).

Horowitz also criticizes constructivists for seeing ethnicity as an altogether opportunistic and infinitely malleable affiliation (Horowitz, 1998). The constraints of the field in which group interactions occur limit what elites can do and what interests they can pursue (Horowitz, 1985: 64–75). By the same token, the freedom of elites to foment conflict and violence is limited by their followers' definition of the situation and what they are willing to fight over. Hindu nationalists in India often attempt to incite attacks on Muslims, but they rarely succeed in the southern states of Kerala and Tamil Nadu, where caste affiliations have more resonance than the Hindu–Muslim polarity (Wilkinson, 1997). Where there are no charismatic leaders, the blame is put on intellectuals who create mythologies to be used by the masses (Kaufman, 2001). The fact is that, in many conflicts in the post-Soviet world, there were no charismatic leaders, and the Soviet Union was brought down in its peripheral colonies by intellectuals, some of whom later rose to prominence in politics but none to a profile comparable to leaders in the former Yugoslavia. When analyzing the factors of nationalist mobilization that led to the collapse of the Soviet Union, Mark Beissinger (2002) finds no prominent role for elites. Boris Yeltsin and the intellectuals in the Baltics or Moldova played a role, but they were just part of a broader context favoring the nations against the multinational state, which included both the masses and international actors.

To bridge the endless debate between those who blame the leaders and those who blame the masses, a political communication approach may be useful. Political communication started in the first half of the twentieth century with simplistic, unilateral models of communication, in which the public was often seen as the passive receptacle of manipulative messages. Contemporary models have evolved to form a circular shape, illustrating the way messages are created to appeal to an audience with its own beliefs, and how messages are transformed during the communication process and fed back to communicators as reactions from the public. The communicators then adjust their messages accordingly and resend them, at which point intermediates (media, public opinion leaders) adjust them again and so forth (see, for instance Dennis McQuail for a review of such theories). Forcing a choice between leaders and followers, between elites and masses, is incorrect. The ball circulates too much to be able to identify to whom it actually belongs in the end, or to grant any meaning to the question of who launched it first. Unappealing balls do not circulate at all; they just slip quietly out of public attention. Nationalist messages, obviously, do not belong to this category.

"West Civic, East Ethnic"

The next—and last—false antinomy we will address is the famous classification of Western European nationalism as civic and of Eastern European nationalism as ethnic. The classification in itself of civic and ethnic nationalisms has come under intense criticism recently, and the idea has gained grounds that any successful nationalism must necessarily draw on principles of both civic and ethnic nationalism, although at different historical moments. The succession wars in the postcommunist world identified Eastern Europe as a perennial area of ethnic conflict, and intellectual archaeologists embarked on rearranging historical facts to promote, once again, the false opposition between the alleged ethnicist Eastern behavior and the alleged ethnically neutral Western one. As the focus was on emancipated postcommunist Europe, the border between East and West was pushed to fit the contemporary, post-1989 border, thus separating Europe in a civic camp, sometimes including Germany, and an ethnic one, comprising the whole of the postcommunist world. This recent division obliterated the classic distinction of civic versus ethnic, as historians of nationalism have always treated Germany in opposition to France and Britain. As this distinction of East versus West often informs policy, one cannot rule out arguments based on such confusions on the simple grounds that they are not credible. A thorough discussion is needed.

Civic nationalism implies that the people's sovereignty is located in the individual or (the citizen). It requires that people and territory belong together and that the people possess a single political will. Within civic nationalism, citizenship can be elected and determines one's nationality. The starting point for civic nationalism is the state, and its focal point is the nation-state, promoting the belief in a society united by the concept and importance of territoriality, citizenship, civic rights, and legal codes transmitted to all members of the group. Ethnic nationalism refers to nationalism as determined by descent. Attachments are inherited and not chosen, representing the exclusivist element of nationalism. The ethnic concept of nationalism also implies a more collectivistic identity.

These are ideal-types, of course, and the reality falls only roughly—at best—within the lines of such classifications. The classifications also do not completely agree with each other. When portraying historical nationalism in five European countries, Liah Greenfeld follows the tradition that emphasizes the dichotomy of the individual and the collective. Collectivism, although of various types, seems to be the mark of continental nationalism, from France's revolution in 1789 to the German and Russian cases. Individualism, the grounds for civic nationalism, underpins only the British experience. Classic liberals, such as John Stuart Mill, expressed skepticism about the existence of a state which is both democratic and multinational. "Free institutions are next to impossible in a country made up of different nationalities" (Mill, 1977: 547), Mill wrote, explaining that people must trust the same leaders and read the same newspapers to form a political community. What he meant was that a unity of culture is necessary to have a democratic polity. Mill viewed the Habsburg Empire with skepticism, and he considered that "it is, in general, a necessary condition of free institutions that the boundaries of government should coincide in the main with those of nationality. . . Where the sentiment of nationality exists in any force, there is a *prima facie* case for uniting all the members of the nationality under the same government, and a government to themselves apart. This is merely to say that the question of government is to be decided by those governed" (Mill, 1977: 547).

This implies that a government should rest in the boundaries of one culture but also that each culture should have its own state when possible. When this is not possible, assimilation or some form of government providing for minority representation are the next options. This was the case in Habsburg-era multinational Hungary, where nationalities were too intermingled to be separated. In this case, Mill concluded, no alternative is available but "making virtue out of necessity;" some form of democratic cohabitation must therefore be designed. Mill's distaste for multicultural polities is as illuminating for contemporary readers as it is sensible, especially because he acknowledges that even the oldest nations in Western Europe were far from homogenous (Mill, 1997: 547–56). In the nineteenth century, democracies needed homogenous or dominant cultures to be born. Both after 1918 and 1989, the new countries that emerged from self-determination processes tried to reproduce these processes.

Hans Kohn coined the "East ethnic, West civic" distinction between Eastern and Western types of nationalism in total disregard of the dichotomy of individualism and collectivism, or any acknowledgement that Western European history presents the nuances described by Mill. Kohn's main criteria for the different types of nationalism are the relationship between nation and state, and his stress on the type of nation building was accepted by a large number of scholars. Accordinto to Kohn, where the nation comes first historically, and the state only follows, nationalism is more likely to be civic. The nation precedes the state in the West, but the state came first in the East. Nationalism in the West was therefore a reality, meaning that states emerged to accommodate already existing nations. In the East, it was based on myths and dreams; the state had to invent the nation, often at the expense of other ethnic groups.

> While nationalism in the West arose in an effort to build a nation in the political reality and struggle of the present without too much sentimental regard for the past, nationalists in Central and Eastern Europe created, often out of myths of the past and dreams of the future, 'an ideal fatherland, closely linked with the past, devoid of any immediate connection with the present and expected to become sometimes a political reality. Then they were at liberty to adorn it with traits for the realization of which they had no immediate responsibility, but which influenced the nascent nation's wishful image of itself and its mission (Kohn, 1961: 330).

The main focus of Kohn's distinction is, therefore, on nation building, a process seen as entirely natural and organic in the West, but inorganic and state sponsored in the East. But more recent research—from Eugen Weber to Eric Hobsbawn—illustrates beyond a doubt that Western nations were also achieved with at least a helping hand from governments and intellectuals. (Mill already knew that as well.) Similar to East Europeans peasants, many French peasants did not have a French identity at the end of the nineteenth century. The French peasants thought of themselves as Christians rather than nationals. The difference between East and West may lie then in the percentage of illiterate peasants in the total population, but again this is not a difference in their degree of nationalism.

Nationalism, as both Deutsch and Gellner agreed, needs literates to create citizens. The East-West distinction should therefore be placed closer to its origins, in the realm of a *difference in development*. Catching up with the West, what the small liberated East European countries were trying to achieve after the First World War, led by ambitious, Western educated elites, requires concentrating evolution in a short space of time. Any process rushed and concentrated in such a fashion risks becoming a caricature of itself. Undeveloped states have politicians who are also writers, intellectuals, and nation builders. This does not happen because they are more xenophobic than their counterparts in developed countries, but because they feel they must recuperate all the delay in one generation. Gellner provided the caricature with his depiction of Ruritania, and his own classification is only a step away from Kohn's. For Gellner, Western nationalism remains good and Eastern bad. Gellner wrote:

> Roughly speaking and allowing for certain complications Europe falls into four times zones. ...The Westernmost time zone is that of the Atlantic coast of Europe. The point about this zone is that from the late Middle Ages, if not earlier, it was occupied by strong dynastic states, which roughly, even if only very roughly, correlated with cultural areas. If nationalism requires the marriage of state and culture, then in this zone the couple has been cohabiting long before their union was acclaimed by nationalist Manifest Destiny. ...Nationalism did not draw on peasant cultures so as to invent a new literate one: rather it strove to replace peasant idioms by an existing court or urban speech. ...Peasant had to be turned into proper speaking nationals, but no national High Cultures had to be forged from peasant materials. ...
>
> The next zone to the East was different. Far from possessing ready-made dynastic states, it was an area of quite exceptional political fragmentation, endowed with effective political units much smaller than the geographical extension of the two locally dominant High Cultures. The major meta-political unit of the area, the Holy Roman Empire, had long ago lost any effective reality, and by the time of the coming of the age of nationalism had ceased to exist even in name. But if the region lacked pre-existing political units ready for the nationalist requirements, it was exceedingly well equipped with pre-existing, codified, normative High Cultures. ...So here was indeed a need for polity-building, though not for culture-building.It was the next time zone to the East which presented the greatest problems from the viewpoint of the implementation of the nationalist principle of one culture, one state. ...Many of the peasant cultures were not clearly endowed with a normative High Culture at all. Some even had no name. High Cultures

had to become co-extensive with entire societies, instead of defining a restricted minority. Here both cultures and politics had to be created, an arduous task indeed. Nationalism began with ethnography, half descriptive, half normative, a kind of salvage operation and cultural engineering combined. If the eventual units were to be compact and reasonably homogenous, more had to be done: many, many people had to be either assimilated, or expelled, or killed (Gellner, 1994: 115–117).

The model correctly stresses the difference between the widespread so-called high culture in the West and its confinement to a much smaller, elitist group in the East. It also correctly points out that both polity and culture had to be created in the East, polity only in Central Europe proper, and only minor adjustments needed to be made to the two in the West. However, there are important points which Gellner's model fails to address.

- Gellner does not foresee, and consequently does not account for, the strong recurrence of ethnic revival movements in the West. He sees Ireland as an exception and notes with some satisfaction the *failure* of the new Irish state to create a new culture. He was far from anticipating the spread of the new Celtic identity and its growing appeal. His model does not account for the Welsh, the Scots, the Basques, the Catalans, and the Corsicans, all following Ireland in their effort to find a suitable political form to express their—perhaps minor—cultural difference from their fellow citizens within their mother countries.
- The model fails to explain the nationalistic behavior of British and French beyond the limits of Western Europe, such as in Algeria or Northern Ireland.
- The model does not explain why a particularly virulent strain of European nationalism developed in Germany, Spain, or Italy.
- Gellner claims that Eastern Europe lacked political models of states, unlike the West. This strong statement should also be considered with some reservation. In Eastern Europe, the Byzantine model persisted throughout the Middle Ages, as the rulers of Russia, Bulgaria, Serbia, and Romanian principalities tried to reproduce it in their own polities and even to expand it to the neighboring areas under their political domination. There is no notable difference between this Byzantine tradition and the one of the state of Charlemagne that Gellner depicts for Western Europe. Only the Ottoman occupation ended this development. Poland and Hungary also had a long state tradition before being incorporated into larger supranational political units. In short, while conjectural factors clearly prevented the state model from being followed in borderland Eastern Europe, there is no evidence of a structural difference. A model did exist.

Peter Sugar (1969) does more justice to Eastern European nationalism by stressing the importance of development. Eastern European elites pitted against reactionary empires—Russia, Ottoman, and Habsburg—viewed nationalism as inseparable from modernization but also as a strategy for it. Sugar identifies important similarities between the Eastern European nationalism and the Western one in its anticlerical, egalitarian, and constitutional approach. But the degree to which the model was pursued in Eastern Europe was dependent on the development of Eastern European societies. Sugar states that the Czechs came closer to a Western version of nationalism, labeling it "bourgeois nationalism." Poland and Hungary lacked a middle-class as developed as the Czech one, so their nationalism could only be aristocratic, as it remained until the end of World War Two. In Romania, nationalism was a state project, in fact a government one. Indeed, Sugar sees it as "the project" of the government, subordinating all others. Romanian, Greek, and Turkish nationalism are therefore seen as bureaucratic, since the state, using its bureaucracy, including educators, played the major role in nation building. Finally, Serbia and Bulgaria, which lacked an aristocracy, a bourgeoisie, and a state, developed a populist, mass nationalism, animated by the low peasant clergy and small traders.

By and large, historical evidence points out that the Eastern European elites copied the West, and the moment when the Western model simply exploded in the East was the 1848 revolution. This pragmatic desire of bringing independence and prosperity by means of a model already tried in the West was the driving factor in the East. Ideology was secondary, and accounts blaming East European nationalism on German romanticism are greatly exaggerated. Ideology was built to mobilize the masses. The elites' development plans were otherwise too abstract to have found any followers. The abstract doctrine of collective self-determination, as derived from Rousseau and the French revolutionaries, was the main inspiration for the modernizing elites in Eastern Europe. Thus it was a self-conscious act of building an ideology for instrumental purposes, but those who initiated it in the East—such as Hungary's Lajos Kossuth and Romania's Ion Bratianu—were pragmatic men. They were liberals guided by a liberal idea, which was certainly imported from the West. Poised against both imperial minded aristocrats and populists, these modernizers of Eastern Europe were not ethnicists. This also accounts for their severe defeat in some of these countries.

Little is left of the distinction of West as civic and East as ethnic in the more refined classifications of either Greenfeld or Sugar. There is also little empirical evidence is to support this theory. More proof is emerging daily that even civic states, such as the United States, could hardly be seen as such until the 1970s. Even the most civic of nationalisms had strong ethnic elements, which have gradually diminished (Kaufman, 1999). The end of the British Empire brought about an ethnic revival, not ethnic tolerance, even in the core of so-called old Europe, although at least some of the varieties of ethnic nationalism (such as in Scotland) have evolved to become more civic (Keating, 2001). In postcommunist Europe as well, new states have become increasingly civic-oriented once one culture establishes itself as the dominant one, and the process of state and nation building is brought to completion (Kuzio, 2002). There is also empirical evidence illustrating that Eastern Europeans are more eager to embrace a European identity than those in Western Europe and tend to support less, not more, the state's assimilationist cultural policies.[3] (Shulman, 2000). In fact, as Shulman points out, Eastern Europe bought the Western model of civic nationalism, even if it was based more on rhetoric than fact, the same way it bought the model of liberal capitalism after 1989.

Due both to their traumatic experiences with nationalism and communism and the strong will to pursue a Western model until their countries are fully integrated into Europe, Eastern Europeans have shown considerable resistance toward assimilationist nationalism in some recent surveys. In 2000, even the Serbs, for example, scored lower values on every nationalism survey compared to their neighbors who had not been through ethnic wars (see Mungiu-Pippidi in this volume). If the risk of nationalism remains high in some parts of the former Yugoslavia or Soviet Union, this is because of unsettled problems of borders or armed ethnic entrepreneurs, but the difference between these focal points and the ones in the West (such as the Basque country, or Northern Ireland) gradually becomes obscured. A *conjectural* difference in the legacies of independent states in the West and of multinational empires in the East is responsible for the most striking differences in the recent history of the two parts of Europe. Leaving aside states such as Spain or Germany, Kohn's false dichotomy between a *structural* ethnic character of Eastern European nationalism opposed to a civic Western character is surely flawed. "The dichotomy is fallacious and misleading for it does not represent the true nature of nationalism as both political expression and cultural declaration, it perpetuates notions of Western and Eastern nationalism and 'good' and 'bad' nationalism" (Nikolas, 2000: 5).

How, then, can we explain the enduring popularity of this dichotomy (Ignatieff, 1994; Brubaker, 1996)? It is mainly on the grounds of convenience. Clear-cut classifications have always been simpler to understand, especially when they flatter the audience. The Kohn model also seemed extremely convenient for policy making. It is enough, common wisdom has claimed, to transplant the model of civic nationalism from West to East, solving the problem of ethnic clashes in the East.

---

3. Both findings are based on the International Social Science Program Survey on Nationalism (1995).

Such illusions still persist, despite the fact that, as Will Kymlicka observed, there is no such common Western model, and the practice is extremely different in various Western countries (Kymlicka, 2000: 184).

In addition, attempts to transplant the so-called Western variety of nationalism ended badly. The international community strongly discouraged any attempts at nation building, which was clearly needed to strengthen the new successor states of the former Soviet Union. Where policies of nation building were nevertheless pursued, such as in the Baltics, where locals knew better than to take bad advice from foreign experts, strong states did ultimately emerge that were able to secure individual rights. Just a decade later, the new states entered a more inclusive, civic phase of state building. Where nation-building policies were pursued incessantly and incoherently, due to the weakness of governments which were caught between Russian imperialism and the double standards of Western Europe, the new states remained weak, bordering state failure. This was the case, for example, in Moldova or Georgia, both of which were plagued by separatism promoted by predatory elites (see the chapter by Charles King in this volume) and often treated as legitimate claims for *cultural* self-determination, despite the proof that self-appointed Russian-speaking agents were acting on behalf of the ethnic minorities who had lost their language and were now culturally Russian. Wherever states were strong and the national problem was addressed as a *minority* problem, so not touching the essentials of state organization, it was solved, and former Warsaw Pact countries have all emerged closer to civic nationalism after the first decade of transition (Shulman, 2000; Kuzio, 2002).

Theories of development are far from explaining everything when ethnic conflict is concerned, but they come close to providing an essential clue of both the difference and similarity between the East and West. Most of the East European nationalism was an answer to underdevelopment and the need to catch up with Western Europe. Nationalism was both the gate to modernization and one of its key vehicles. Struggling still today with unfinished modernization, states of the East embark on nation-building processes, which look ethnic from contemporary Western Europe. Moreover, state- and nation-building processes in Eastern Europe at the end of nineteenth century and in the first decades of the twentieth century are also criticized in retrospect. The core question here is if some nation building is not unavoidable for the creation for a viable state, and whether another type of development can unfold than the succession of phases with a more ethnic-oriented one first and a civic one later—similar to the Western European sequence, although more concentrated. It is highly unusual that success is met in state building without one culture playing a dominant role, unfair as this may be. The one grand exception, Switzerland, has arisen out of a very special context. While the most successful part of its story is widely known, the wars among its ethnic and religious groups—the last no older than 1848—are now largely forgotten. This may explain why the quest to recreate new Switzerlands has failed so far.

Eastern Europe's political development was also determined by another factor, more and more underevaluated today: the external pressures (German, Russian, Byzantine, Ottoman) that "never ceased" (Sugar, 1969: 35). This external factor, decisive in many cases, has somehow been obliterated from the Western discourse on the Balkans lately, despite vigorous reminders (Todorova, 1997). If one looks at the roots of conflicts between nationalities in the Balkans, for instance, one will always discover the Ottoman Empire's manipulation of elites. It is a grave delusion to indulge the idea that these empires were tolerant political entities struggling to keep peace among small savage tribes. They were autocratic underdeveloped states themselves playing *divide et impera*, encouraging conflict and political corruption to dominate (Glenny, 1999).

Those who see East European nationalism as a vicious psychological drive tend to forget how poorly these nations were governed when part of the empires. Seeking a state of one's own was almost always an answer to a problem of bad governance, as well as the need for cultural assertiveness. Merging the latest ethnic conflicts in the former Yugoslavia in a sort of permanent trend toward the ethnicism of the broader region is mistaken. Eastern Europe, due to its long foreign domination, presents simply far less favorable grounds for state building than the West. Abrupt democratization in conditions of differing and often diverging cultures entailed a need to share common resources, such as the state. This need prompted the succession wars in the former Yugoslavia. Apart from that, tensions in the broader region do not even qualify as conflict. Ethnic conflict is a fight among ethnic groups to attain objectives and simultaneously to neutralize, affect, or eliminate rivals (Horowitz, 1984). Political conflicts should not be misread as ethnic ones. Ethnic conflicts are so ubiquitous, anyway, that there is no need to add pseudo ones to the tally.

From Nationalisms to Ethnic Conflict.
In Lieu of a Conclusion

If nationalism is neither good nor bad, but can simply have good or bad consequences depending on the context, context becomes essential. Empirical evidence provides good grounds for a theory making justice equal to some anthropological truths on identity, as well as to some sociological facts on social mobilization. It also provides enough grounds to consider that violent ethnic conflict is not the inevitable station at the end of a road Eastern European countries cannot change. Can we, however, predict when an ethnic conflict would be mild and when violent, and can we emerge with a value free classification of nationalism to fit both majorities and minorities, both historical and contemporary events?

So far, the contemporary literature on violent ethnic conflict has produced a few solid conclusions. Among the facts commonly accepted are that conflict is more likely when minorities are spatially concentrated, there is a previous history of conflict, and the country is transiting from authoritarian rule. Evidence on the role of ethnic heterogeneity is mixed, with one group of scholars arguing that it has a significant relation to conflict, while another argues that it does not and the only variable that matters is the size of the dominant group.[4] There is some agreement that neighborhood and regional context matters importantly, as does international intervention. On internal democratic conditions, there is less agreement, with Collier claiming that political rights, democracy, and dictatorship make no difference in triggering ethnic war, while Sambanis argues that a democratic neighborhood decreases the likelihood of civil identity war. Clearly, political instability matters, and transition regimes are more at risk than stable regimes, be they democracies or dictatorships. On development, views are again rather divergent, with Collier arguing that ethnic wars are a phenomenon of low income countries, and what matters is the overall level of development and the dependency on natural resources as the main export commodity, not income inequality. Others see development as a factor second in importance to ethnic structure and political conditions. The Balkans emerge as fairly atypical in any of these multicountry classifications, which renders the value of the entire exercise rather doubtful. According to Sambanis, Cyprus should not have experienced an ethnic conflict, while Yugoslavia clearly falls outside Collier's cluster of criteria, being among the most economically developed and liberal in the former communist bloc, although there was great inequality among the constituent republics of the Yugoslav Federation.

Combining these empirical findings with our sketchy theoretical review, two essential variables emerge. One is a favorite instrumentalist variable—development. By development, we must, however, understand more than just economic development, as a society's entire development, including the civil and political society, is needed to explain why the institutions of consociative democracy have functioned in the Netherlands better than in Lebanon or elsewhere. More than just overall political and economic development, the degree to which development differs among groups was

---

4. For evidence along the two lines, see Nicholas Sambanis (2001) "Do Ethnic and Non-Ethnic Civil Wars Have the Same Causes? A Theoretical and Empirical Inquiry." World Bank and, respectively, Paul Collier (2001) "Economic Causes of Civil Conflict and Their Implications for Policy." World Bank.

often invoked to explain conflict. When reviewing all the evidence in favor of development, Horowitz (1995) concludes that economic inequality seems to matter more for elites than the rank-and-file ethnic group members. If elites, however, are then instrumental in mobilizing constituencies around this issue, its importance should not be overestimated, despite failing to show up in the World Bank models.

The second variable, the type of contact among groups, is closer to the primordialist approach, being at the core of psychological explanations of ethnic conflict. The more two ethnic groups have to share poorly separated resources (such as the state), or the more resources of two spatially concentrated groups are uneven, the higher the chances of conflict. Contact works inversely with groups, simply because when groups are in contact, some form of sharing is necessary, and sharing is the source of troubles. Groups with no contact do better regardless of the levels of prejudice, simply because they have nothing to share and are separated by a safe distance

Table 1

Likelihood of Ethnic Conflict
by Development and Type of Contact Among Groups

Development		Contact			
		Groups share a territory within a state	Groups in neighboring states	Foreign rulers	Immigrant groups, diasporas, other
Low	Uneven	e.g. Macedonia, Kosovo	e.g. India and Pakistan, Kuwait and Iraq	e.g. Rwanda	e.g. 19th century US (gangs of New York)
	Even	e.g. Georgia	e.g. Ethiopia and Eritrea	—	—
High	Uneven	e.g. Serbia and Croatia, Baltics	e.g. Germany and France prior to WWII	—	e.g. Brooklyn, L.A. riots
	Even	e.g. Belgium, Transylvania	e.g. Western Europe	—	—

A matrix resulting from crosstabulating the two essential variables—contact and development—would look as in table 1. The likelihood of conflict increases the more two groups have to share common resources and the more development is low and uneven. The degree of violence in a conflict also depends on other variables, of which international context becomes a more and more crucial factor. Soviet intervention in the Baltics could have ended up as violent as the one in Chechnya had not the West given clear signs that the Baltics were protected territory. The matrix explains historical conflicts, as well as contemporary ones, can accommodate liberation revolutions, and invasions of neighboring countries or diaspora conflicts. It predicts that sharing will always produce conflict, and that, although development eases the consequences of conflict and developed societies are better equipped to control it, development cannot eliminate conflict.

As it takes many years as well as ethnic peace to foster development, a sound policy of ethnic-conflict prevention and management would then have to manage contact intelligently, through case by case institutions adjusted to the specific conditions on the ground. The lessons learned from the experience of the past decade and the consequences for the people and states of the institutional experiments in nation and state building in the postcommunist world make the substance of the rest of this book.

References

Allport, Gordon (1954) *The Nature of Prejudice*. New York: Double Day Anchor Book.

Anderson, Benedict (1991) *Imagined Communities. Reflection in the Origins and Spread of Nationalism*. London: Verso.

Barry, Brian M. (1987) "Nationalism" in *The Blackwell Encyclopedia of Political Thought*. Oxford: Blackwell.

Beissinger, Mark R. (2002) *Nationalist Mobilization and the Collapse of the Soviet State*. Cambridge: Cambridge University Press.

Bell, Daniel (1975) "Ethnicity and Social Change." In N. Glazer and D. P. Moynihan (eds.) *Ethnicity: Theory and Experience*. Cambridge: Harvard University Press.

Biberaj, Elez (1999) *Albania in Transition: The Rocky Road to Democracy*. Boulder: Westview.

Brass, Paul R. (1985) *Ethnicity and Nationalism: Theory and Comparison*. Newbury Park: Sage Publications.

Breuilly, John (1984) *Nationalism and the State*. Chicago: University of Chicago Press.

Brewer, Marilynn B. (1979) "In-Group Bias in the Minimal Intergroup Situation: A Cognitive-Motivational Analysis." *Psychological Bulletin* 86(2): 307–24.

—— (1991) "The Social Self: On Being the Same and Different at the Same Time." *Personality and Social Psychology Bulletin* 17(5): 475–82.

—— (1997) "The Social Psychology of Intergroup Relations: Can Research Inform Practice?" *Journal of Social Issues* 53(1): 197–211.

—— (1997) "The Social Psychology of Intergroup Relations: Can Research Inform Practice?" Paper presented at the meeting of the Midwest Consortium for International Security Studies, December 5, Oak Brook, IL.

Brewer, Marilynn B. and Norman Miller (1996) *Intergroup Relations*. Buckingham, England: Open University Press.

Brubaker, Rogers (1996) *Nationalism Reframed: Nationhood and the National Question in the New Europe*. Cambridge: Cambridge University Press.

Chirot, Daniel and Martin Seligman (2001) *Ethnopolitical Warfare: Causes, Consequences, and Possible Solutions*. Washington, D.C.: American Psychological Association.

Comaroff, John and Jean (1992) "Of Totemism and Ethnicity." In *Ethnography and the Historical Imagination*. Boulder: Westview.

Connor, Walker (1993) "Beyond Reason: The Nature of the Ethnonational Bond." *Ethnic and Racial Studies* 16(3): 373–89.

—— (1994) *Ethnonationalism: The Quest for Understanding*. Princeton: Princeton University Press.

Conversi, Daniele (2002) (ed.) *Ethnonationalism in the Contemporary World. Walker Connor and the Study of Nationalism*. London: Routledege, 271–277.

De Figueiredo, Rui and Barry R. Weingast (1997) "The Rationality of Fear: Politi-cal Opportunism and Ethnic Conflict." Unpublished paper, Stanford University.

Deutsch, Karl (1966) *Nationalism and Social Communication: An Inquiry into the Foundations of Nationality*. Cambrdige: MIT Press.

Doise, Willem (1990) "Les Representations Sociales." In Bonnet,G., Ghighlione, R. and Richard, J.F. (eds.) *Psychologie Cognitive*, vol. 3, Paris, Bordas.

Eiser, J. Richard (1990) *Social Judgment*. Pacific Grove: Brooks/Cole Publishing.

Eller, Jack David and Reed M. Coughlin (1993) "The Poverty of Primordialism: The Demystification of Ethnic Attachments." *Ethnic and Racial Studies* 16(2): 183–202.

Fearon, James D. and David D. Laitin (1996) "Explaining Interethnic Cooperation." *American Political Science Review* 90(4): 715–35.

Firth, Raymond (1957) *We, The Tikopia*. 2d ed. London: Allen & Unwin.

Fiske, Susan and Shelley Taylor (1984) *Social Cognition*. New York: Random House.

Forbes, H.D. (1997) *Ethnic Conflict: Commerce, Culture, and the Contact Hypothesis*. New Haven: Yale University Press.

Geertz, Clifford (1973) *The Interpretation of Cultures*. New York: Basic Books.

Gellner, Ernest (1983) *Nation and Nationalisms*. Oxford: Basil Blackwell.

—— (1994) *Conditions of Liberty: Civil Society and Its Enemies*. London: Penguin Press.

Giles, Howard and Bernard Saint-Jacques (1992) (eds.) *Language and Ethnic Relations*. New York: Pergamon Press.

Glenny, Misha (1999) *A History of the Balkans*. London: Penguin.

—— (1999) *The Balkans: Nationalism, War & the Great Powers, 1804–1999*. London: Penguin.

Greenfeld, Liah (1991) *Nationalism, Five Roads to Modernity*. Cambridge: Harvard University Press.

Hardin, Russell (1995) *One for All: The Logic of Group Conflict*. Princeton: Princeton University Press.

Hobsbawm, Eric (1983) "Mass Producing Traditions. Europe." In Eric Hobsbawm and Ranger Terence (eds.) *The Invention of Traditions*. Cambridge: Cambridge University Press, 263–307.

Hogg, Michael A. and John C. Turner (1985) "Interpersonal Attraction, Social Identification and Psychological Group Formation." *European Journal of Social Psychology* 15(1): 51–66.

Horowitz, Donald L. (1985) *Ethnic Groups in Conflict*. Berkeley: University of California Press.

—— (1998) Structure and Strategy in Ethnic Conflict. Paper prepared for the Annual World Bank Conference on Development Economics, Washington, D.C., April 20–21.

Htun, Mala and Smita Singh (2001) "Identity, Meaning and the Institutions of Ethnic Politics." Paper prepared for the 2001 Annual Meeting of the American Association of Political Science, San Francisco, August 29–September 2.

Ignatieff, Michael (1994) *Blood and Belonging*. New York: Farrar, Straus, and Giroux.

Kaufman, Stuart J. (2001) *Modern Hatreds. The Symbolic Politics of Ethnic War*. Ithaca: Cornell University Press.

Kakar, Sudhir (1996) *The Colors of Violence: Cultural Identities, Religion, and Conflict*. Chicago: University of Chicago Press.

Kedourie, Elie (1985) *Nationalism Revived*. London: Hutchinson.

Kohn, Hans (1965) *Nationalism: Its Meaning and History*. Malabar: Robet E. Krieger Press.

—— (1974) "Nationalism." In *Encyclopedia Britannica*. Encyclopedia Britannica.

Kuzio, Taras (2002) "The Myth of the Civic State: A Critical Survey of Hans Kohn's Framework for Understanding Nationalism." *Ethnic and Racial Studies* 25(1): 20–31.

Kymlicka, Will (2000) "Nation-building and Minority Rights Comparing West and East." *Journal of Migration Studies* 26(2): 183–212.

Laitin, David (1998) *Identity in Formation: the Russian-speaking Populations in the Near Abroad.* Ithaca: Cornell University Press.

Lanca, Margaret and Christine Alksnis (1994) "Effects of Language Choice on Acculturation." *Journal of Language & Social Psychology* 13(3): 315–31.

McGarry, John and Brendan O'Leary (1993) *The Politics of Ethnic Conflict Regulation.* London: Routledge.

McQuail, Dennis (1983) *Mass Communication Theory.* London: Sage.

Melluci, Alberto et al. (1989) *Nomads of the Present.* London: Hutchinson Radius.

Mill, John Stuart (1977) "Considerations on Representative Government." In *Essays on Politics and Society.* Toronto: University of Toronto Press.

Milne, R.S. (1980) *Politics in Ethnically Bipolar Societies.* Vancouver: University of British Columbia Press.

Nikolas, Margareta Mary (2000) *The Nationalism Project: False Opposites in Nationalism.* Madison: The Nationalism Project.

Oomen, T.K.(1997) *Citizenship, Nationality and Ethnicity.* Cambridge: Polity Press.

Pandey, Gyanendra (1992) "In Defense of the Fragment: Writing About Hindu-Muslim Riots in India Today." *Representations* 37 (Winter): 27–55.

Rabushka, Alvin and Kenneth R. Shepsle (1972) *Politics in Plural Societies.* Columbus: Charles E. Merrill Publishing.

Shils, Edward (1957) "Primordial, Personal, Sacred and Civil Ties." *British Journal of Sociology* 8(2): 130–45.

Shulman, Stephen (2002) "Challenging the Civic/Ethnic and West/East Dichotomies in the Study of Nationalism." *Comparative Political Studies* 35(5): 554–85.

Sidanius, Jim and Felicia Pratto (2000) *Social Dominance: An Intergroup Theory of Social Hierarchy and Oppression.* Cambridge: Cambridge University Press.

Sugar, Peter and Ivo Lederer (1969) *Nationalism in Eastern Europe.* Seattle and London: University of Washington Press.

Sugar, Peter (1980) *Ethnic Diversity and Conflict in Eastern Europe.* Santa Barbara: ABC-Clio.

Sugar, Peter (ed.) (1995) *East European Nationalism in the Twentieth Century.* Maryland: University Press of America.

Tajfel, Henri et al. (1970) "The Development of Children's Preference for their Own Country. A Cross-national study." *International Journal of Psychology* 5: 245–53.

—— (1974) "Intergroup Behavior, Social Comparison and Social Change." Katz-Newcomb Lectures, University of Michigan, Ann Arbor.

—— (1981) *Human Groups and Social Categories*. Cambridge: Cambridge University Press.

Tajfel, Henri and J.C. Turner (1979) "An Integrative Theory of Social Conflict." In W. Austin and S. Worche (eds.) *The Social Psychology of Intergroup Relations*. Monterrey: Brooks/Cole.

Todorova, Maria (1997) *Imagining the Balkans*. Oxford: Oxford University Press.

Weber, Eugen (1976) *Peasants into Frenchmen: The Modernization of Rural France 1870–1914*. Stanford: Stanford University Press.

Weinrich, Uriel (1974) *Languages in Contact, Findings and Problems*. Mouton: Hague.

Wilkinson, Steven I. (1997) *The Electoral Origins of Ethnic Violence: Hindu-Muslim Riots in India*. Ph.D. dissertation. Massachusetts Institute of Technology, Cambridge, Mass.

II.
The 'Subjective' Grounds
of Ethnic Conflict

Milosevic's Voters:
Explaining Grassroots Nationalism in Postcommunist Europe

Alina Mungiu-Pippidi

An Analytical Framework to Study Contemporary Nationalism

This chapter deals with the grassroots of ethnic conflict in postcommunist Europe, with a special focus on the Balkans. In other words, it is concerned with Milosevic's voters (and others like them) rather than with the historical circumstances that have the potential to generate ethnic conflict, political environments that allow nationalist leaders to win votes, and institutions that favor certain outcomes in specific conflict circumstances. Declaring the voters a primary interest is not to avow some preference for the hypothesis that mass attitudes or mass behaviors are the main causes of the Balkan ethnic conflict, or of any other ethnic conflict for that matter. While the theory of ethnic conflict remains divided over almost every important issue in two camps that are difficult to reconcile (Horowitz, 1998; chapter one of this book), ethnic favoritism and discrimination against out-groups figure largely in both, although in different explanatory frameworks. Therefore, one can hardly deny the legitimacy of the grassroots approach for Eastern Europe's nationalism. From the general condemnation of the region by Gellner or Kohn as a mere collection of Ruritanias, to Robert Kaplan's "Balkan ghosts" or George F. Kennan's ancient tribal hatreds, nationalism has been largely blamed on the masses in Eastern Europe. Some grounds for this are obvious: in the fall of 2002 alone, when the Balkans seemed extremely peaceful compared to previous years, ethnic-based or nationalist parties won elections in Macedonia, Montenegro, Bosnia and Herzegovina, and, of course, Kosovo, where only such parties exist. Ultranationalist Vojislav Seselj made a good score in the Serbian elections. In their time, Slobodan Milosevic and Franjo Tudjman were elected repeatedly by their citizens. Nationalism varies greatly across the region, however. Not every postcommunist country has nationalist leaders who run in elections and make headlines in the domestic and international media; neither are all East Europeans nationalistic, even when nationalists are successful in elections. In some countries, nationalism becomes the dominant ideology, whereas in others it remains only secondary. This variation also justifies a grassroots comparative approach.

What causes support for nationalism in postcommunist societies? Explaining widespread nationalistic attitudes is the main goal of this chapter. Nationalism is defined as the *individual subscription to the political ideology advocating the perfect congruity of the political unit with the national (ethnic) unit*. This definition places the phenomenon at the individual level while retaining the main elements of the common definitions of nationalism as belief-system or ideology (Barry, 1987), which is centered on an ethnic identity, based on race, language, culture, and history (Smith, 1991), an internalized ideology shaped by the social representation of a common historical experience. Ethnic identity is defined here, simply, as an individual's ethnic self-ascription (Breakwell, 1982; Giles, 1982). This definition serves our present purpose since we can fairly predict it for most individuals, as well as rely on their ethnic identification, as declared in the surveys discussed in this chapter. Ethnocentrism is defined by the drive to view one's own ethnic group under a favorable light and to disfavor other groups.

This chapter is divided as follows: in the first section, I will clarify my approach and sketch a general theoretical model for the empirical study of nationalism. In the second, I will present my panel of countries, explain why I chose those countries, and provide some background for understanding their particular contexts. In the third section, I will present the surveys used and discuss the main results. In the fourth, the main theoretical hypotheses will be put forth. The fifth section will discuss the results for the main group of countries—Serbia, Bulgaria, Romania, Hungary, and Slovakia. The sixth section will be dedicated to Kosovo, and the seventh will summarize the main findings and sketch a model of postcommunist nationalism.

Nationalism is seldom studied at the individual level, although efforts were made, notably by Horowitz, in his masterful *Ethnic Groups in Conflict* (1985) to make a bridge between social psychology and political science. Generalizations from an individual to a group, and from a small group to society, are the source of many errors and biases in ethnic-conflict theory. Among other things, these generalizations generated the paradox of contact theory (Forbes, 1997). As phrased initially by Allport (1954), contact theory claims that contact reduces prejudice among groups. Yet decades of amassed evidence illustrates that individuals who enjoy more contact with another ethnic group tend to be less prejudiced, but that groups with more contact tend to engage in conflict more often. Generalizing from Allport's theory for individuals to larger groups proved catastrophic, as many other variables that are irrelevant for individuals do indeed matter for group behavior. Groups are more than the sums of individuals, and societies are not just the sum of the various social groups within them.

But this does not mean that inferences from the individual level are not valuable to understanding what happens at the societal level. It only means they are insufficient. Clearly, one cannot understand what happens at the society level without a comprehension of the dynamics at the individual level. It is crucial to understand why Serbian voters elected Milosevic repeated times, even after most of the world had denounced him as a new Hitler. The model in figure 1 attempts to capture the relationship between the two levels of analysis—societal and individual—as well as horizontal causal relationships, which public opinion models try to capture. The societal level forms the upper level of the figure (which is a mirror) and consists of the formal institutions, which are borders, power-sharing arrangements, state structure (federal or unitary), the ethnic group's status (as state holder or state seeker). It includes the informal institutions, consisting of practices and informal arrangements with other groups (for example, cooperation, competition, or violence). These usually reflect both current and previous formal institutions. If a group historically has enjoyed an inferior position, and its status is equalized with the dominant group at some point, informal institutions or practices need a period of time to catch up with the legal developments. Finally, we have the public opinion on the ethnic matter, which is an aggregate of majority opinions on the status of other groups or nations and relations with them. All these layers then have their correspondents at the individual level. An individual has his or her own attitudes toward one's nation, borders, and neighbors; his or her own status as member of a dominant, inferior, unique, or equal national constituent group; and a personal social position, which renders this status more or less acceptable. An individual also behaves in a certain way toward the national question. He or she may vote for Jean-Marie Le Pen, plant bombs to liberate the Basque country, or simply ignore the matter.

Correspondences between the two levels are obvious. If many individuals espouse prejudice, a majority will support a law restricting immigration. If a large group of people vote for a nationalistic leader, the leader will be elected. If too many members of the minority decide to mingle in the larger society to acquire a superior social status, a minority group can be assimilated and disappear. Furthermore, all the formal institutions and most informal institutions are historical products. Unlike public opinion, which can shift after a dramatic event in almost no time (like a majority supporting a foreign war after the bombing of the World Trade Center), institutions are more durable and produce long-lasting effects. As Douglas North wrote in the aftermath of the fall of communism, "today's and tomorrow choices are shaped by the past" (North, 1990: vii). In addition to historical data, information on formal and informal arrangements, as well as on individual's opinions on them, allows inferences that are clearly placed at the individual level. The theory *directly* relevant for this chapter is therefore limited to the one inferring from individual attitudes and behavior, although much of the larger theory from various disciplines on nationalism works with assumptions about human behavior and its consequences.

The most important psychological theories that have tried to shed some light on the human propensity toward discriminative behavior that can be extrapolated to nationalism are: Allport's prejudice/contact theory, the theory of authoritarian personality (Adorno et al.), social-identity theory (Henri Tajfel and the Bristol school), and social-dominance theory (Sidanius and Pratto). Although largely discarded today, the theory of real interests conflict can still be traced at the roots of many policies (Becker, 1957; Sheriff, 1967; Sowell, 1981). Horowitz draws on social-identity theory, descending from the society level to seek an explanation at the individual or small-group level. I will journey in exactly the opposite direction.

Figure 1
A Tripartite Model for the Study of Nationalism

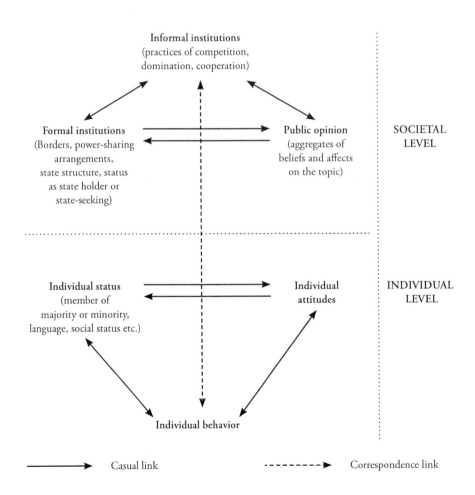

The Region: The Balkans and Beyond

The chapter surveys a region broader than the Balkans, also including Hungary and its Central European neighbors. Thus, the panel includes Serbia, Kosovo, Bulgaria, Romania, Hungary, and Slovakia. To a large extent, the countries in the area share a long history of foreign occupation, late state formation in their present makeup, and a communist regime for the second half of the twentieth century. Diplomats and scholars have argued repeatedly on the substantiation of including these countries in either Central or Eastern Europe. Equally disputed is the composition of the ill-famed Balkans to which no state, except Bulgaria, fully acknowledges belonging. Hungary and Slovakia, the latter a new state, are clearly Central European by geography. Excepting Hungary, a special case, none of these five countries is ethnically homogenous. Their share of minorities varies, but, on the average, it is considerably higher than in Western Europe. Of course, a country can have nationalism without minorities and border problems, as it seems one can have anti-Semitism without Jews. And, indeed, in many Western European developed countries, immigration plays the same role as the presence of indigenous minorities in Eastern Europe, prompting national self-awareness and xenophobia. The agenda in the West, however, is utterly different, as are the stakes. Borders and sovereignty issues, crucial in Eastern Europe, are seldom a topic in the West, except for very special cases (the Basque country or Northern Ireland, for example). The issues of ethnic minorities, borders, and sovereignty are closely interlinked in Eastern Europe. Centuries of foreign occupation have frozen, to a large extent, the organic development of social communication on the basis of one language (Deutsch, 1953). The consequence of this evolution, in Brubaker's words, is a "triadic nexus," involving national minorities, nationalizing states, and external national homelands, which all contribute to the escalation of national awareness (Brubaker, 1996: 6). Each and every state of the region declares that it is responsible for its kin living in the near abroad. Politically organized Hungarian minorities are found in Slovakia, Serbia, and Romania. Macedonian Slavs in Macedonia, a successor state of Yugoslavia, speak a language close to Bulgarian, as most Moldovans in Moldova, a successor state of the Soviet Union, speak Romanian (which the Moldovan Communist Party calls Moldovan). Borders have shifted repeatedly, and identities have followed suit as well. Not every regional identity is equally old and stable. There are Albanians living in Macedonia, Serbia and Montenegro, as well as Serbs living in what is now the international protectorate of Kosovo, where Albanians form the majority. The intricacies of these patterns of cohabitation are shown in table 1.

Table 1

Majorities and Minorities

	Total Population in State or Unit	Largest Ethnic Group's Share of Population [%]	Minorities
Bulgaria	8,200,000	83	Turkish 697,000; Roma 213,200; Other 246,000
Bosnia	3,800,000	44	Serb 1,178,000; Croat 646,000; Other 266,000
Czech Republic	10,300,000	81.2	Moravian 1,369,900; Slovak 309,000; Other 309,000
Hungary	10,000,000	89.9	Roma 400,000, German 260,000; Other 300,000
Kosovo	1,600,000–1,800,000	88	Serbs 7% (uncertain); Bosnians 2%; Roma 1.68%
Macedonia	2,000,000	66.6	Albanian 454,000; Turkish 8
Moldova	4,300,000	64.5	Russian 593,400; Ukrainian 559,000; Gagauz 150,500; Other 215,000
Romania	22,400,000	89.5	Hungarian 1,590,400; Other 448,000
Serbia	10,700,000	63	Albanian 1,498,000; Montenegrin 535,000; Hungarian 428,000; Other 1,177,000
Slovakia	5,400,00	85.7	Hungarian 572,400; Other 162,000
Slovenia	2,000,000	88	Croatian 60,000; Other 120,000

My choice of countries has a twofold explanation. First, as I am looking at the interplay between communism and nationalism, the populations must have had experience of both in sufficient degree. All of the countries selected share both considerable common experience and considerable variation of national diversity and the problems it underwrites. Romania and Bulgaria have large ethnic minorities, but they are unitary states. Romania borders the Balkans, but it is sometimes considered

Eastern Balkan, sometimes Central European. State building has been more intense in Slovakia, a fully independent state only from 1991, as well as in Kosovo, which, although formally still part of Serbia, is learning self-government under the tutorship of the international community. In Brubaker's terminology, my panel of countries includes four nationalizing states, a minority state (Kosovo), and a homeland state—Hungary.

The nature of communist regimes in these countries also varied substantially. Romania's totalitarian regime and Serbia's authoritarian one were considered as national communist. Unlike the other countries, they were not occupied by the Soviet Army (in the case of Romania, only in the last 30 years of Ceausescu's regime), and their domestic leaders resorted to nationalist and patriotic rhetoric to boost their legitimacy. The retreat of the Soviet Army from the rest of the countries was celebrated as a major symbolic event, clearly tying communism with foreign occupation. Although the situation is complex in every country, resisting simple categorization, some of them did emerge after the first decade of postcommunism as successful in dealing with multiethnicity (Romania, Bulgaria, and Slovakia), while others were plagued by ethnic war (Serbia and Kosovo). All the countries in the sample have formally expressed their decision to join the European Union, with Hungary and Slovakia already in, Romania and Bulgaria negotiating for 2007, and Serbia and Montenegro on the path for an association agreement in 2003.

The reason for limiting the choice to these countries is of a different nature. Surveys on nationalism are not common, and survey capacity in some of these countries is weak because of an absence of reliable demographic data. As a result, sets of national data are either unavailable or difficult to homogenize for the purpose of comparative analysis. This restricted choice of countries (missing the other former Yugoslav republics) is, therefore, driven partly by the necessity to have reliable data for comparison. It is compensated, hopefully, by the fact that this is original data, reported here for the first time, based on similar questionnaires and sampling designs for the purpose of comparative analysis.

Measuring Nationalism

Although widely debated and extensively studied, nationalism in the postcommunist world is still something of a mystery. Some authors argue that it is a positive phenomenon, responsible for the defeat of communist ideology, a response to a need for an identity related to freedom (Nodia, 1997). Other scholars claim that it is a ideology leading to totalitarianism, which has been in bed with communism more than once, and is fundamentally directed against individual freedom and democracy

(Michnik, 1991; Brubaker, 1996). In the first instance, nationalizing policies are benign and necessary for nation building (Taras, 2001). In the second, they are malign and threaten the peace of ethnically mixed regions. Surveys measuring the appeal of nationalism in postcommunist countries (Times Mirror, 1991; Miller, White, and Heywood, 1998; Colton, 1999; Gordy, 1999) revealed its attractiveness, with, as the Times Mirror survey put it, Eastern Europeans disliking both their borders and their neighbors (Times Mirror, 1991: 202). Due to historical circumstances, the successor states of Yugoslavia were missed by these surveys. But these past studies remain important because they bring considerable evidence that grassroots nationalism, far from being confined to the Balkans, is widespread throughout the postcommunist world.

The surveys used in this chapter were sponsored by Freedom House in Bulgaria (2000), Slovakia (2000), and Serbia (2002), and by UNDP in Romania (2001) and Kosovo (2002) and executed by national pollsters. The data on Hungary comes from a survey, conducted in 1993, for the Values and Political Change in Post-Communist Europe Project and is courtesy of the UK Data Archive. Details on the surveys are outlined in appendix 1 of this chapter.

The method employed here is not so common in comparative politics. In a world increasingly dominated by regions rather than spheres, in-depth regional understanding probably lies in an intermediate approach somewhere between an exhaustive country specific knowledge and broader testing of particular hypotheses (Katzentstein, 1996: 14). So rather than simply observing what varies between the countries, I cast a thorough look within each of them, building separate national models of nationalism, and comparing determinants of nationalism across the region. With this, we can preserve in the models the specificity of each environment, which is so important in explaining nationalism and ethnic conflict. This comparison is based, therefore, on the study of each population—Romanians, Bulgarians, Serbians, Slovakians, Hungarians, and Kosovars. Minorities were included in the original samples (with the exception of Kosovo and Serbia, where separate samples were drawn) creating a dummy variable to account for one's position as a member of the majority group.

Nationalism was operationalized in these surveys by a common battery of a minimum of four variables (six in the lengthier questionnaires in Serbia and Romania). The congruence sought between the ethnic unit and the political unit usually manifests itself through territorial nationalism (the idea that state borders and the borders of the cultural nation should be one and the same) and cultural nationalism (the idea that within borders political rights should be granted only to speakers of the language of the dominant ethnic group). My first question was a common one, asking respondents if they felt that territories of neighboring countries do in fact belong to their own country. The second phenomenon, cultural nationalism, was measured by agreement with the statement that only people who speak the official or national language are entitled to vote. To explore the issue further, I added two more variables. One, adjusted from the classic authoritarian personality questionnaire, asked respondents if they perceived minorities as a threat to their country's sovereignty and borders. Finally, the fourth question measured attitudes toward the West by querying respondents on their willingness to concede that international organizations can tell their nation how to run its affairs. This is relevant since, during the Cold War, the West was the identified enemy and now also imposes, more or less, the rules of the transition in every country, making democracy and a free market the norm. The question is even more necessary in view of the loss of sovereignty implicit in the European integration process. This battery of questions addressed therefore all the features of postcommunist nationalism signaled in literature, its anti-Western, antineighbors and antiminority components. As the four variables turned out to be strongly correlated, I then created a nationalism factor out of them, extracting principal components. This factor was then used as a dependent variable for multivariate linear regression models explaining nationalism (see table 4). For Romania and Serbia, I submitted another group of variables to the same treatment, measuring authoritarian or autocratic attitudes to create a factor of authoritarianism. For the rest of the countries, a proxy for authoritarianism was used. The components of these factors are broken down in appendix 2, while results are displayed below in table 2.

Table 2

Nationalism as a Broad Regional Phenomenon

Agreement with the following statements:	Romania [%]	Bulgaria [%]	Kosovo [%]	Serbia [%]	Slovakia [%]	Hungary [%]
Parts of other countries belong to us (territorial nationalism)	67	45	81	50	na*	60
Those who cannot speak the state's language should not have the right to vote (cultural nationalism)	50	26	na	45	58	61
Foreigners should not be able to tell us how to run our own country (In Hungary, there is a danger of becoming a colony of the West.)	64	72	72	74	76	40
Minorities are a threat to sovereignty and borders	44	43	78	75	72	na*

Source: Polls conducted in Serbia in 2002; Bulgaria, 2000; Slovakia, 2000 (SAR-Freedom House data); Romania, 2001; Kosovo, 2002 (UNDP data); Hungary, 1993 (MODUS data).

* not available

Results point to strong territorial nationalism in the entire region, with the least amount of people answering affirmatively in Bulgaria and the most in Kosovo. Serbia falls behind Romania and Hungary, with only half of the population considering that Serbia has territories within other states. Cultural nationalism is, again, the lowest in Bulgaria, with respondents evenly divided in the rest of the countries. Hungary's high score is probably explained by the absence of sizeable minorities speaking alternative languages (Miller et al., 1998), but it completes the regional view that citizens should speak the official language. What state language means is not clear in every situation, so pollsters received detailed instructions on a country-by-country basis on how to phrase this question. Bulgaria and Hungary have only one national state language; in Slovakia, Hungarian has the status of a second official language, and, despite fierce legal battles during the Meciar era, the language has retained this status during most of the transition. In Romania, the Constitution gives official status to Romanian only, while specifying that other languages can be used in the judicial and administrative systems in areas where minorities live. More recent legislation has made Hungarian a de facto second official language in the counties with large numbers of Hungarians. Imperfect language pluralism in the former Yugoslavia ended when the country split into the component republics, with different solutions in each republic, and the Albanian language retaining the least recognized status.

Increasing minorities' rights or concessions over sovereignty seem, therefore, not too popular with segments of the public. Bulgaria's macroeconomic policy may be run by a foreign currency board, but its public is strongly opposed to the idea that foreign organizations, such as the EU or IMF, should have a role in the country's political scene. The same feelings are shared by Kosovars who are de facto governed by the international community through UNMIK, and by citizens of Slovakia, Serbia and, to a lesser extent, Romania, all of whom have been granted membership in the EU or are potential members. Minorities are perceived as a threat everywhere, especially in Serbia and Kosovo, but also in Slovakia, and, to a lessen extent, in Romania and Bulgaria. Awareness of the issue is high, with a long conflict history. After liberal treatment of the minorities in the first decades of their regimes, by the 1980s, both Nicolae Ceausescu in Romania and Todor Jivkov in Bulgaria had imbued their national communist regimes with a clear antiminority stand. Attempts to assimilate Turks in Bulgaria and Hungarians in Romania through a range of denationalization policies during the last decade of the communist era attracted, for the first time, the attention of the international community, signaling that these countries had become a serious danger to segments of their own citizenry. In 2001, Viktor Orban's right-wing government in Hungary promoted the Status Law that granted a Hungarian identification card to all ethnic Hungarians in neighboring countries, allowing them to travel to Hungary without a visa and entitling them to welfare benefits in their so-called homeland. The policy was disputed by Romania and Slovakia and made headlines for more than a year.

Table 3

Trust in Other Ethnic Groups in Serbia and Romania

Serbs trust...	Mean (standard deviation)	Romanians trust...	Mean (standard deviation)
Serbs	7.76 (2.37)	Romanians	7.48 (2.31)
Bosnian Serbs	6.66 (2.72)	Transylvanians (Romania)	7.70 (2.44)
Macedonian Slavs	5.90 (2.49)	Moldovans (Romania)	6.70 (2.78)
Hungarians	4.53 (2.53)	Germans	5.70 (3.07)
Romanians	4.24 (2.41)	Moldovans (Moldova)	5.08 (3.05)
Austrians	4.80 (2.63)	Jews	4.61 (3.11)
Germans	4.40 (2.82)	Serbs	4.65 (3.06)
Americans	3.63 (2.82)	Bulgarians	4.38 (2.97)
Roma	3.42 (2.19)	Hungarians (Romania)	4.28 (2.88)
Bosnian Muslims	3.38 (2.48)	Roma	4.26 (3.12)
Kosovar Albanians	2.35 (2.27)	Russians	4.25 (2.97)

Legend: Scale from 1 to10, with 10 as maximum trust.

Even deeper than these political attitudes toward nationalism, measurements of ethnocentrism (using a scale of trust from one to ten in one's ethnic group as well as the other neighboring groups) show the expected in-group favoritism, albeit with some nuances. Romanians view various minorities differently, as well as their conationals, ranking Transylvanians higher than Moldovans, while distrusting Moldovans across the border in the former Soviet state of Moldova, but less so than Hungarians or Roma. In Serbia, Bosnian Muslims and Kosovar Albanians are at the bottom of public trust, both falling below the Roma. But Westerners are also distrusted in Serbia. The war waged against Milosevic by the rest of the world may be responsible for that, as many Serbs perceived it as a war against all Serbs. The distance between the most trusted and the least trusted is higher in Serbia than Romania, as well as the distance between one's own ethnic group and the next most trusted group. The conclusions seems to be that Romanians are less ethnocentric than Serbs.

Hypothesizing Nationalism

Mancur Olson once remarked that "human beings rarely act out of unmixed motives," (Olson, 2000: 3). Finding one clear-cut explanation justifying the endorsement of nationalism by large numbers of East Europeans might be, in this case, just a delusion. There are many competing explanations. Is it that old ethnic resentment is strong enough to resurface, despite fifty years of forced homogenization and repression of ostentatious nationalism during the communist regimes? Or is it the fear that minorities will secede, breaking away with national territories? Or are we dealing with plain authoritarianism, a legacy of communist socialization, requiring a strict enforcement of conformity on minorities? Is it the appeal of charismatic nationalist leaders?

The first step in answering the above questions is to group the large number of causes of mass nationalism advanced by various scholars in a few more structured categories. Let me start with the first and most popular—the ethnic-hatreds theory, which purports that so-called ethnic tribes distrust and hate those who do not belong to their same blood community. This is what George Kennan described as the "tendency to view the outsider, generally, with dark suspicion and to see the political-military opponent, in particular, as a fearful and implacable enemy to be rendered harmless only by total and unpitying destruction" (Kennan, 1996: 201). This theory has become a default explanation, as well as the most popular one, for everything that has occurred in the Balkans since 1989. It assumes that the causes of nationalism are psychological givens. People are inclined to trust only those of the same kin and to distrust foreigners. This structural predisposition toward the distrust of foreigners is all the more natural in rural and underdeveloped societies. In this case, nationalism should be associated with social contexts of poverty and underdevelopment, as well as with distrust of foreigners and minorities.

According to social-identity theory, negative perceptions of others as inferior to one's own serve the purpose of boosting a group's positive social identity (Tajfel, 1981; Brewer, 1987). Tajfel attributed the intensity of feelings over these matters to the challenge to one's self-esteem. Self-esteem comes to be associated with national identity through a variety of socializing experiences. Self-esteem was also important in the contact theory, elaborated by Allport, which assumed that individuals who enjoyed less contact with other ethnic groups should be more discriminative. Discriminative behavior is also implicit in the social-dominance theory, which postulates that every multiethnic society tends to produce a hierarchical assignment of groups with the one on top, closer to the nation (Sidanius and Pratto, 1998). In accordance, nation comes to be associated with the dominant group (the majority or the ruling elite). Therefore, it follows that this specific group would espouse more nationalism or patriotism.

Even though there are important differences among these theories, they tend to cluster around one hypothesis postulating that nationalism is only a form of in-group favoritism. The classic authoritarian personality theory, on the other hand, dealt more with individuals than groups. For convenience, its argument can be separated in two parts. The first asserts that discriminative behavior is part of a syndrome which also includes rigidity, paranoia, conspiratorial thinking, and low self-esteem, all conclusions which emerged from applying the authoritarianism questionnaire. The other speculates that the causes for this syndrome lie in an individual's personality, a product of very early socialization, and therefore impossible to change. The personality aspect is not testable in a research design such as mine and has been the object of disputes ever since it was first published. The syndrome aspect, namely, the empirical finding that these psychological features tend to be found together rather than separately, is of great interest for research on nationalism in Eastern Europe.

To test these hypotheses, each survey had at least one statement measuring trust toward one's kin versus trust toward foreigners. Statements included: "Only your kin can be trusted," "Only your ethnic group can be trusted," and "Most people can be trusted," as well as questions on household welfare and regional development. The longer Romanian and Serbian questionnaires included a scale of trust in other ethnic groups (from one to ten), and, in Kosovo, a measurement of social distance as perceived by Kosovars toward every neighboring group was included. These were used as ethnocentrism scales.

The next category of explanations emerges from regional and postcommunist studies. The reappearance of nationalism on the ruins of communism led several analysts to allege a causal link between them. As synthesized in the phrase of Adam Michnik, "Nationalism is the last word of Communism. A final attempt to find a social basis for dictatorship. Kim Il Sung, Castro, but also Milosevic, the leaders of Serbia's communists, are good illustrations of that" (Michnik, 1991: 565). This political hypothesis sees nationalism not as a remote inheritance of historical conflicts and structural distrust, but as a purely residual phenomenon, essentially communist determined, a form of authoritarianism that emerged because of communist socialization. The source of this idea can be found, unexpectedly, even in historical theory, for instance in the Greenfeld argument (1992), which alleges that far from being cosmopolitan, communism was founded on the old dichotomy between East and West, and contributed to forging a national Russian identity in opposition to the West. So one explanation is that communism might have laid the grounds for nationalism through its anti-Western socialization. The second places the blame on communist ideology, a worldview that explained everything, and whose failure left, in Michnik's words, an "ideological vacuum." Combined with the challenge the transition poses to identity, this vacuum generates the insecurity that leads large masses to adopt nationalist and populist ideologies. This implies that people ultimately found some use for communist ideology, as a provider of identity and even a stabilizer of mood. If valid, this hypothesis implies that an association exists between communist ideology and nationalism.

An alternative powerful explanation, although more difficult to test in a public opinion research design, regards the role of former communist leaders. Many nationalist leaders, including Milosevic, Tudjman, and Vadim Tudor of Romania, were active in the communist regime either as apparatchiks or propagandists. Yet it is also true that Tudjman, as well as Vladimir Meciar in Slovakia, had long fallen from the grace of the Communist Party by 1989. In addition, other nationalist leaders, such as Gheorge Funar in Romania or Hungary's Viktor Orban did not have a connection to the Communist Party. Former communist leaders were accused of having unleashed nationalism to mobilize popular support and ensure their control, even when their communist party was clearly losing popular appeal. To do so, these leaders unscrupulously employed the entire arsenal of communist manipulation to attain their goal of preserving power (Gordy, 1999; Mungiu-Pippidi, 1999; Gallagher, 2000, in Pridham and Gallagher). This explanation must somehow combine with another. No matter how manipulative and shrewd a leader, his message must find some echo in the public opinion to get votes. In Slovakia's parliamentary elections in 2002, Meciar garnered the largest number of votes, even when he was in the opposition and no longer in control of the party propaganda apparatus. Funar and Tudor were always in the opposition but received many votes. In Romania, Funar won the race for the mayor of Cluj, the capital of Transylvania, three times, and Tudor managed to enter the second round of the presidential election in 2000 (although he never received more than a third of the vote). Bulgaria is the only country where a strong nationalist leader has not emerged during the last decade, and the postcommunist party recorded good electoral scores without resorting to nationalism. There seems to be evidence, in other words, that, in many countries, communist leaders and successor communist parties used the former propaganda arsenal to instrument the passage from "enemy of the regime" to "enemy of the nation." The challenge is how to separate their personal appeal from their ideological appeal. But surely one should be able, at least, to find a positive correlation between nationalism and the popularity of certain leaders who openly promote intolerant and xenophobic attitudes.

Finally, communism may have laid the grounds for nationalism by creating an authoritarian syndrome of its own. Ordinary life under communism, in addition to the heavy repression of dissent and blame on the West for economic hardship, produced shortages of essential goods. This made people compete for everything, from food to toilet chapter. As a result, even neighbors and friends were perceived as either competitors or informants of the secret service, making paranoid attitudes thrive. Similarly, the total inability to shape one's life, fully regulated by the communist state, is likely to have left scars, such as fatalistic and passive political attitudes. Socialization in this environment meant promotion of social envy and distrust, paranoid and selfish attitudes. By authoritarianism, I understand, therefore, a complex of closely correlated attitudes, a syndrome not so different than the one described by the authors of the authoritarian personality, involving antidemocratic beliefs, passive and fatalistic attitudes about participation in politics, and the propensity to perceive enemies and blame them for the country's problems. The richer questionnaires used in Romania and Serbia allowed for building more complex factors, but all the questionnaires included at least one identical proxy to test this hypothesis.

In the country-by-country analysis, three other important variables were used to test Michnik's "blame communism" hypothesis: self-assessed ideology (placement on a left-right scale), appreciation of communism as a good idea poorly implemented, and trust in the political system (factor score of trust in parliament, government, president, and prime minister). This entire group of variables can account for a generic residual communism hypothesis. If this hypothesis is correct, nationalism should be associated with antidemocratic and paranoid attitudes, low trust in politics, and a positive evaluation of communism.

The third group of explanations regards the context. Basic nationalistic attitudes are present at high levels in all these countries, but nationalism mobilizes majorities and leads to violence only in some countries. It is likely that the triggers and stakes, which vary in the specific environment, account for the different outcomes, even if attitudes are rather uniform. People are mobilized when the stakes increase, for example when new borders are to be drawn, rights already secured are denied, and so forth. In other words, they are mobilized by the perception of threat. Threat varied greatly among the countries surveyed. Serbia, menaced by separatism from Kosovo and Montenegro, and Kosovo, uncertain of its final status, compare against Hungary and Slovakia, neither of which have threats to their borders or stability, and Bulgaria or Romania, whose minorities are peaceful and do not have a delimited territory they can secede with. All the surveys had open questions on the main problems and challenges faced by the countries in transition. The secession of Kosovo from Serbia, Kosovo's final status, as well as Romanian fears of a war similar to that in the former Yugoslavia, came about spontaneously. Nothing of the sort was invoked in Bulgaria or Slovakia. A follow-up question to measure the intensity of the threat mentioned was then added. This accounts for our threat variable. Also under context, one should test the frustration with transition hypothesis, which has also been popular in literature. Poverty, unemployment, and the serious decline in living standards since the communist era are all thought to enhance ethnic competition and nationalism.

To test these hypotheses, models were designed using the nationalism factor as a dependent variable for every country, including Hungary and Slovakia, where its composition was slightly different. As a general rule, all scales included elements of territorial nationalism, attitude toward the West, and cultural nationalism. Attitude toward minorities were included everywhere except Hungary, which practically does not have minorities. While final multivariate models emerging from linear regressions are outlined in table 5, the history of each model based on testing predictors separately is of equal importance.

"State" Nationalists ...

Nationalism depends little on social status. Milosevic's voters in Serbia were more likely to be poor, but no other social structure variables predict if a Serb will turn nationalistic or not. In the region in general, nationalists are more likely to be recruited among the poor, old, and less educated, with males (in status models only) more nationalistic than women. Nationalists are more likely to come from the ranks of unemployed only in Slovakia, and from villagers in Bulgaria and, to some extent, in Serbia (status model only). But overall, social status items explained little of nationalism. Not only were many findings not robust and disappeared in more complex variants of the models (see table 4), but they also explained little of the variance, even with media consumption added. The effects of the media are visible in the Romanian, Bulgarian, and Kosovar models, and they tend to be positive, despite the difficulty of interpreting them in the absence of some indication of the specific media people watch or read. As a general rule, individuals who read more political reports in newspapers tend to be lower rather than higher on the nationalism scale, but this variable should be seen more as an indicator of individual political sophistication than of the press's influence. There was also no association between having been a member of the Communist Party and having a nationalistic attitude. However, as both common sense and social-dominance theory predict, members of the ethnic majority are more likely to have nationalistic views.

Structural psychological factors were also disappointing as predictors. The main common variable tested in all models was interpersonal trust, measured as agreement with the statement "only your kin can be trusted." In bivariate models, there was an association between believing that only one's kin is trustworthy and the nationalism scale. When more controls were added, however, this variable lost its significance in all the models, except Romania and Kosovo, where it explained little of variance but was robust enough to feature in the final model. The scale of trust (ethnocentrism) factor turned up as a predictor in the final models for Romania and Serbia, but also explained little (see table 4). Unlike interpersonal trust, a basic variable, the trust factor indicating ethnocentrism, built either from trust in other ethnic groups (Romania and Serbia) or social distance toward others (Kosovo) is in itself a complex indicator, needing separate explanation. Finally, structural factors combined with status controls in the Romanian and Serbian models, the most complex, including interpersonal trust and trust in other ethnic groups, accounted for less than a third of the total variance explained.

The next group made of residual communism elements—authoritarianism, ideology, and trust in politics—accounted, when added to status controls, for almost all the variance and was very significant in each and every country model. People who believe that ideology is irrelevant for their political choice or are ignorant on ideology altogether (Hungary) are likely to score higher on the nationalism scale in every country in the status models. This finding was robust enough to feature in the final models for Hungary, Romania, and Bulgaria. The authoritarian syndrome, formed by paranoid attitudes, endorsement of undemocratic alternatives, and fatalism ("people cannot influence politics"), is present in almost every country and is the most powerful predictor where tested as such. Similarly, low trust in the political system (factor scores of trust in the executive and legislative branches) predicts nationalism consistently across all countries. In Hungary, where the questionnaire was slightly different, the most consistent predictor among residual attitudes was the feeling that no political party represents the views of the respondent. In Slovakia, where the questionnaire was shorter, the two existing components of authoritarianism were tested separately, and both political fatalism and rejection of democracy turned out to be powerful predictors. It becomes evident that nationalism is more about politics and democracy than about ethnic attitudes.

Context factors vary greatly from one country to another, as we would expect. Threat is a very powerful predictor in the Serbian models and a weak one in the Kosovar and Romanian models. In the words of Dostoevsky's hero Stavroguine, "one needs a rabbit to cook a rabbit dish, and one needs a God to believe in God." In Serbia, the rabbit is quite big—the threat of separatist Kosovo and Montenegro. In Romania, it is hardly enough to make an appetizer, and in Kosovo, the international peacekeeping force acts as a strong deterrent of fears. The subjective threat varies from one region and one individual to another, but it originates in an actual threat.

Comparing one's present living standards to communist times ("frustration with transition") emerges as a determinant, especially in Hungary and Slovakia, the better off countries in the panel, which enjoyed better living standards even during communism. But it is also a determinant in Bulgaria, the poorest country in the panel. Leaders were tested only in the countries where they ran in elections under nationalistic programs, and in bivariate models, they turned up as predictors. This was the case for Tudor in Romania, and for both Kostunica and Seselj in Serbia. These models explained very little, however, and when adding additional controls, trust in leaders lost significance. On the contrary, when explaining trust in leaders as a dependent variable, the nationalism scale featured as a predictor in all models with status controls.

Table 4

Determinants of Nationalism

Predictors	Bulgaria	Romania	Serbia	Slovakia	Hungary	Scales for independent variables; for dependents, see appendix 1
Status						
Education	–.076*	–.076*	NS	–.064*	–.168***	Below 8 grades (1); secondary (2); high school and vocational (3); university (4)
Wealth	–.065*	NS	–.086**	–.114***	–.109***	Individual income last month. For Slovakia, subjective assessment of household economic situation from very poor (1) to very good (4)
Age	.080**	.067**	NS	.063*	.100 ***	4 steps: 18–30 (1); 30–45 (2); 45–60 (3); over 60 (4)
Village	.126***	N/S	N/S	N/S	NS	Village (1), else (0)
Majority member	.167***	.238***		.322***	NS	Belong to majority (1), else (0)
Structural-psychological						
Trust only your kin	NS	.081**		NS	NS	Likert scale, from strongly disagree (1) to strongly agree (5)
Ethnocentrism	—	.072**	–.277***	—	—	Factor score of ratings on a scale of 1 (least trust) to 10 of attitude toward other ethnic groups
Residual communism						
Authoritarianism and proxies	079**	.454***	.354***	.096**	NS	Higher scores mean higher authoritarianism; Principal component for Romania and Serbia, see appendix 2; Disagreement with the statement "democracy is the best system of government" for Bulgaria and Slovakia on a scale from 1 to 4; Agreement with the statement "politics was better during communism" for Hungary

Predictors	Bulgaria	Romania	Serbia	Slovakia	Hungary	Scales for independent variables; for dependents, see appendix 1
Ideology irrelevant	.136***	.061*	NS	NS	.111***	Dichotomous, ideology does not matter or does not know (1), else (0)
Trust in politics	–.110***	NS	–.085**	–.163***	—	Factor score of trust in government, parliament, president, and prime minister. Coded from minimum trust (1) to maximum (4)
Communism good idea	.151***	.059*	NS	—	—	Likert scale, from disagreement (1) to full agreement (5)
No party represents views					.141***	Likerst scale, from disagreement (1) to full agreement (5)
					Context	
Threat		NS	.102***	—	—	For Serbia, Likert scale, from no threat (1) to important threat persists (5). For Romania, Likert scale, for approval with statement "Do you think something similar to what happened in the former Yugoslavia could occur in Romania?" from disagreement (1) to full agreement (5)
Frustration with transition	.093***	NS	—	.114***	.085**	Life compared to communist times. From better now (1) to better during communism (4)
Media consumption	–.200 ***	NS	NS	–.066 *	NS	Factor score of following politics on television, newspapers, radio. The higher values indicate more frequent use.
Nationalist leaders		NS	NS			Trust in Seselj and Kostunica for Serbia (Likert scale). Dichotomous variable (preference for Vadim Tuodr) for Romania with Tudor (1) and else (0)
Adjusted R square	27	39.5	35.3	18.4	12.8	

Legend: Entries are standardized coefficients (betas).

*** significant at 0.000;

** significant at 0.00;

* significant at <0.05–0.00;

NS: nonsignificant item.

Nationalism in Hungary and Slovakia, the two Central European countries, is clearly grounded in the current performance of regimes in addition to the authoritarian legacies of communism. Unlike Bulgaria and especially Romania, which could be considered totalitarian regimes during the communist era, Hungary and Slovakia, as well as Serbia, enjoyed variants of goulash communism, a softer version of that political system. The discontent with the political class, with politicians as well as institutions, and the feeling that politics do not address one's problems is common in all these countries and feeds nationalism. The contrary is not true: the nationalism scale does not turn out a determinant in models predicting political trust, which is determined by personal experience with governance. It seems, therefore, that distrust and disappointment with politics and politicians feeds nationalism, not the other way around. When deconstructing the more complex predictors of authoritarianism and distrust in other groups, one discovers a stronger social determinism. The authoritarian and the distrustful tend to be worse off, inactive, less educated, and old. Trust in other ethnic groups proves, when treated as a dependent variable, to be influenced by self-esteem, more in Romania than in Serbia, but significantly in both. Individuals with more self-esteem tend to show more trust in other ethnic groups, whether minorities or neighbors. In both Romania and Serbia, trust in other ethnic groups improves with education, but is not dependent on age and income. Personal acquaintance with at least one individual from the main rival group increases trust in Romania and decreases social distance in Kosovo. Contact does not discriminate between those with low trust and those with high trust in Serbia, where an individual's personal experience with others may be overridden by recent collective experiences. Psychological theory of ethnic conflict seems to work better when explaining ethnocentrism, a more basic attitude based on social comparison between groups, than nationalism, a complex social representation of self, country, and world.

Communism's most important legacy in regard to nationalism is therefore neither the readiness of leaders to make unscrupulous use of propaganda tools for their political survival (such leaders can be found anywhere) nor the unfreezing of so-called structural hatreds among nationalities long in conflict. It is the communist socialization of people into a culture of distrust and the strong enforcement of conformity, collectivism, and social envy, all of which foster nationalism. The object seems less important than the need it answers, which is a need to assign blame rather than provide identity. This overall distrustful attitude (nationalists are more suspicious toward minorities, more conspiracy-minded, and more likely to believe that the transition did not change much but enriched the same people as did the communist regime) is combined with the perception of ethnic conflicts with other groups. Nationalism is a general distrustful and paranoiac orientation that does not really discern among its objects, which could include neighboring countries, minorities, the outside world, politicians, and even the winners of the transition, who could be conationals. The focus of postcommunism nationalism is poor.

The nationalistic syndrome does not explain why some people are mobilized to vote for nationalistic leaders and others are not, since those who vote for radical nationalists, such as Seselj in Serbia or Tudor in Romania, number fewer than the amount of people in the nationalist group. What differs among nationalists, making more than half of them more passive than the others? A look at the constituencies of the two leaders mentioned may provide some answers.

Table 5

Determinants of Voting for Radical Nationalists

Determinants	Vojislav Seselj		Vadim Tudor	
	Standardized coefficients (betas) Scales and wording		Standardized coefficients Scales and wording	
Income	NS	Cash individual income last month	NS	Cash individual income last month
Education	.139***	Below 8 grades (1); secondary (2); high school and vocational (3); university (4)	NS	Below 8 grades (1); secondary (2); high school and vocational (3), university (4)
Age	NS	4 steps: 18–30 (1); 30–45 (2); 45–60 (3); over 60 (4)	>45 1.14*	4 steps: 18–30 (1); 30–45 (2); 45–60 (3); over 60 (4)
Male	NS	Dichotomous, male (1)	1.76*	Dichotomous, male (1)
Village	.073**	Dichotomous, village (1); rest (0)	1.76*	Dichotomous, village (1); rest (0)
Active	NS	Actively employed (1); else (0)	−.405**	Actively employed (1); else (0)
Interest in politics	.239**	Factor score of reading, watching, and discussing political news from never (1) to daily (4)	NS	Factor score of reading, watching, and discussing political news from never (1) to daily (4)
Nationalism (variant 1)	.192***	Index, see appendix 2	NS	Index, see appendix 2
Adj. R²	.071		—	
Authoritarianism (variant 2)	.073***	Index, see appendix 2	.706**	Index, see appendix 2
Adjusted R²	.087		.10	

Legend: For Seselj, linear regression, with dependent trust measured from 1 to 4. For Tudor, logistic regression, with vote preference as dependent (1 vote, 0 other candidates).

*** significant at 0.000; ** significant at 0.00; * significant at <0.05–0.00; NS: nonsignificant item.

Social status explanatory models of the preference for Seselj or Tudor illustrate some similarities, as well as some important differences. Seselj's voters are less educated. In the case of Tudor, education does not discriminate among voters and non-voters. Income also does not predict preference. Tudor's voters are more likely male and reside in villages; those employed, rather than the retired or unemployed, are less likely to prefer him. Seselj's followers are more likely to be recruited among those who follow politics closely, while, in the case of Tudor, media consumption makes no difference in his acceptance or rejection. The most important finding, however, is not based on the social structure of these constituencies. The scale of nationalism, although a predictor with basic status controls only, loses significance when tested in more complex models in the case of Tudor, and accounts for less variance in the case of Seselj than the scale of authoritarianism, which is also a powerful predictor in the Tudor model. The conclusion is thus that authoritarianism is at least as important as nationalism when predicting support for national mobilization. Authoritarianism and nationalism are of course correlated, and authoritarianism is a determinant of nationalism. Still, when tested separately, authoritarianism proves more powerful in explaining the vote for radical nationalists. Both leaders are actually running on programs that are overtly antidemocratic, in addition to being nationalistic.

And State-Seeking Ones...

After this review of nationalism among majorities, those who have a state of their own, the time has come to examine Kosovo more closely. Kosovo is a different story, requiring different treatment. In the Brubaker triad, Kosovo stands as a national minority, similar to Hungarians in Serbia, Romania, or Slovakia, and Turks in Bulgaria. Yet unlike these minorities, due to various historical circumstances (Malcolm, 1998), Kosovars became concentrated in one region. Although formally a part of Serbia, this region enjoyed a status similar to that of a republic in the former Yugoslavia prior to 1989. It was later stripped of its autonomous status, and the reaction to that led to the escalation that ultimately brought the recent war. Due to their history of conflict with a communist Yugoslav state dominated by a Serb policy, Kosovars built a separate society within the borders of the communist state, an island with informal institutions—from schools to courts—substituted to the formal ones. Kosovo is now an international protectorate and a would-be nationalizing state itself, with a shrinking Serb minority and international peacekeepers standing between what is left of the minority and the Albanian majority. While Kosovars definitely aspire to a state of their own and will not settle for anything less, they do not have one yet. And while Kosovars and their institutions have opinions on the province's relationship with the West and a sense of what Kosovar citizenship means, at this moment, they do not set their own domestic or international policies. Because of this, the four-step nationalism scale used for consolidated states does not fit Kosovo well. Kosovars do not have an official language, and even their borders are not yet formally their own. While I did test three of the components of the scale separately, a model to explain Kosovar nationalism, *a state-seeking nationalism of a former minority*, called for a different approach. Results from the survey in Kosovo show how an embattled minority can transform itself, given the proper conditions, into a nationalizing state. Presently, only a small minority (18 percent) of Kosovars are interested in reuniting with Albania. Instead most want their own state protected, but not patronized, by the international community. Many also aspire to reunite with the Albanians in Macedonia. (Our respondents indicated Macedonia as the reason they agreed with the question asking whether Kosovo has territories in other countries.) Few Kosovars see any chance for cohabitation between Serbs and Albanians in the future. Nor do Kosovars—Serbs and Albanians alike—aspire to the solution preferred by the international community, a loose confederation on the model of Serbia and Montenegro, with Kosovo as the third element. From the entire sample, including Serbs, less than 1 percent of both ethnic groups endorsed this solution (see table 6). This seems to back the argument that the conflict is between states and minorities rather than between ethnic groups (Caplan and Pfeiffer, 1996).

Table 6
Kosovo: Attitudes Toward Cohabitation and the State's Future

Agreement with ...	[%]
Members of one's own ethnic group are more trustworthy than other people	67
The conflict between Kosovars and Serbs still exists	77
Blame for the conflict belongs with Serbs (including Serbs from Kosovo, Serbia, and Serbian political leaders)	89
History matters for present lives (agree fully and to a great extent)	77
Parts of other countries should belong to us (fully agree only)	79
Good Serbian-Albanian cohabitation is still possible in the future (agree fully and to a great extent)	27
It is time to run own affairs (agree fully and to a great extent)	80
Independence in the present borders is the best solution	74
Unification with Albania is the best solution	18

While the Kosovars' situation as a minority protected by an international peace force and governed by an international government is exceptional, their situation as a minority with a clear territorial base is far from uncommon in Eastern Europe, and compares well with many similar enclaves in the former Soviet Union. Even Kosovo's symbolic status is not singular. Transylvania plays a similar symbolic role for Hungary, even though the majority population has been Romanian since the eighteenth century. Macedonia is in a comparable situation toward Greece. What makes Kosovo unusual is its long history of dissent and its recent parallel life within the communist Yugoslav state. Starting with the demonstrations in 1968, Kosovars had a high awareness that the political arrangements were not equitable to them when compared to the proper Yugoslav republics. Most Albanians in both Kosovo and Macedonia organized their existence separately from, and at times in opposition to, the state, especially after 1970. The legacy of this existence on the borderlands of the communist society is still apparent in the difficulty of making sense of demographic data in Kosovo. For example, high numbers report having graduated from ten classes of school, but there is no way to check this, due to the informal status of the schools. Similarly, income figures from Kosovo are unreliable, as well over a third of the active population is unemployed, registered work contracts are not the norm, and remittances from abroad are the main source of income for many families. Due to the high birth rate, the population is young, an unusual feature, as Kosovo's neighbors share the West European pattern of aging populations with a large share of the population retired. Not only ethnicity and religion (Muslim), but also demography and culture, make Kosovars different from many in the region. Even other Muslims, such as Bosniacs, do not share their clan-type organization and large families. Kosovars make a distinctive society, one differing not by a few traits exaggerated by nationalists (such as the difference between the Serbian and Croatian languages), but by many features. When measuring social distance between Kosovars and other ethnic groups, the results are striking. Most Kosovars would not want to share a town with any Slavs, regardless if Serbs, Montenegrins, or Macedonians. They are better disposed toward Americans and Germans and show moderate acceptance toward Bosnians. But they strongly disapprove of any marriage outside their ethnic group. A representation of average ethnic tolerance toward each group (consisting of acceptance of others through sharing a town, immediate neighborhood, workplace, and marrying into one's family, each given equal weight) is reproduced in table 7.

The results are very eloquent. They show a tolerance of almost 100 percent toward Albanians, followed by large tolerance toward Germans and Americans, groups known mostly by Kosovars who have worked abroad and also as members of the international community working in Kosovo. The acceptance of these two control groups is rather high, but the likeliness that Germans or Americans any will settle in

Kosovo is, of course, low to zero. Of groups living in close proximity, Bosnians fare better, being considered acceptable to share both town and neighborhood, while the Roma are acceptable to share town or village only. Acceptance of the presence of any of the southern Slavs—be they Macedonians, Montenegrins, or Serbs—is very low, even when it comes to sharing the same town or village. Even though these three groups may consider themselves different and have taken steps to live in separate states in the past decade, for Kosovars, there is little difference among them. Social distance toward any potential neighbors likely to share the premises with Kosovars is therefore quite high. This is a closed community. Answers to the question asking if a conflict among Serbs and Albanians continues confirm the high perception of conflict. Minorities, such as Serbs (96 percent), and Bosnians (94 percent) answer affirmatively, compared to the slightly more moderate perception of Albanians (76 percent "yes," and 9 percent "no").

Table 7
Ethnic Acceptance in Kosovo

Ethnic group	Mean	Standard deviation
Albanian	3.90	0.49
American	2.50	1.27
German	2.42	1.30
Bosnian	2.08	1.47
Roma	1.18	1.40
Macedonian	0.75	1.20
Montenegrin	0.96	1.31
Serb	0.66	1.10

Legend: Social distance scale reversed, with 4 as maximum acceptance and 0 as minimum acceptance.

Table 8

Determinants of Nationalism in Kosovo

Predictors	Want own state	Scale nationalism	Ethnic acceptance	Cohabitation optimists	Scales and wording
Welfare	NS	NS	NS	.107**	Scale from minimal satisfaction (1) to maximum (5) with the economic situation of household
Education	NS	NS	NS	-.082**	Did not finish 10 grades (1); else (0)
Age	-.136*** (under 35)	NS	NS	NS	4 steps; 16–25 (1), 24–35 (2), 35–45 (3); over 45 (4)
Urban	-.073*	NS	-.115*	NS	Urban (1), else (0)
Regional development	NS	NS	NS	NS	Cumulative scale built by simple addition of facilities in one's community, from 1 to 12.
Threat	NS	126***	—	—	Likert scale, from no threat (1) to important threat (5)
Trauma	.058*	.124*	NS	NS	Dichotomous violence during the war in one's community (1); else (0)
Nationalism scale	NS	—	—	-.104***	Factor score, see appendix 2
Tolerance Serbs	-.099**	NS	—	396**	Social distance scale, with maximum acceptance (4) and minimum acceptance (0)
Ethnic tolerance	—	NS	—	—	Factor score, principal component from distance toward Serbs, Bosnians, Montenegrins, and Macedonians; KMO = 0.74; from minimal tolerance to maximum
Acquainted with Serbs	—	—	.135***	—	Dichotomous, knows at least one Serb (1), else (0)

Blames Serbs	.099**	—	—	—	Dichotomous, blame attribution of the past violence, blame of Kosovar Serbs, Serbs from Serbia, and Serb leaders aggregated and coded (1), else (0)
History matters	—	—	—	.095***	History matters for present lives, from agreement (1) to disagreement (4)
Trust only your kin	NS	.060*	.069**	−.082** (trust only your ethnic group)	Likert scale, from 1 to 4, 4 is maximum trust with no intermediate step
Variance explained [%]	14.5	4.7	6.5	20.1	

Legend: Multiple linear regression models, except "want own state" (logistic regression, dependent dichotomous).

Cohabitation optimism was worded as "Do you think Serbs and Albanians will be able to live together peacefully in Kosovo from now on?"

*** significant at 0.000;

** significant at 0.00;

* significant at <0.05–0.00;

NS: nonsignificant item.

Figures are standardized regression coefficients.

Using ethnic tolerance as a dependent variable in a multiple regression model, we find that higher tolerance is associated with political sophistication (regular reading of political reports in newspapers), residence in larger settlements rather than villages, and distrust of strangers. The most important determinant, however, is acquaintance with at least one member of the other ethnic group. People who have known a Serb personally are more likely to show acceptance than those who do not. Social distance toward Serbs predicts attitude toward independence: those with higher rates of tolerance are less likely to prefer independence. Those who do prefer independence, moreover, also blame only Serbs for the degradation of the reciprocal relationship. *Villagers and older people are significantly more in favor of independence than unification with Albania.* An important determinant of both nationalism and opting for independence is past violence in one's community during the war. Perception of a current threat is associated with people high on the nationalism scale. Finally, and most importantly, optimism about future cohabitation, though confined to a narrow section of the population, is associated with superior wealth and education, lower scores on the nationalism scale, and more trust beyond the borders of one's kin. Regional development and political trust did not turn out as predictors. *On the whole, Kosovar nationalism seems deeply rooted in recent history, with the gradual separateness of the community from the official state, followed by the trauma caused by the war.* At this point, it is impossible to discern if hostility toward Serbs is due to the war trauma and the preceding years of discrimination or is a more archaic attitude opposing Slavs and Albanians. The attitude toward other Slavs, such as Montenegrins and Macedonians, suggest that Albanians do not get along with any Slavs. But it is also true that each of these groups had its own republic in the former Yugoslavia, in which Albanians were still at the bottom of social hierarchy. As social-dominance theory predicts, the group in this lower position has little to no loyalty toward the state and its other constituents.

Conclusion: Nationalism as Ideology and Nationalism as Pathology

What emerges from the two previous sections is the confirmation of the idea that nationalisms, rather than nationalism, is what we are dealing with. They have much in common but many differences as well. One variety, the most widespread in the postcommunist world, is conformist nationalism, the nationalism of majorities who identify themselves with their states, have high rates of residual communism, and feel threatened by those who are different, especially when those people pose some challenge to the state and push for political or legal changes. This includes Brubaker's nationalizing states as well as homelands such as Hungary. The second variety is one that characterizes minorities, of which Kosovo is the extreme case. This brand of nationalism is also, in many ways, a legacy of communism, but it is also closer to minority nationalisms in Western Europe, sharing their main feature of development in opposition to the state. To resist communist conformism, strongly promoted by communist states, ethnic minorities retreated into their communities, and their social distance toward other groups grew. Their nationalism looks less political and more psychological because they have lived outside politics for so long. Similarities are remarkable, however, in the models of countries that are proper states. Throughout the postcommunist world, Balkans or not, the communist legacy, more than anything else, seems to drive the adherence to the nationalistic ideology. Communism was, with some exceptions (Romania, Albania, and North Korea) a universalistic ideology, preaching internationalism and brotherhood among socialist countries. As a result, its strong linkage with nationalism in every country is, to some extent, surprising. Yet this is not the case when we examine the residual communist attitudes one by one. The type of political attitudes fostered by communism—conformity, distrust, fatalism, a political culture where the individual is a subject—are all excellent grounds for nationalism. Collectivism (the idea that "communism is a good idea badly put into practice") is associated with both nationalistic and antidemocratic attitudes, overriding freedom and individualism. Similarly, the rejection of politics in its traditional sense, of the left-right spectrum, is a communist leftover, which feeds directly into nationalism. This socializes people into autocracy and conformity. Because of all this, communism laid the grounds for the nationalism of the nineties.

Due to its positive association with political fatalism and distrust in politics, nationalism emerges from our models as *a substitute ideology, a form of distinctive political identity*. Frustration and helplessness over the difficult transition, basic distrust in the outside world, lack of proper political information, and the habit of having one's political thinking done by others all combine with residual collectivism, a collectivism so basic it does not identify with the left. Nationalism is the ideology of non-ideologues, a form of political assertiveness of the less informed and more frustrated, popular because it puts the blame on foreigners or social groups viewed as secretive or occult-like, reactive because it draws on the real frustrations of transition and the presence of threats. But most of all, its essence is residual, as it draws on those with communist attitudes, authoritarianism, and nostalgia for the former regime.

The model in figure 2 sums up these findings and places them in the larger social context. An individual's personal status, such as the number of years lived under the communist regime, education, and the opportunities to be socialized in a larger world (determined by personal income and the region or place of residence) shapes his or her attitude as a rigid authoritarian or a more open-minded democrat, as well as the propensity to trust or distrust. The complex of attitudes related to communist socialization, labeled residual communism, has the strongest influence in determining nationalism. A weaker role is played by more basic psychological factors, such as reticence to trust foreigners and perception of other ethnic groups as inferior to one's own, grounded in an individual self-esteem. But these two groups of factors combined still need a specific context to produce nationalism, instead of, say, left-wing populism. Each and every one of the countries surveyed has these conditions, as they all have a national issue, be it minorities perceived as separatist, neighbors suspected of being unsettled with borders, or conationals living in neighboring states as minorities. As such, each has a perceived threat.

Figure 2
A Model of Nationalism

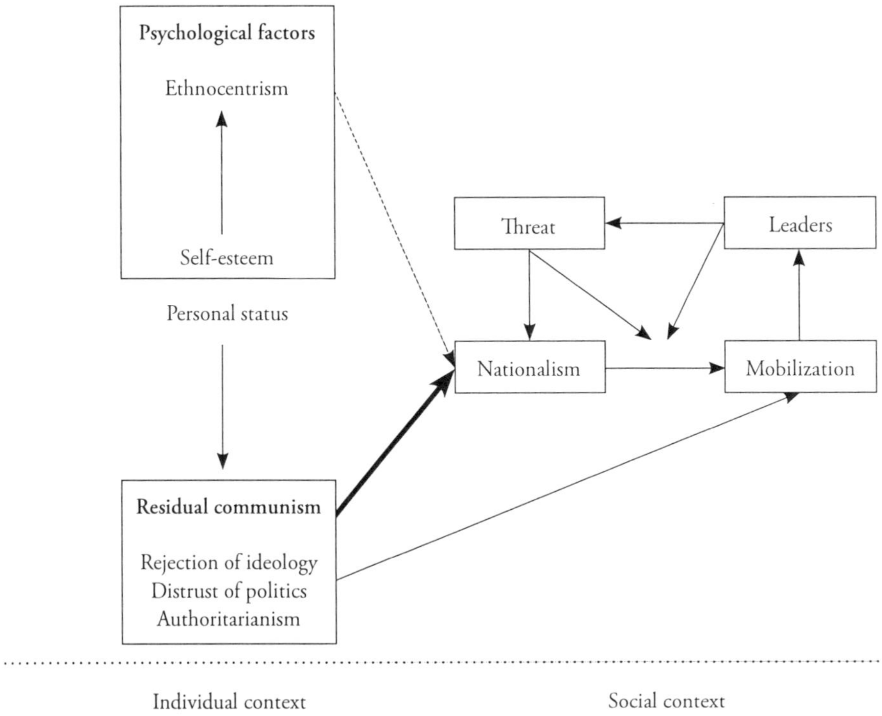

Individual context   Social context

Once this considerable mass of nationalistic attitudes is known to exist, the issue of mobilization of passive individual attitudes into some form of actual social behavior—or, on the contrary, of preventing mobilization—becomes the crucial issue. And here is where leaders matter. Wherever we have basic nationalistic attitudes, leaders are bound to use them when everything else fails. In the case of Milosevic, this occurred when economic reforms failed to revive the communist economy. In other cases, it happened when leaders saw their popularity drop, or sometimes simply because the left and right positions were already occupied by other leaders. This is not to belittle their manipulative skills. Milosevic had an exceptionally favorable situation as a prime secretary of the Communist Party, and he was able to manipulate the circumstances to pass from this nonelected position to an elected one. But had he not enjoyed this privileged position, it is likely that another nationalist leader, from the ranks of the noncommunist opposition perhaps, would have tried successfully to capitalize on the generalized perception of threat in the aftermath of secessions shaking the former Yugoslavia. Attitudes and contexts together simply favor nationalist leaders over other leaders. But once empowered, they will call for further mobilization. They will increase the threat that empowered them in the first place.

Both former communists and political newcomers extensively relied on nationalistic rhetoric during the transition. The only parties that resisted this are the smaller liberal parties, which usually draw on urban and educated constituencies, such the late Zoran Djindjic's party in Serbia, former president Emil Constantinescu's party in Romania, the Slovakian Christian Democrats, Bulgaria's Liberal Party, and the Alliance of Free Democrats in Hungary. These parties have never formed the government, except in the framework of larger coalitions, which included at least one party drawing on nationalistic constituencies. By including these parties in the coalitions, nationalism was tamed. Moreover, in Bulgaria, Romania, and, more recently, Slovakia, parties representing the ethnic minority were also included in these broad coalitions. The experience of these three states, which are unitary states, illustrates that once an ethnic party is given a share of power in central and local governments, it becomes an important third actor in the game, making it more likely that parties from across the spectrum will consider some alliance with it. The positive experience of Bulgaria and Romania illustrated that even former communists, those whom Gallagher (1995) considers national communists, adopted such alliances with parties of minorities, originally initiated by liberals with antinationalistic constituencies. Of course, external conditionality and the EU accession process created a strong incentive for political elites to behave in such a liberal fashion. Nonetheless, in this way, even parties drawing on nationalistic constituencies were able to cheat their voters and contribute to liberalization. The contrary was true in the former Yugoslavia, where the stake was not sharing the state, but partitioning it. The manipulation of threat there allowed leaders to increase nationalism and to mobilize large numbers of followers to vote or even fight in the war. *Similar figures of public support for nationalistic attitudes can therefore lead to very different outcomes in different contexts.*

Context is essential for both basic nationalist attitudes and mobilization. If a threat is not present, or if there is a consensus among political elites that the manipulation of a threat is unacceptable (for instance, on the topic of European integration and national identity), grassroots nationalism may linger with little political consequence. The electoral outcome of mobilization also depends on the political status of politicians (it works better for members of the opposition in democracies and incumbents in autocracies) and the political alternatives. Whenever political alternatives are perceived as attractive and realistic (for example, European integration), nationalists lose elections to pro-European parties. In other words, there is considerable room for manipulation of electoral outcomes through the manipulation of contexts, that is, the reduction of threat and increase in incentives.

Nationalist and populist leaders fare well in the Balkans. But seeing the issues and the people, the question is actually why they do not fare even better. Not even Milosevic had absolute majorities. He benefited from the majority system when first elected through a popular vote, and he was never again able to win the support of more than relative majorities. In Bulgaria, no politician appeals to nationalism; such issues simply do not exist. In the second round of Romania's presidential election in 2000, the opposition to Tudor's returns in the first round led to an intense mobilization against his candidacy. As a result, in the second round, he garnered fewer votes. In that case, an extensive media campaign showed the public how a Tudor victory would affect the country's European accession, the main political project of domestic elites. The same happened in Slovakia, in the 2002 elections, when strong pressure from the international community determined that Meciar, a populist-nationalist leader, ended up as an isolated opposition politician, despite the fact that he received the largest share of the votes (although just 20 percent). Hungary's Viktor Orban showed his nationalist stripes during debate backing the Status Law, when he vowed to extend citizenship to all Hungarian-speakers in the region. Ultimately, he lost both the legislative and local elections, despite scoring high percentages of the vote.

Nationalism becomes dangerous when everything else, both politics and policy, fails. It is *preceded* by a perceived drop in political choices, even if later it itself subverts political choice. Where choice exists, grassroots nationalism is not powerful enough to compete with it. Invited to join Europe in 2004, both Slovakia and Hungary may retain nationalistic publics and politicians, but their importance is bound to decrease as the stake becomes minimal to nonexistent. If Romania and Bulgaria manage to stay on course of European integration, they are likely to follow the same path. However, as long as some voters still do not believe that politics works or the state can deliver the goods, discourses ranging from populism to nationalism through a spectrum of combinations will continue to appeal. Their importance will vary with the threat. It is larger in Serbia, minimal in Romania, and absent in Bulgaria.

The model pictured in this chapter is a model of banal nationalism. It was not designed to explain atrocities, as a survey is clearly not the tool to do that. The contribution of most people in creating exceptional circumstances is small—and is manifested mostly through voting nationalist in elections or referenda. Most people would not commit atrocities, although in any society there are groups who feel dispossessed and are aware of the opportunity of the spoils of ethnic war. The circumstances that empower such groups are beyond the scope of this chapter. The passive nationalists pictured in this chapter are not criminals, but they are insensitive to a certain category of crimes when committed in the name of their values. But is this blindness different from any other ideology? Nationalism is not more powerful than other ideologies. This is apparent in the many elections it loses, as well as in the bloody records of two other authoritarian ideologies—communism and fascism. To defeat nationalism, one has to manipulate contexts (from the political agenda to the political alternative) rather than people. Many of the region's nationalists, including Milosevic's voters, can recognize a good political choice when offered one.

References

Adorno, T.W., E. Frenkel-Brunswick, D. Levinson and R. Newitt-Stewart (1982) *The Authoritarian Personality.* New York: Norton.

Allport, G. (1954) *The Nature of Prejudice.* New York: Addison-Wesley.

Barry, B.M. (1987) "Nationalism" in *The Blackwell Enyclopaedia of Political Thought.* Oxford: Blackwell.

Becker, G.S. (1957) *The Economics of Discrimination.* Chicago: University of Chicago Press.

Breakwell, G.M. (1992) *Social Psychology of Identity and the Self Concept.* Surrey University Press.

Brewer, M.B. (1997) "The Social Psychology of Intergroup Relations: Can Research Inform Practice?" *Journal of Social Issues* 53(1): 197–211.

Brubaker, Rogers (1996) *Nationalism Reframed: Nationhood and the National Question in the New Europe.* Cambridge: Cambridge University Press.

Bunce, Valerie (1999) *Subversive Institutions: The Design and the Destruction of Socialism and the State.* Cambridge: Cambridge University Press.

Caplan, R. and J. Feffer (1996) *Europe's New Nationalism. States and Minorities in Conflict.* Oxford: Oxford University Press.

Chirot, Daniel and Martin Seligman (2001) *Ethnopolitical Warfare: Causes, Consequences, and Possible Solutions.* Washington, D.C.: American Psychological Association.

Colton, Timothy (1999) *The Russian Voter.* Cambridge: Harvard University Press.

Connor, Walker (1994) *Ethnonationalism, the Quest for Understanding.* New Jersey: Princeton University Press.

Deustch, Karl (1953) *Nationalism and Social Communication. An Inquiry into the Foundations of Nationality.* New York: Wiley.

ESI (2002) "Western Balkans 2004. Assistance, Cohesion and the New Boundaries of Europe." Berlin: European Stability Initiative, www.esiweb.online.de.

Forbes, H.D. (1997) *Ethnic Conflict: Commerce, Conflict and the Contact Hypothesis.* New Haven: Yale University Press.

Horowitz, Donald (1985) *Ethnic Groups in Conflict.* Berkeley: University of California Press.

——— (1998) *Structure and Strategy in Ethnic Conflict,* Chapter prepared for the Annual World Bank Conference on Development Economics, Washington, D.C., April 20–21.

International Crisis Group. "After Milosevic. A Practical Agenda for Lasting Balkans Peace," www.icg.org.

Gallagher, Tom (1995) *Romania after Ceausescu: The Politics of Intolerance.* Edinburgh: Edinburgh University Press.

Gellner, Ernest (1983) *Nation and Nationalism.* Oxford: Basil Blackwell.

Giles, H. and Saint-Jacques, B. (1992) *Language and Ethnic Relations.* NY: Pergamon Press.

Greenfeld, Liah (1992) *Nationalism: Five Roads to Modernity.* Cambridge: Harvard University Press.

Gordy, Eric D. (1999) *The Culture of Power in Serbia. Nationalism and the Destruction of Alternatives.* Philadelphia: Pennsylvania State University Press.

Katzenstein, Peter J., et al. (1996). "The Role of Theory in Comparative Politics. A Symposium." *World Politics* 48(1): 1–49.

Kaufman, Stuart J. (2001) *Modern Hatreds. The Symbolic Politics of Ethnic War.* Ithaca: Cornel University Press.

Kennan George F. (1996) *At a Century's Ending: Reflections, 1982–1995.* New York and London: W. W. Norton and Company.

King, Charles (2001) "The Benefits of Ethnic Wars. Understanding Eurasia's Unrecognized States." *World Politics* 53(4): 524–52.

Kohn, H. (1965) *Nationalism: Its Meaning and History.* Malabar: Robet E. Krieger.

Kuzio, Taras (2001) "Nationalizing States or Nation-Building? A Critical Review of the Theoretical Literature and Empirical Evidence." *Nations and Nationalism* 7(2): 135–54.

Los Angeles Times Mirror (1991) *The Pulse of Europe: A Survey of Political and Social Values and Attitudes.* Los Angeles, CA: Times-Mirror.

Luhtanen, R. and Crocker, J. (1992) "A Collective Self-esteem Scale: Self-evaluation of One's Social Identity." *Personality & Social Psychology Bulletin* 18 (2002): 302–18.

Malcolm, Noel (1994) *Bosnia. A Short History.* London: Macmillan.

—— (1998) *Kosovo. A Short History.* London: Macmillan.

Michnik, A. (1991) "Nationalism." *Social Research.* 58(4): 757–564.

Miller, W., S. White and P. Heywood (1998) *Values and Political Change in Postcommunist Europe.* London: Macmillan 1998.

Mungiu-Pippidi, Alina (1999) *Transilvania subiectiva* [Subjective Transylvania]. Bucharest: Humanitas.

Nodia, Ghia (1994), "Nationalism and Democracy." In Larry Diamond and Marc F. Plattner (eds.) *Nationalism, Ethnic Conflict, and Democracy.* Baltimore: The Johns Hopkins University Press, 3–22.

Olson, M. (2000) *Power and Prosperity. Outgrowing Communist and Capitalist Dictatorships.* New York: Basic Books.

Pavkovic, A., H. Koscharsky and A. Czarnota (1995) *Nationalism and Postcommunism. A Collection of Essays.* Aldershot: Dartmouth.

Pridham, Geoffrey and T. Gallagher (2000) *Experimenting with Democracy : Regime Change in the Balkans.* New York: Routledge.

Roeder, Philip (1999) "Peoples and States after 1989: The Political Costs of Incomplete National Revolutions." *Slavic Review* 58: 4 (Winter).

Sidanius, J. and F. Pratto (2000) *Social Dominance: An Intergroup Theory of Social Hierarchy and Oppression.* Cambridge: Cambridge University Press.

Smith (1991), A. D. *National Identity.* London: Penguin Books.

Smith, David (2002) "Framing the National Question in Central And Eastern Europe: A Quadratic Nexus?" in *The Global Review of Ethnopolitics* 2:1, 3–16.

Sowell, T (1981) *Markets and Minorities.* New York: Basic Books.

Sugar, Peter (1980) *Ethnic Diversity and Conflict in Eastern Europe.* Santa Barbara: ABC-Clio.

Sugar, Peter (ed.) (1995) *East European Nationalism in the 20th Century.* American University Press.

Tajfel, H. (1981) *Human Groups and Social Categories.* Cambridge: Cambridge University Press.

Verdery, K. (1991) *National Ideology Under Socialism: Identity and Cultural Politics in Ceausescu's Romania.* Berkeley and Los Angeles: University of California Press.

Woodward, S. (1996) *Balkan Tragedy.* Brookings.

Appendix 1

The Six Surveys

Country	Number questioned	Interview dates	Pollster
Bulgaria (all)	1,161	March 2000	CSD (Center for the Study of Democracy)
Hungary (all)	988	November–December 1993	MODUS
Kosovar Albanians	911	July–August 2002	RIINVEST (UNDP/EWR)
Romania (all)	1,001	October 2001	CURS-SAR (UNDP/EWR)
Serbia (Serbs)	1,200	May 2002	CPS (Center for Policy Studies)
Slovakia (all)	1,011	March 2000	GFK

Appendix 2

Scales for Nationalism and Authoritarianism

Nationalism	Principal component. Factor loadings		Keiser-Meyer-Olin
Slovakia	People who cannot speak the official language should not have the right to vote.	.764	KMO = .610
	No foreign country or international organization should be able to tell us how to run our own country.	.715	
	There are ethnic groups living within this country that pose a threat to our sovereignty and borders.	.688	
Bulgaria	There are ethnic groups living within this country that pose a threat to our sovereignty and borders.	.771	KMO = .710
	People who cannot speak the official language should not have the right to vote.	.689	
	There are parts of neighboring countries which should belong to us.	.756	
Serbia	There are parts of neighboring countries which should belong to us.	.756	KMO= .710
	People who cannot speak the official language should not have the right to vote.	.689	
	No foreign country or international organization should be able to tell Serbians how to run their own country.	.611	
Kosovo	There are parts of neighboring countries which should belong to us.	.651	KMO = .586
	No foreign country or international organization should be able to tell Kosovars how to run their own country.	.771	
	There are ethnic groups living within this country that pose a threat to our sovereignty and borders.	.692	
Hungary	People who cannot speak the official language should not have the right to vote.	.677	KMO = .550
	There is a risk of turning into a colony of West.	.597	
	There are parts of other countries which should belong to us.	.652	

Nationalism	Principal component. Factor loadings		Keiser-Meyer-Olin
Romania	There are ethnic groups living within this country that pose a threat to our sovereignty and borders.	.657	KMO =. 687
	People who cannot speak the official language should not have the right to vote.	.744	
	There are parts of neighboring countries which should belong to us.	540	
	No foreign country or international organization should be able to tell Romanians how to run their own country.	.759	

Legend: All variables initially coded with agreement (1) to disagreement (4) for analysis codes were reverted.

Authori-tarianism	Principal component. Factor loadings		Keiser-Meyer-Olin
Romania	Most people behave properly only when led by a strong hand.	.773	KMO =. 790
	The same people enjoy privileges now as during communism.	.509	
	Romania is a country both rich and beautiful but its many enemies prevent the country from achieving the prosperity it deserves.	.690	
	No point in holding election if the country is run by the same small group at the top.	.758	
Serbia	Serbia is a country both rich and beautiful but its many enemies prevent the country from achieving the prosperity it deserves.	.800	KMO =. 540
	Most people behave properly only when led by a strong hand.	.706	
	This country would be better off if inferior groups stayed in their place.	.554	

Legend: Authoritarianism questions adjusted after Adorno et al., 1982. Self-esteem question ("Sometimes I feel I am no good at all") adjusted from Luhtanen and Crocker, 1992.

III.
The 'Objective' Grounds
of Ethnic Conflict

The Economics of Disintegration and Reintegration: The Case of Yugoslavia

Vladimir Gligorov

Introduction

In my book, *Why Do Countries Break Up? The Case of Yugoslavia,* I argued that economic reasons were not among the main ones that led to Yugoslavia's disintegration (Gligorov (1994). In some of the follow-up work, I argued that economic reasons will not be among those that will drive the reintegration process of the political entities that emerged on the territory of the former Yugoslavia (Gligorov, 1995a, 1998, 2002). As the process of disintegration has not yet ended, and while the reintegration process is still just beginning, it might be interesting to revisit the issue of why countries break up and then turn around and make up. In this paper, I will begin by discussing some of the theoretical reasons that were advanced to explain the break up of countries and then examine the theoretical reasons for their integration. I will then review some of the economic developments in the newly established countries and other political entities on the territory of the former Yugoslavia. I will also look into the prospects for trade and investment integration as well as the various strategies of further integration, especially connected with the EU accession. I will close with a discussion of the role of states and markets in the region's future development.

Why Do Countries Break Up?

In the aftermath of Yugoslavia's break up, at least two economic explanations of disintegration have been advanced. The first is that disintegration is a consequence of the large economic diversity that existed in the country. More generally, there is a level of diversity beyond which the political integration does not make sense. In the case of the former Yugoslavia, it was often pointed out that, in terms of GDP per capita, the most developed region, Slovenia, was perhaps six or seven times richer, depending on the year in question, than Kosovo, least developed region. Table 1 gives an indication of regional differences in GDP per capita[1] between the states

---

1. Or rather Gross Social Product per capita, which is something similar to the Gross Material Product used in other socialist countries.

and provinces in the former Yugoslavia over a long period of time and among the newly established states (as well as the provinces of Vojvodina and Kosovo) in the late 1990s. As can be seen, the differences were rather stable throughout most of the history of the former Yugoslavia with the exception of Kosovo.[2] There is, however, marked divergence after the break up that took place in the early 1990s.

Table 1

Gross Social Product Per Capita in the Former Yugoslavia

	1952	1965	1974	1980	1989	1997[1]	1999[2]
Slovenia	100.0	100.0	100.0	100.0	100.0	100.0	10,078
Croatia	66.7	65.8	62.5	64.1	64.1	48.0	6,464
Vojvodina	49.1	60.9	58.0	57.1	59.6	24.3	6,006
Serbia (proper)	56.7	52.2	48.0	49.5	52.0	18.9	5,243
Serbia (incl. Vojvodina and Kosovo)	51.5	50.0	45.0	45.5	46.0	17.1	4,632
Montenegro	48.5	41.3	34.0	39.9	36.9	16.1	3,716
Bosnia and Herzegovina	52.6	39.1	33.0	33.3	34.3	10.2	3,461
Macedonia	39.2	36.4	34.0	33.8	33.3	20.3	3,359
Kosovo	25.7	19.6	16.0	14.1	12.6	5.1	1,272

Legend: Slovenia = 100 unless otherwise indicated.

Notes: 1. In 1997, data refer to GMP per capita for Serbia, Montenegro, Vojvodina, and Kosovo and to GDP per capita for other countries.

2. Actual GDP per capita (in USD at exchange rate) for Slovenia, and hypothetically attainable level of GDP per capita (in USD at exchange rate) for other republics, under the assumption that regional discrepancies (as measured in GDP per capita) are the same as in 1989.

Assuming that there were significant transfers from the richer to the poorer regions in the former Yugoslavia, the richer regions would have had an incentive to become independent. Even if it turned out, as indeed it did, that it was some of the poorer regions that were more interested in independence, a modified explanation from diversity could be applied. It could be argued that the common level of taxation could be higher or lower than the poorer regions would need with the transfers

2. There the divergence was mostly due to the rapid growth of population rather than to the lower growth rate. On that more in Gligorov (2001).

not being high enough to make up for the difference. In that case, the poorer region would have incentives to seek independence even though it would have to give up on transfers from the richer region. Indeed, an argument could be made that disintegration could be better for everybody, in other words, could be Pareto-improving, if the tax rates and transfers differed too much from what they would be if these regions were independent states. It could indeed be the case that disintegration would emerge as a Pareto-improving option if the level of diversity was high enough (Bolton and Roland, 1997).

This theory takes the state to be simply a fiscal agent. This makes sense if the state is a small open economy. In that case, markets determine almost everything else. Thus, perhaps the only thing left to a state as an economic policy agent is fiscal policy (in the broader sense that adds the fiscal effects of regulations to taxes and their rates). Then, different preferences over the level of public spending and the distribution of the fiscal burden would provide incentives to consider the trade-off between fiscal independence and integration. The theoretical question then is whether there is much room for fiscal divergence for a small open economy. The answer is likely to be negative. Indeed, as a rule, less developed countries would tend to have smaller public sectors than more developed ones, partly for reasons of competitiveness and partly because of the differences in demography. In any case, it cannot simply be assumed that independent small open economies would be able to set their taxes independently of the rest of the world.

The crucial assumption here is whether the country in question is a small open economy. In fact, the former Yugoslavia was not such a country; it was small but not very open (see table 2). Clearly, liberalization was one of the goals of the transition process that the country was entering at the moment of its dissolution. So, the argument regarding the Pareto-improving fiscal arrangements that dissolution would bring have to be seen as expected benefits. This is where the second explanation comes in. Many have argued that Yugoslavia's dissolution occurred because of the difference in expected gains from transition and integration into the world economy and especially into the European Union.

For instance, it is conceivable that the more developed regions could expect to benefit from the external markets more than the less developed regions. In other words, it might be the case that the richer and poorer regions do not form an optimal customs union. It might be that the level of protection that a less developed region needs is higher than what the more developed region needs. In that case, the more developed region would have an incentive to secede because gaining access to the larger outside market would be enough to compensate for the loss of the internal market.

Table 2

Exports of Goods as a Percentage of GDP in the Former Yugoslavia

	1970	1976	1983	1987
Slovenia	17.7	17.1	41.9	22.2
Croatia	15.6	14.9	25.5	14.3
Vojvodina	10.9	11.1	22.7	13.1
Serbia (proper)	17.4	14.9	31.4	20.3
Serbia (incl. Vojvodina & Kosovo)	15.0	13.9	28.2	17.6
Montenegro	8.6	17.5	24.6	17.5
Bosnia and Herzegovina	12.9	15.9	32.3	19.8
Macedonia	13.7	15.0	26.6	17.8
Kosovo	7.7	17.5	22.6	11.4
Yugoslavia total	15.1	15.1	30.0	17.9

Source: OECD

This, of course, assumes that the less developed a country is, the more protection it needs. Clearly, one needs to make an argument to prove this assumption correct. Though it is true that in the former Yugoslavia, protectionist interests were rather strong in the less developed regions, they were also strong in some of the more developed regions as well. In any case, those interests cannot be easily rationalized with the help of economic theory. It is rather the case that economic theory advises openness rather than reliance on protection and self-sufficiency. Of course, political incentives may differ from the economic ones, which indeed has been the case in the former Yugoslavia.

Thus, economic explanations for political disintegration either rely on the idea that this is:

- a Pareto-improving move because all of a country's regions stand to benefit when they become independent states (although the distribution of benefits may not be equal), or
- that the preservation of the common country is a Pareto-optimal situation in which disintegration benefits some regions (usually the richer ones) and disadvantages others, mostly the poor ones; in other words, it is Pareto-optimal but not an equilibrium state of affairs.

These two explanations can be put into a variety of more general theoretical models to determine the influence of a number of other political and economic developments on the country's stability. Clearly, if a country is closed, it may be destabilized when it liberalizes its foreign economic relations. Thus, as it has been argued, globalization of free trade may lead to an increase of the number of countries (Alesina and Spolaore, 1997; Alesina, Spolaore, and Wasziarg, 2003; Alesina, Angeloni, and Etro, 2003). This is because access to the world market makes any advantage of closed local markets disappear. Then, the state's size ceases to matter.

Democratization has a similar effect. It takes into account the political preferences of the citizens, revealing the differences in desirable tax rates. This assertion is sensitive to gerrymandering, however. Therefore, it is often assumed that diversity increases with size. For instance, any state within the United States should be more homogeneous than their union is. Or, every member state of the European Union should be less diverse than the EU itself. If that is the case, then at some point, the diversity will be much larger than a common state can accommodate. Thus, incentives to disintegrate will emerge, and such a movement cannot be suppressed if decisions are made democratically.

There are other economic accounts for the break up of states, but they collapse into these two, in one way or another. As long as the world is not globalized, larger states have advantages over the smaller ones. Once there is free trade, a state's size becomes irrelevant except in terms of the level of redistribution that different agglomerations of individuals are ready to accept. Then, there are two possibilities: either disintegration is Pareto-improving or it is not. In the latter case, there may exist a conflict of interests, a lack of equilibrium, which can be resolved in a number of ways, one being integration into a wider economic and political area or union.

Why Do Countries Make Up?

The theory of integration is almost a precondition of that of disintegration, at least in the economic theories discussed above. Countries have an interest to disintegrate their fiscal policies if they are diverse enough and if other advantages of integration have already been internalized. The theory of integration looks at the reasons why these other advantages would be internalized. Thus, it mostly looks at the advantages of joining customs and currency unions.

The benefits from customs unions related to the more efficient allocation of resources. The removal of tariff and nontariff barriers should increase the opportunities to trade, leading to better allocation of goods and services. Assuming that customs unions are created voluntarily, they would not come into existence if they are not Pareto-improving, in other words, if all parties to the customs union did not stand to benefit from their membership in that union.

Those benefits can also apply to the prospects of growth. There is an advantage for the less developed country to join a more developed one in a customs union because that should accelerate its growth, leading to faster convergence. This is even more so if the customs union is supplemented by a currency union. Here, the benefit is the consequence of the increased mobility of capital between different countries.[3]

This is a point worth discussing in some more detail. It has been argued traditionally that joining currency unions could have an effect on the stability of prices but will not have significant other effects. This is the case primarily because it was assumed that there is a close correlation between domestic savings and investments, so that monetary integration will not affect significantly the level of investment in a country and will thus not affect its growth rate. This would be surprising, however. It might be true that a currency union that is not also a customs union may not have any additional benefits beyond the increased price stability. However, if countries form a customs union, joining the same currency area may be an advantageous move. This is because it will increase the attractiveness of investments, both direct and debt-creating. This is because the less developed country would be able to benefit from the lower interest rate that would, as a rule, exist in a large currency area. Thus, investments could outpace domestic savings significantly without necessarily causing too much concern (Blanchard and Giavazzi, 2002). As a consequence, the less developed country could grow faster if it joins a customs and currency union.

There are other benefits from integration. Those most discussed have to do with the effects that integration has on the development of infrastructure and human capital in the broadest sense of that concept. The effect of the size of a country or a region on investments in infrastructure are well known from the literature on development economics.[4] Those can be connected more generally with the existence of increasing returns as the consequence of the "extent of the market," to use the expression of Adam Smith. Most models of growth from the so-called new growth theory predict rather quick convergence for less developed countries that join a union of more developed countries. To that, important contribution comes from the growth of human capital. An easy way to see this is to consider a production function in which the average level of knowledge adds significantly to total factor productivity. Then, a less developed country could increase the average level of knowledge by

3. For a detailed recent treatment of currency unions see Alesina and Barro (2000) and also Alesina, Barro and Tenreyro (2002).
4. Early statement in Rosenstein-Rodan (1943), a recent one in Murphy, Shleifer and Vishny (1989).

simply joining a more developed country. This is, of course, just an arithmetical trick, but is not completely devoid of meaning if it is taken into account that the costs to knowledge and information decrease significantly with the improvement of the institutions designed to distribute them. Assuming that integration would also involve institutional harmonization, there should be a rather fast accumulation of human capital in the less developed countries that have joined a more developed union.

These arguments do not apply directly to the countries that were created on the territory of the former Yugoslavia. Clearly, their integration within the former Yugoslavia was an inferior alternative to the integration with the European Union. However, as they were already integrated within the former Yugoslavia, the real question was whether their disintegration from Yugoslavia and integration into the EU was superior to their joint EU integration. At the time, the former alternative was chosen. However, with all the countries of former Yugoslavia advancing to EU integration, the latter answer, in a modified form, seems to be more appropriate.

Developments so Far

The theory suggests that countries tend to prefer disintegration on fiscal grounds but integration on trade and investment grounds. If we look at the development after the disintegration of the former Yugoslavia, it becomes clear that the fiscal argument cannot be applied directly. The public spending of Slovenia and Croatia, the two more developed nations, was either the same or indeed larger than it was in the former Yugoslavia. Less developed regions, with the exception of Montenegro, tended to downsize their public expenditures. Serbia and Montenegro tend to have large governments, though in the case of Serbia this is partly because it inherited the large federal structure, especially a large and costly army. In the case of Macedonia, public expenditures were downsized—at least until the near civil war in 2001—while in Bosnia and Herzegovina and Kosovo, the state collapsed, and international intervention was required.

Thus, the fiscal argument does not fare all that well in the case of Yugoslavia's dissolution, at least when it comes to the overall fiscal burden. Intraregional transfers are a different matter, of course. Those do not exist any more, but it would be hard to argue that the former Yugoslavia broke up because of the existence of the transfers from the more developed to less developed regions. Those were being phased out at the moment of disintegration anyway.

Table 3 shows data on public expenditures in the last three years. Albania is included here because it can stand as a proxy for Kosovo, where the current situation is quite unrepresentative. Similarly, the situation in Bosnia and Herzegovina is exceptional, though the level can be compared to that of Croatia and Serbia and Montenegro with which it is more similar than to Macedonia. These data cannot be compared easily with the level of public expenditures in the former Yugoslavia, as the later was a socialist country, and public finances were in a mess. Still, taking Slovenia as a benchmark, which is now publicly spending at least as much as it did in former Yugoslavia, it could be concluded that public spending has not decreased in most new countries and that less developed countries tend to spend less than the more advanced ones.

Table 3
General Government Expenditures [Percent GDP]

	2001	2002	2003
Albania	31.5	31.0	31.0
Bosnia and Herzegovina	56.7	56.7	53.1
Bulgaria	38.6	38.9	36.3
Croatia	51.5	51.5	50.0
Romania	33.7	33.1	33.1
Serbia and Montenegro	43.6	48.4	47.6
Serbia	43.2	48.0	47.5
Montenegro	50.9	45.7	—
Slovenia	44.6	45.2	—

Sources: IMF and national statistics.

Note: Serbian and Montenegrin expenditures are shares of Serbia's and Montenegro's GDP respec tively.

When it comes to trade, it can be argued that the less developed regions were interested in higher protection. This was disadvantages to the more developed regions, which saw the prospects for growth to be found in the trade integration with the EU.

If that were true, it could be expected that the more developed new states would increase their trade with the EU while decreasing it with the former Yugoslavia states. The evidence is, however, mixed at best. Slovenia, the most developed country in former Yugoslavia did indeed shift its exports toward the EU. Though for a long time Slovenia's exports lagged to what they had been when Slovenia was part of the former Yugoslavia, they grew throughout the entire period of independence (Gligorov,

1995b). Croatia, another more developed region, on the other hand, did not do as well. Indeed, both exports of goods and of services stagnated for a long time, with tourism recovering, and not completely, only after 2000. Exports of goods, however, stagnated. In that respect, Croatia is not doing much better than when it was part of former Yugoslavia and is probably doing worse when exports to former Yugoslavia countries are subtracted. Of the less developed countries, Macedonia has not done much better than Croatia, while the rest—Serbia, Montenegro, Kosovo, Bosnia and Herzegovina—have seen significant decreases of exports. In general, except for Slovenia, the loss of intra-Yugoslav markets has not been compensated with the growth of exports to other markets in all the other former Yugoslavia countries.

Figure 1
Exports in CEE and SEE [EUR mn]

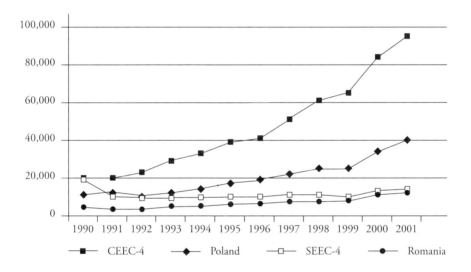

Figure 1 shows the development of exports in Central European (CEEC) and Southeast European (SEEC) transition economies. In the SEEC-4, Croatia, Macedonia, and Serbia and Montenegro are included together with Bulgaria. If added, Bosnia and Herzegovina would not make much of a difference. Slovenia is included in CEEC-4. From this, it is clear that SEECs did not benefit from the disintegration of the former Yugoslavia, at least in terms of exports. If shares of exports to GDP in SEECs are calculated, they are somewhere between 20 and 25 percent, which is not much more than those were when they were integrated within former Yugoslavia. Only they tended to trade much more among themselves than they do now. Thus, the overall exports have in fact declined, except in the case of Slovenia. Figure 2 shows that trade deficits that SEECs run are much larger than those in CEECs. Thus, exports have suffered much more than imports.

Figure 2
Trade Balance in Percentage of GDP in SEE and CEE 2001[5]

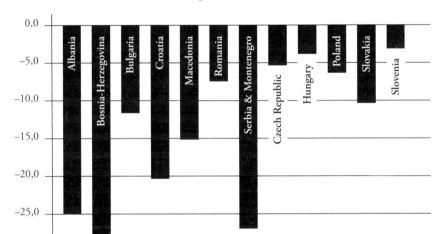

Indeed, in the last few years, integration has proceeded via intraregional trade liberalization. There is also no doubt that there is strong support for that in the business community. As a consequence, there has been some increase in intraregional trade. It is, however, difficult to assess how sustainable that is because some of the less developed former Yugoslavia countries are still not altogether integrated into the European and world markets, and thus their trade patterns can change. This is especially true for Bosnia and Herzegovina, which is an important exporting destination for a number of countries in the region.

5. WIIW is the source for the data in the figures.

Investments are following similar developments as trade. In the former Yugoslavia, most internal investments went from more developed to less developed regions. Those were discontinued with the dissolution of the common country. With trade liberalization, however, larger flows of investments from more developed former Yugoslavia states to less developed ones can be observed. Again, it is difficult to assess whether this is an instance of the more developed states taking advantage of historical ties, in which case this may prove to be a temporary development.

Figure 3
Current Account in Percentage of GDP in SEE and CEE 2002

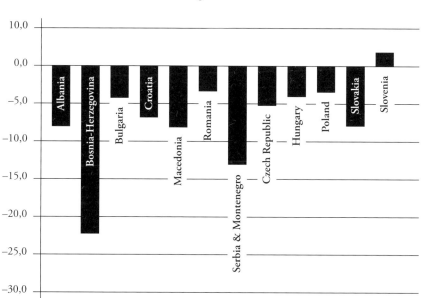

The possibility of the increased intraregional investments depends also on the previously discussed dissociation of savings and investments in cases of the creation of customs and currency unions. In the case of the former Yugoslavia countries, large current account deficits are the rule, with the exception of Slovenia, as can be seen in figure 3.[6] Thus, practically all these countries import savings. Therefore, their capacities to invest are quite limited. Still, there is no doubt that integration is conducive to investments. Though those may come from outside of the region.

6.   On that and on other data see Gligorov, Holzner, and Landesmann (2003). On intraregional trade, see Gligorov (2002).

Assessing the Theory

The economic theory of integration and disintegration of states discussed above proposes that break-ups are political (in the sense of political economy), while make-ups are economic. The theory also suggests that political nationalism is compatible with economic cosmopolitanism. Thus, it can be expected that with the more free trade and globalized investments, the number of countries should be larger than the number of customs and currency unions.

As argued above, the theory is difficult to apply to the break-up of Yugoslavia. One reason is that the costs of disintegration are not taken explicitly into account. The same is with the costs of integration. Both can be quite important.

Most of the break-ups of countries have been quite costly. Here, the break-up of the Soviet Union and of Czechoslovakia contradict the overwhelming historical evidence. The break-up of Yugoslavia, however, is more in line with what could have been expected on the basis of the historical evidence. Most of the evidence mentioned above is probably not relevant for the theory because it is distorted due to the very high costs of disintegration. Where these costs have been less important, for instance in the case of Slovenia and Macedonia, the evidence is more useful, but is not altogether supportive of the theory. In other instances, both political and economic costs are so high that the theory is not applicable at all.

It is similar with integrations. The role of the European Union will be commented on presently. But creation of customs and currency unions usually takes time, and their stability is not assured. The reason is that these unions are political and not simply economic ventures. Their survival also depends on political agreements. Trade negotiations tend to be long and arduous and also reversible. Giving up monetary sovereignty tends to be even more difficult to accept which is why, again with the exception of the European Union, currency unions are not so common.

The neglect of these costs of integration and disintegration are the consequence of the belief that political nationalism and economic cosmopolitanism are compatible. This is not the case from the political or as economic points of view. The development of the European Union illustrates the connection between politics and economics of integration. The idea is to start with the customs union, introduce the currency union, and finally have a political union. This development seems sustainable because every new step of economic integration requires an additional step of political integration. In other words, economic cosmopolitanism requires the states to give up their political nationalism.

This works in the opposite direction too. Political disintegration tends to lead to economic disintegration too. In that sense, the example of the break up of Yugoslavia is quite representative. Trade and investments between the former Yugoslav countries plummeted after their political disintegration. Also, free trade agreements and other measures of economic integration between these countries are not being implemented consistently and irreversibly because political accommodation is lagging. Thus, there is a trade-off between economic cosmopolitanism and political nationalism.

This observation can be applied to so-called delayed integrations (Gligorov, 2000a). Those are cases where economic and political preferences are not consistent. This is one way to interpret the developments in the region of the former Yugoslavia. After Yugoslavia's disintegration, the dominant trading partner for almost all the new countries became the European Union. The same is true for investments. Thus, it could be argued that the region revealed economic preferences for integration with the EU. However, as the EU is also a political union, political nationalism in the new post-Yugoslavia states also led to political disintegration from the EU. Even in the case of Slovenia, the establishment of contractual relations with the EU were delayed. Thus, political nationalism was not in fact consistent with the economic Europeization.

This inconsistency is not stable, and either political nationalism or economic internationalism have to give. This inconsistency can be expressed with the proposition of the interconnection of political and economic interests that states simply that price-taking implies policy-taking (Gligorov, 2000a). There are several ways to see why this is the case. Going descriptively through some of them may be helpful. Looking at the issue of trade integration first, free-trade arrangements or customs unions require significant harmonization of economic regulation. Otherwise, the arrangement will either not work or will not be sustainable. The stability of the single market of the European Union is premised on that, while the imperfect functioning of free trade agreements in the Balkans verify the same statement in the negative sense. This is even more the case once currency union is contemplated. Then, financial regulation has to be harmonized and even institutional integration is necessary.

The remaining issue is that of fiscal harmonization. There is no doubt that the level of public expenditures and thus of the fiscal burden will depend on local characteristics that, in one way or another, can be reduced to those of local preferences. However, if trade and investment integration is significant, certain significant fiscal harmonization will be necessary either because there will be a regulatory need to be satisfied or because the competition in the financial and product markets will work in that direction. There will be some scope for divergence to reflect different levels of development and the size of a country (assuming that there is some economy of size in the production of public goods), but these differences will be limited. The European Union relies more on explicit harmonization than on tax competition, but the outcome of both reflects the same mechanism of market integration requiring political integration too.

The converse is also true. If a country cherishes political nationalism, then it will have to disintegrate economically from the union it is in or may be expected to be a part of. This is quite clearly seen in the evidence of the dissolution of the former Yugoslavia. As already argued, most countries have grown more closed after dissolution. Also, regional integration has become an important issue and has gained momentum with the interest and expectation of EU accession. Both—regional and EU integration—will have to precede in economic as well as in political domains. There is a price of economic cosmopolitanism in terms of political nationalism.

Future Disintegrations and Integration

The region of the former Yugoslavia is still interesting to analyze. This is because the processes of disintegration and integration are not yet finished. On one hand, there is the process of regional integration that has to be a part of EU integration. On the other hand, there is the process of nation and state building that is still unfinished in a number of states or state-like political entities.

One example is the Union of Serbia and Montenegro. These are two states of which Serbia is more than ten times larger than Montenegro, in terms of population, and somewhat larger than that in terms of GDP. This case is interesting because it can be used to test the theoretical assumption mentioned above that homogeneity decreases with size. It can be argued, however, that the former Yugoslavia was less heterogeneous than the Union of Serbia and Montenegro. This is because the preferences change when the set of alternatives changes. Thus, political preferences for integration over disintegration are not the same for both Serbia and Montenegro depending on whether it is the integration into a larger union of the former Yugoslavia that is considered or that into a much smaller Union of Serbia and Montenegro. Montenegro seems to have preferred Yugoslavia over independence, but independ-ence over the union with Serbia. In Serbia, preferences may be different. It may have preferred the union with Montenegro over that of the former Yugoslavia with independence being the least preferred alternative.[7]

This may explain the interest in reintegration of the region within the process of EU integration. It may generally be the case that former Yugoslav countries preferred independence to the former Yugoslavia but prefer regional integration to independence if this is the consequence of EU integration. This goes against the

7. It could be argue that Serbia preferred independence to the former Yugoslavia, but this does not make any difference for the point being made here.

96

argument from diversity when diversity is seen in cultural terms. As most people on the territory of the former Yugoslavia speak the same language, there is a sense that they are more similar to each other than to any one of the EU countries. Indeed, this was one of the original reasons for the initial creation of Yugoslavia at the beginning of the twentieth century.

Another argument can be made in the case of Bosnia and Herzegovina. That country all but disintegrated and now consists of a very loose union of two entities. It would be difficult to argue that these two entities have separated because of the significant diversity between them. The level of development is the same, they speak the same language, and have similar interests in regional and European integration. They seem to show an interest to integrate if the level of diversity in fact increases. They feel more comfortable inside an integration that includes both Serbia and Croatia. As the latter two can integrate if that is the consequence of the EU integration, Bosnia and Herzegovina also prefers that integration to independence. Thus, in case of Bosnia and Herzegovina, the increase of diversity would increase the possibility of local, regional, and EU integration.

Finally, wider integration would support regional integration in the case of Kosovo as well. Clearly, diversity would suggest that Kosovo should be an independent state, while economic interests would suggest at least regional integration. The latter seems impossible without EU integration and indeed without even wider integration which includes the United States in some kind of a security role.

Given the existing public preferences in the region of the former Yugoslavia, it can be expected that the process of disintegration will continue. However, not because it is a Pareto-improvement for the political entities involved and not as a consequence of the liberalization of trade. In fact, liberalization would sap political nationalism and support the process of regional and EU integration. Diversity of preferences is not a factor that systematically works for either integration or disintegration. Thus, regional reintegration can be expected once the process of EU integration advances far enough.

Conclusion

Models of integration and disintegration of countries have difficulties explaining disintegrations like those that are still going on in the Balkans and integrations like those going on in the European Union. In other words, they are inapplicable to processes of balkanization and Europeization. In the former case, there is an interest in political independence, but not as a consequence of either liberalization or democratization. In fact, it mostly takes place against those two processes. In the latter case, it is the political motive that is behind economic integration. The European Union is designed to sap political nationalism. As it always goes together with economic nationalism, it is economic integration that is taken as the first instrument to achieve that goal. In the case of the former Yugoslavia, political nationalism was clearly motivated by economic nationalism as well. Not just in terms of the control over the tax base, but also over the markets, both domestic and foreign. An important role was played by the collapse of socialism and the expectation of the huge redistribution that privatization was to bring about, but these issues cannot be entered into here. In any case, balkanization was accompanied with authoritarianism (Gligorov, 2000b) and economic nationalism together with huge redistribution of resources. This process is not yet finished in the area of the former Yugoslavia. It will be partly overshadowed by the process of euroization that will lead to the region's reintegration. That will sap political nationalism and open the possibility for liberalization and other forms of economic integration.

References

Alesina, Alberto, Ignazio Angeloni and Frederico Etro (2003) "International Unions." www.economics.harvard.edu.

Alesina, Alberto and Robert Barro (2000) "Currency Unions." NBER Working Paper No. w7927.

Alesina, Alberto, Robert Barro and Silvana Tenreyro (2002) "Optimal Currency Areas." NBER Working Paper No. w9072.

Alesina, Alberto and Enrico Spolaore (1997) "On the Number and Size of Nations." *Quarterly Journal of Economics* 112(3): 1027–56.

Alesina, Alberto, Enrico Spolaore, and Romain Wacziarg (2003) "Trade, Growth and the Size of Countries." *HIER Discussion Paper* No. 1995.

Blanchard, Olivier and Francesco Giavazzi (2002) "Current Account Deficits in the Euro Area: The End of the Feldstein Hurioka Puzzle?" http://econ-www.mit.edu/faculty/blanchar/files/draft1f3.pdf.

Bolton, Patrick and Gerard Roland (1997) "The Break Up of Nations: A Political Economy Analysis." *Quarterly Journal of Economics* 112(3): 1057–90.

Gligorov, Vladimir (1994) *Why Do Countries Break Up? The Case of Yugoslavia.* Uppsala: Acta Universitatis Upsaliensis.

—— (1995a) "Bosnia and Hercegovina: Small, War-Damaged Economy." *The Vienna Institute Monthly Report* No.11.

—— (1995b) "Reorientation of Foreign Trade in Slovenia." *Communist Economies and Economic Transformation* 7(4): 543–54.

—— (1997) "Trade in the Balkans." The Vienna Institute Monthly Report No. 12.

—— (1998) "Trade and Finance in the Balkans." In Vladimir Gligorov and H. Vidovic (eds.) *On the Way to Normality: The States on the Territory of Former Yugoslavia in the Postwar Period*. Wiener Institut fur Internationale Wirtschaftsverglieche [WIIW] Research Report No. 250.

—— (2000a) "Delaying Integration." WIIW Research Report No. 267.

—— (2000b) "The Role of the State in the Balkans." In Vladimir Gligorov (ed.) *Balkan Reconstruction: Economic Aspects*. WIIW.

—— (2001) "Economic Future of Kosovo." European Centre for Minority Issues.

—— (2002) "European Union Enlargement and the Balkans." In Andrew Warner (ed.) *European Competitiveness and Transition Report*. Oxford: OxfordUniversity Press, 114–25.

—— (2003) "Serbia and Montenegro: Transition with Organized Crime." *WIIW Current Studies* 19.

Gligorov, Vladimir, Mario Holzner and Michael Landesmann (2003) "Prospects for Further (South-) Eastern EU Enlargement: From Divergence to Convergence?" WIIW Research Report No. 296.

Murphy, Kevin, Andrei Shleifer and Robert Vishny (1989) "Industrialization and the Big Push." *Journal of Political Economy* 97: 1003–26.

Rosenstein-Rodan, P. N. (1943) "Problems of Industrialisation of Eastern and South Eastern Europe." *Economic Journal* 53(210/211), 202–11.

The Political Economy of Interethnic Relations: Ahmeti's Village or the Macedonian Case

Knaus Gerald, Kristof Bender, Marcus Cox

Most travelers in Macedonia pass through Kicevo, on the road from Skopje to Ohrid by way of Tetovo. But many of them will barely notice the town, let alone the intense social drama of contemporary Macedonia being played out in this region. Entering the Kicevo region from the north, the traveler first reaches the village of Zajas, home to the guerrilla leader turned party politician, Ali Ahmeti. The uprising led by Ahmeti brought the country to the brink of civil war in 2001, and his new party, the Democratic Union for Integration, has since emerged as the Albanian community's preeminent political force. On the left side of the road stands the house of his uncle, Fazli Veliu, who formulated the ideology of the Kosovo Liberation Army and the National Liberation Army (associated with Macedonia's ethnic Albanians) from his diaspora home in Switzerland. The village of Zajas has no real center, just a scattering of cafés and shops along the main road. The old iron-ore mine of Tajmiste lies to the right but has been closed down since the mid-1990s. A sign on the left points the way to the region's largest employer, the thermal power station in Oslomej.

On the outskirts of Kicevo town, the traveler enters the heart of the region's industrial zone, with all the premier companies of the socialist era lined up along the road like pearls on a string. Turning off the main road into Kicevo, the traveler enters the main street, Liberation Boulevard, which divides the town into two distinct quarters: the Muslim (mainly Albanian but also Turkish) on the left and the ethnic Macedonian on the right. What makes the basic pattern so visible is that, during

First published as "Ahmeti's Village. The Political Economy of Interethnic Relations in Macedonia" by the European Stability Initiative (ESI): in October 2002. ESI is an independent nonprofit research and policy institute based in Berlin, with regional offices in Sarajevo, Pristina, and Skopje. Reports are available free of charge on its website (www.esiweb.org). In 2002, ESI received support from the German Marshall Fund of the United States, the Swedish Government, the Swiss Government, the UK Department for International Development, the Körber Foundation, the British Government, and the European Union Pillar of UNMIK in Kosovo.

the summer months, the Albanian quarter is much livelier. Along the left side of the main shopping thoroughfare, Aleksandar Makedonski Street, the shops and cafés are doing a lively trade. On the ethnic Macedonian side, customers are sparse. Most of the building projects on Liberation Boulevard are Albanian financed, including the former socialist-era shopping mall, which is being converted into a reception center for Albanian weddings.

Continuing along the main road, the visitor passes a defunct furniture company and the large grain silo of the bakery, Zito Karaorman, before reaching the empty fields of the former agricultural cooperative that mark the edge of the urban area. Drive another few minutes, and the traveler is in the ethnic Macedonian village of Drugovo, where the entire municipal administration is housed in a red, temporary-looking shelter and the local office of the Ministry of Justice is dilapidated as well, marked by its broken windows. Next comes the small, visibly impoverished village of Izvor, with its textile company and a fish farm. And then comes Kicevo—apparently just another unremarkable Macedonian backwater.

What the traveler hurrying through Kicevo may have missed are the complex social dynamics between two communities—ethnic Macedonian and Albanian—pursuing very different development paths, and the profound implications of this story for the country's future.

There has been no communal violence in this region for decades, and it remained peaceful even at the height of the fighting in 2001. Like much of Macedonia, Kicevo has a deeply rooted tradition of ethnic coexistence. Although Macedonians, Albanians, Turks, and Roma live largely separate lives, there are countless areas where they interact. The mayor, who is from the Internal Macedonian Revolutionary Organization–Democratic Party of National Unity (IMRO-DPNU), which is associated with ethnic Macedonians on the national level, was elected in 2000 with the support of Kicevo's Muslims. For years now, the municipal gazette has been published in two languages, and the high school has approximately equal numbers of Albanian and Macedonian students.

But the story of Kicevo is central to the ethnic Macedonian conflict in a much deeper way. This region of 52,000 people contains an extraordinary diversity of social and economic patterns. Its different ethnic groups are undergoing deep social changes which are pushing them along widely divergent paths. It is a pattern of development (and decline) which seems programmed to generate interethnic suspicion and fear.

This chapter on Kicevo's economic and social life is written to explore the political economy of ethnic tension and highlight the other conflict (ESI, 2002)—that of diminishing resources and collapsing lifestyles, which so often goes unnoticed by international observers and threatens to undermine the important peace arrangements.

Context

The west Macedonian region of Kicevo (in Albanian, Kercova), home to 26,000 ethnic Albanians, 21,000 ethnic Macedonians, 2,500 ethnic Turks, and 1,300 Roma, is a mirror of contemporary Macedonian society.[1] Driving through its villages, strolling its streets, visiting its factories, and talking to its people brings one face to face with a society in the midst of a social and economic revolution.

Kicevo's social landscape has been shaped by the rise and fall of the industrial society created by Yugoslav socialism. In the decades following the Second World War, most Macedonians left the harsh, traditional life of subsistence agriculture and moved to Kicevo, drawn by jobs in the new industrial sector and the lure of an urban lifestyle. Many rural areas were left completely depopulated, and the town became home to three-quarters of all ethnic Macedonians in the region.

In contemporary Kicevo, one can see the remnants of this process of industrialization lined up along Ilinden Street (also known as Industry Street)—the formerly proud companies, once the backbone of a new industrial society. With privatization largely complete, most of these enterprises are either closed down or clinging to a precarious existence. Of some 6,600 jobs in socialist companies in 1990, half have already disappeared, and further decline is inevitable.

The local economy of Kicevo's ethnic Macedonians now depends heavily on the thousand jobs (even more than in socialist times) provided by the state-owned, thermal power station in Oslomej, part of Macedonia's state electric utility, ESM. There are also a number of residential construction projects funded by the public-housing company in Skopje, which is headed by a former IMRO–DPNU mayor of Kicevo, Ilija Kitanoski. The directors of these two public enterprises are childhood friends and, at this moment, considered to be the most influential figures in the small world of Kicevo's political economy. Under the outgoing central government, their connections in business and politics helped to sustain the remaining socially owned enterprises (SOEs), which are firms owned by their employees, closely linked together by a network of subcontracts.

Without this continuing flow of public funds, there is no economic dynamic to be seen in the industrial sector. The ethnic Macedonian managers of the former SOEs foresee a grim future. Gathered in a hotel owned by the company Tajmiste, whose iron-ore mine was shut down a decade ago, the managers speak of awaiting the arrival of a big foreign investor to regenerate the local economy ("FIAT," suggests one; "BASF," says another). They complain of the encirclement of their town by Albanians and the instability of the region as a whole. Under the present conditions

---

1. Census data of 1994 (which is contested by Albanians, Turks, and Roma).

of "fear and insecurity," they tell each other, even the most competitive enterprises with the best managers in the world would be failing.[2]

Table 1

Demography and Ethnic Structure in the Kicevo Region[3]

Municipality	1948	1994			
		Total Population	Macedonians [%]	Albanians [%]	Other [%]
Kicevo	8,761	27,543	58.55	26.12	15.33
Drugovo	9,824	3,555	87.43	3.68	8.89
Oslomej	7,401	9,170	1.74	98.16	0.10
Vranestica	4,203	1,650	79.94	0.48	19.57
Zajas	5,949	10,055	2.79	97.12	0.09
Total	36,138	51,973	40.39	50.22	9.39

Source:　Census data from 1948 and 1994, projected according to 1996 municipal boundaries.

The economic reality which Kicevo's ethnic Macedonians now face is not merely one of stagnation but of a slow and relentless decline. This process has generated a deep fear of social relegation on the part of urban Macedonian households, who have seen their living standards collapse over the past two decades. Their sense of insecurity is acute (UNDP, 2001b). Each job that disappears pushes another household into poverty. Former SOEs have long since stopped hiring, and the public administration is under pressure both to downsize and to make space for more minority representation. There is almost no new private sector in the ethnic Macedonian parts of Kicevo, with the exception of a few small construction firms, shops, and cafés.

The chief accountant of the metal-working SOE "Tane Caleski", whose first name is Vesna, is a typical case of what economic transition has meant at the household level. Until the early 1990s, her family had two incomes from SOE jobs and enjoyed the high standard of living common to the urban middle class across the former Yugoslavia. In the early 1990s, her husband's position at Kikotex, the textile company, was made redundant while he was still too young to receive a pension. His severance

2.　ESI interviews with the managers of many of Kicevo's privatized and state companies, May and June 2002.

3.　Under the 1996 Law on Territorial Organization, the former municipality of Kicevo was divided into five new municipalities. In this report, "Kicevo region" refers to the pre-1996 municipality and "Kicevo municipality" to the post-1996 municipality of the same name, made up of Kicevo town and six villages.

package has long since been spent. Occasionally, he finds casual work as a waiter for €5 per day. Vesna's salary is €125 per month but is months in arrears. As Vesna explains, the most basic living costs in Kicevo come to at least €90 per month: food (€60), electricity (€15), telephone (€10), and water (€5). The middle-class privileges she once took for granted—a car, modern household appliances, an annual vacation at the seaside—are a thing of the past. Vesna's company faces a highly uncertain future and is likely to slide into bankruptcy. If that happens, it will tip another family over the line into genuine poverty.

The new private sector is on the other side of Liberation Boulevard, and it is overwhelmingly young and Albanian. There are 184 shops crammed into the Albanian end of Aleksandar Makedonski Street, selling carpets, furniture, jewelry, and wedding gowns. The shops make most of their annual turnover during the summer months, when thousands of Albanian migrants return to get married or build houses in their villages. In this period, the Albanian quarter bustles with activity, and Cadillacs and other impressive cars with Chicago and Alaska license plates are parked along the sidewalks. Many of Kicevo's 300 private taxi drivers make a living shuttling the diaspora to and from the Skopje airport. The heart of the Albanian economy is made up of traders, restaurateurs, construction workers, money changers, tradesmen, and a few lawyers and private doctors.

The Albanian economic engine is fuelled almost entirely by remittances. By conservative estimates, the modern-day *Gastarbeiter* (migrant workers) send home or spend more than €16 million in Kicevo annually—more than the total salaries paid to Kicevo's ethnic Macedonians in the public sector and the former SOEs combined. Interestingly, the largest new private-sector employer of ethnic Macedonians in Kicevo is the textile company Himara, owned and managed by an Albanian who returned from France.

Kicevo's Albanians have been forced to channel their energies into this new private sector because of their traditional exclusion from jobs in the public administration and SOEs—largely the preserve of the ethnic Macedonian community. Although making up 50 percent of the population in the Kicevo region, Albanians hold only a third of the jobs in the public administration, or just 14 percent if one leaves out school teachers. Of the 1,000 workers in the power station in Oslomej, an almost entirely Albanian municipality, there are fewer than 60 Albanians. The trend is the same across the rest of the former SOEs.

Interethnic relations in Kicevo are framed by this paradox. As the primary beneficiaries of four decades of industrial development, ethnic Macedonians have been left cruelly exposed to its rapidly declining fortunes. At the same time, the exclusion of Albanians from the socialist sector and the benefits it offered have forced them to seek out economic strategies, chiefly labor migration and small-scale trade, which have left them much better equipped to survive the collapse of the socialist system.

These divergent experiences explain the very different perceptions among the two communities as to *how* the Macedonian state is failing, and who is paying the price for its failure. With one foot abroad, the Albanian community sees the state as alien and unresponsive to its needs. Despite their relative prosperity, the Albanian viewpoint is colored by a lifetime's experience of exclusion. For their part, ethnic Macedonians feel under siege, both socially and economically. The state's machinery is growing weaker and out of touch with developments in this postsocialist, postindustrial society. As the economic privileges that were once attached to the administration disappear, ethnic Macedonians are unable to comprehend the abrupt reversal of their fortunes.

This difference in perception helps to explain why education has become such a heated topic in Macedonian politics. Barely 10 percent of Albanians in the municipality of Zajas have advanced beyond primary education.[4] For these Albanians, forced either to remain in the village or to leave the region in search of work, their lack of formal education is enduring proof of discrimination at the hands of the Macedonian socialist republic. The situation is now changing, and today there are almost equal numbers of Albanians and ethnic Macedonians in Kicevo's bilingual secondary school, Mirko Mileski. But change necessarily takes time, needing a generation to filter through the Albanian community.

For many ethnic Macedonians, the educational profile of Albanians is a sign of their backwardness and their inability to participate in modern society. The majority of urban Macedonians in Kicevo have acquired secondary or higher education. Their privileged access to the education system was the key to participating in the benefits of the socialist economy, in which jobs were strictly graded according to educational requirements. Now, they are baffled by the new rules of the game, in which the link between education and standards of living has been severed.[5] They find it incomprehensible that uneducated Albanians are in a position to purchase prestigious buildings in the center of town. This devaluation of education is an affront to their social status and is all too often rationalized as evidence of criminality among the Albanians.

Blagoje Despotoski, the director of the Oslomej power station remembers the Albanian political leader Ali Ahmeti from the time they attended the Kicevo gymnasium, the only source of secondary education in the area. "He was one class below me.

4. Statistical Office of Macedonia, census data of 1994.
5. A World Bank report noted that the "average rate of return to an additional year of schooling amounts to 7.6 percent, which is in the range typical of industrialized market economies" (World Bank, 1998: 58). However, this is misleading, applying only to the public sector where the state sets the salary levels by reference to education levels. It does not hold for the labor market generally, as the bank noted in another report: "In contrast to most countries, the private sector rewards education less than the public sector. This somewhat surprising fact is attributed to private sector growth in low skilled industries" (World Bank, 1999: 23).

He was a nobody then, he knew nothing. And now he poses conditions and black-mails us. I studied at university, he did not. I cannot respect him" (ESI interview, June 2002).[6]

Albanians of Ahmeti's generation intensely resented their exclusion from the education system, which was conducted exclusively in the Macedonian language at the university level and, during certain periods, at the secondary level as well. Some of the most radical thinkers, including Ahmeti's uncle Fazli Veliu, were teachers who were resentful of Macedonia's intellectual establishment. Veliu taught at the Kicevo gymnasium before going to Kosovo and then to Switzerland. Albanians, even those who left a long time ago and only return for visits, express their frustration at the way access to education and formal qualifications was used to block their careers in the past.

There is an obvious lack of respect between the communities, which emerges time and time again in conversations about the overall economic situation. Many Albanians see Macedonians as lacking initiative and unwilling to work, wedded to white collar jobs and patronage networks. Many Macedonians see Albanians as backward and prone to crime. The new wealth of their Albanian neighbors is seen not as potential investment capital or the results of hard labor abroad, but as the fruits of illicit activity. "When they see my wealth they say I am a drug dealer," shrugs the owner of a large limousine service in the United States who, in his own words, "discovered Alaska in 1971." The language of "rampant corruption" and "organized crime" covers just about any grievances, however diverse they may be, between the two communities.

In reality, however, the weakness of the Macedonian state is as much a constraint on the development of the Albanian community as it is for the Macedonians. Diaspora wealth funds consumption and trade in Kicevo but very little in the way of productive investment. Large sections of the Albanian community remain trapped in a cycle of underdevelopment, particularly in the rural areas. The emigration of Albanians continues to provide the only safety valve for the pressures generated by Kicevo's failing economy. For most ethnic Macedonians in the region, there is no such escape route available.

The Rise and Fall of Industrial Society

Economic transition in Macedonia, in the narrow sense of the range of specific policy measures which the international financial institutions have advocated across all postcommunist countries, is largely complete. The core institutions of the socialist

6.   Ahmeti has in fact studied at Prishtina University.

economy, such as the payments bureau and the central planning organs, have disappeared. Privatization of socially owned companies and banks is far advanced. Most enterprises that could attract a buyer have already been sold, and, although some former SOEs still operate under the protective umbrella of the state, many of them have been liquidated. New entrants into the Macedonian economy are now subject to the discipline of market forces.

However, for the Macedonian people, economic transition has overwhelmingly been experienced as a collapse in living standards and general rise in economic insecurity. According to the UNDP, "transition to a market economy ... has led to a massive rise in unemployment, a sharp fall in family incomes, diminution in official support services and a rise in general poverty levels—widely based and extremely troubling for a large proportion of the population" (UNDP, 2001c).

Since the beginning of the transition, official unemployment has doubled to more than 30 percent, cutting across all social and ethnic groups (UNDP, 2001c). Nearly half of those under 30 years of age have never held formal employment, despite high levels of education. For those still employed, salaries have been decreased and are often heavily in arrears, and 90 percent feel at least some level of anxiety about losing their jobs. Social-welfare programs are failing to provide an effective safety net—49 percent of social-welfare beneficiaries report that, despite frugal lifestyles, their benefits are spent in the first ten days of the month (UNDP, 2001c: 29).

In the industrial sector, which once provided the bulk of employment, economic transition has left most companies limping along at a fraction of their former production levels. In theory, the weeding out of inefficient enterprises should have freed up assets for more productive use in the private sector. Yet the response of the new private sector has been slow, and its employment needs remain very modest. Only the state itself has continued to provide a reliable source of employment, although the social status and standard of living attaching to jobs in the public sector are diminishing every year. For ordinary Macedonians, the question they must be asking is: transition to where?

These trends become much more palpable when one studies a place like Kicevo. The industrial jobs that once provided the backbone of the local economy have contracted by more than half, and the remainder is looking extremely tenuous. The new private sector is mainly a realm of family-run shops and cafés, with a small construction sector heavily dependent on contracts for public works. Only a handful of companies have emerged that are able to offer employment in double figures. As the productive sector contracts, the economic and social significance of the state as an employer actually becomes more important over time.

Table 2
UNDP Opinion Poll in December 2000

What makes you most insecure?	Percent
Unemployment	57.2
Low income, despite being employed	16.2
Poor social assistance from the state	6.2
Ethnic tensions	5.0
Crime	4.3
Negative influences from the international community	2.4
Negative influences from neighboring countries	1.9
Lack of opportunities to use health service	1.7

Source: UNDP, 2001c: 121.

Table 3
Registered Unemployed in Kicevo, Drugovo, Oslomej, Vranestica, and Zajas

Registered unemployed	No.
Male	4,969
Female	3,483
Town	5,371
Village	3,081
Unqualified workers	4,109
Semiqualified workers	741
Qualified workers	1,228
Technicians	1,983
Higher schools and university	391
Up to 30 years of age	3,541
31 to 40 years of age	2,412
41 to 50 years of age	1,431
over 50 years of age	1,068
Total	8,452

Source: Data taken from the Bureau for Employment, December 31, 2001.

Note the age structure of the unemployed (41 percent younger than 30 years), qualification structure (48 percent unqualified), and geographical distribution (63 percent in the town).

Privatization and its Aftermath

As in the rest of Macedonia and throughout the Balkan region, the economic transition in Kicevo has amounted to a painful process of deindustrialization. A quarter of its socialist-era enterprises are already in liquidation, and half of the industrial jobs have gone. Most privatized companies have been sold through a process of insider privatization to their workers and management, who have clung to their jobs while presiding over a steady decapitalization of assets.

Of 32 significant state and socially owned enterprises in the Kicevo region, 13 have already been privatized, two are awaiting privatization, nine are in liquidation, and eight will remain in public ownership.[7] In 1989, socially owned and public companies provided a total of 6,623 jobs. By 2002, this has dropped by half to 3,298. There are still 490 jobs in companies waiting to be privatized, and, in the postprivatization companies, overstaffing is widespread.

Privatization brought very little new capital investment into the socially owned sector. Only four of the 13 privatized companies were bought by external investors. None of the companies headquartered in Kicevo attracted any foreign interest, although there are two local outlets of national companies that have been sold to foreign investors: Macedonian Telecom and Stopanska Banka.

Table 4
Employment in Former Socially Owned and Public Enterprises

	No. of companies	No. of workers	
Socially owned and public enterprises (1989)			6,623
a. companies privatized to date	13	1,145	
b. companies to remain public	8	1,631	
c. companies still to be privatized	2	490	
d. companies in liquidation	9	32	
Former socially owned and public enterprises (2002)	32		3,298

Interest from domestic investors was equally scarce. Only two companies were bought by private interests external to the company. The agricultural combine was

7. This is based on a list by the Skopje-based Agency for Privatization, cross-checked with a large number of economic actors (enterprise directors and representatives of ministries) in Kicevo itself.

bought by Blagoja Gjorgjijoski, Kicevo's premier ethnic Macedonian entrepreneur, after it slid into bankruptcy. The other domestic investment was the purchase of one of Kicevo's two hotels, Hotel Union, by an academic and two entrepreneurs. In addition, a local outlet of the liquidated ceramic combine, the brick factory in Vranestica, was bought by Granit, a subsidiary of one of Macedonia's former construction giants.

Aside from these examples, the limited value of the enterprises available for privatization and the shortage of domestic investment capital have meant that the economic transition in Kicevo has been a process of insider privatization. Shares were distributed to workers, with the value offset against unpaid salaries, or were sold to managers at discounted prices, payable in installments over many years. The process did not attract any new capital for investment or restructuring, leaving the companies to struggle with a severely outdated capital stock. In fact, by transferring ownership to the existing workforce, the privatization process made enterprise restructuring unlikely, as neither the workers nor the management intended to fire themselves. A law in force until 1998 determined that shares could only be traded freely within the existing workforce, while sales to outsiders needed to be approved by the company board (World Bank, 1998: 18).

The aftermath of privatization leaves most of Kicevo's enterprises operating at a fraction of their former capacity, with heavy debt burdens and a severely underemployed workforce. As in the rest of Macedonia, the outcome has been deeply disappointing. In a report of April 2000, the IMF notes: "With the privatization process nearing its end, the outcome has been below expectations. Internal ownership by workers and managers had widened, owing to the predominant reliance on insider privatization ... and, notwithstanding the impact of external factors, the overall financial performance of transformed enterprises failed to improve significantly" (IMF, 2000: 48).

While privatized companies in Kicevo have sought to reduce their workforce through natural attrition and a freeze on new hires, there is still a serious problem of overemployment and inappropriate staffing structures in many of them, indicating the extent of the adjustment that lies ahead.

The management of the bakery Zito Karaorman, which currently employs 153 workers, admits that it could operate at the same capacity with less employees. In 2000, the bakery had a turnover of €3.9 million (Agri Consulting, 2002: 33). By way of comparison, a private Kicevo bakery, Dime dooel, achieved a fifth of this turnover (€783,000) with only seven employees.[8]

---

8. Ibid., p.40.

Table 5

Current Business Activities of AD Tajmiste, Kicevo's Largest Privatized Company

Area	Activities	Location	Employees
Mining	Stone-mining and separation, marble production, subcontracts with the power plant in Oslomej, Feronikel (Kavadarci), Rudnik Bakar CU (Bucim), and Granit, the public-construction company; also active in Albania	Kicevo	150
Metal industry	Mechanical construction (aluminum, motorway guide tracks), locksmith workshops, maintenance, and repair	Kicevo	65
Services	1 hotel, 2 restaurants, 3 workers' restaurants, retail trading, repair workshop for electrical goods, 1 petrol station	Kicevo & Gevgelja	55
Agriculture	fish, apples, honey, mushrooms, meat (beef, lamb, goat); dog and pig breeding	Zajas	25
Construction	Water supply systems, canals, buildings	Kicevo	20 + occasional workers
Total			315

Source: AD Tajmiste (director Vladimir Toleski). Feronikel was bought by French investors and Bucim by Bulgarian investors.

The metal producer Tane Caleski, which is still awaiting privatisation, is another company which has failed to make the transition to a market economy. Ten years ago, it sold its products to the Soviet Union, Czechoslovakia, and Italy. Now that it is obliged to import its raw materials at market prices, the company cannot compete with Chinese, Bulgarian, or Turkish producers. Unable to find a market for its products, it is sliding further and further into arrears and may be heading for bankruptcy.

Kikoteks, a textile company, is assembling half-finished products on behalf of another producer for the German market. It has been forced to reduce its workforce by half but with 260 employees it is still the second largest employer among the privatised companies. In the textile sector, it is forced to compete with low-cost emerging economies in the region and around the world. Across southeastern Europe, where by world standards wage costs are not particularly low, the future of the textile industry looks bleak. A recent review of the sector in Bosnia noted that: "only those companies that are capable of sustained investment in both plant and innovative products will have a share of the international market. Commodities can be bought from low cost emerging economies in SE Asia at prices that Bosnia Herzegovina based textile producers can never hope to match."[9]

Table 6
Kicevo's 13 Privatized Companies

Company	Description of activities	Method of privatization	Estimated employees
Tajmiste	Various	Insider	315
Kikotex	Textiles	Insider	260
Zito Karaorman	Bakery	Insider	153
Granit (Kicevo outlet)	Construction	Insider	110
Izvor DOO	Textiles	Insider	75
Stopanska Banka (outlet Kicevo)	Branch office of Macedonia's biggest bank	Foreign investor	60
MK Telekom	Branch office of Telekom	Foreign investor	57
Zemiodelski kombinat Kicevo	Agricultural combine	Private local investor	45
Keramicki Kombinat Vranestica	Brick factory	Purchased by domestic company after liquidation	30
Agrokop	Trade	Insider	20
Hotel Union	Hotel and Restaurant	Private investor	15
Kicevoprom (kompani DOO)	Reregistered former trading company	Insider	4
Kicevoprom–Klanica	Slaughterhouse	Insider	1
Privatized companies			1,145

Note: The World Bank complains repeatedly, "little information is publicly available on the ownership or financial performance of enterprises, and what is available can be difficult to understand" (World Bank, 1998: 29). As a result, the data in this and the next table was gathered from a wide variety of sources (pension fund, the outlet of Economics Ministry in Kicevo, and municipal administrations) and then cross-checked with managers of most of these companies (Tajmiste, Kikotex, Zito Karaorman, REK Oslomej, Stopanska Banka, Agricultural Combine, and Tane Calevski). It is the best possible estimate available at this moment.

9. FIPA, *Bosnia and Herzegovina Textile and Clothing Industries.* Sarajevo, 2002, p.6.

Finally, there is the case of Tajmiste, the former mining combine whose core business, the iron-ore mine, closed down a decade ago. Following insider privatization, its dynamic director (who is also the biggest shareholder) has worked hard to keep the former workers' collective intact, and Tajmiste remains the largest private employer in the area. The company manages to survive through a range of entrepreneurial activities—a fish farm, pig breeding, a restaurant on the Greek-Macedonian border, a petrol station, a quarry, a locksmith, various retail outlets, and workshops. With such a range of activities all operating within a web of cross-subsidies, it is impossible to gauge which are genuinely profitable—a problem which has always plagued businesses in the former Yugoslavia.

Companies can limp on for quite some time in these conditions. Even after privatization, they have retained their special relationships with state banks, their existing contracts with other public companies as suppliers or customers, and their preferential treatment by tax authorities and public-utility companies. They enjoy soft budget constraints, enabling them to continue operating at a loss. However, by 1998, it had become apparent that liquidity problems in the former socially owned sector were accumulating. According to the IMF, 46 percent of all Macedonian companies in the formal enterprise sector were experiencing a lack of liquidity by the end of 1998, as compared to only 17 percent in 1996. The percentage of workers employed by illiquid firms jumped from 24 to 42 percent over the same period. The IMF found that there was a general decline in the performance of privatized companies as privatization proceeded:

> Continued enterprise sector losses stemmed primarily from insuffi-
> cient labor adjustment and high labor costs *in both privatized and state
> and socially owned enterprises.* ... Operating losses were mainly financed
> by wage arrears, and overdue obligations to suppliers, the government
> and banks. Although during 1996-98, wage arrears for the enterprise
> sector as a whole declined slightly to about 7 percent of GDP in 1998,
> owing to wage arrears reductions by private and state and socially-
> owned enterprises, they *increased further in the transformed enterprises,
> to about 4 percent of GDP"* (World Bank, 1998: 50; emphasis added).

Most recently, the Macedonian National Bank reported that 29.4 percent of employees in Macedonia did not receive their wages in February 2002 (National Bank of the Republic of Macedonia, 2002: 9).

Kicevo's postprivatization economy remains heavily dependent on the continuing state sector, in particular on one company, the thermal power station in Oslomej. Together with Fort and Separacija, two companies only recently separated from the power station, REK Oslomej provides nearly a third of all jobs across the public and formerly socially owned sectors. It pays monthly salaries of 250 euros, well above the average. With almost 1,000 employees, REK now has more workers than during the socialist period and significantly more than required to run a power station of its size. REK is also an important customer of ethnic Macedonian private construction companies. Even the conglomerate Tajmiste is leasing some of its workers to REK at profitable rates. Kicevo's managerial elite all agrees that, without REK, Kicevo would become an economic ghost town.

The power station, which belongs to the state utility Elektrostopanstvo (EMS), has therefore assumed the function not just of employer of last resort, but also of primary customer of other struggling enterprises. By investing most of its income in salaries and subcontracts, EMS is running down its capital stock. It can continue to play this role only so long as it avoids privatization or restructuring and is willing to transfer the costs of its present social policies to the next generation.

Table 7
Kicevo's Ten Publicly Owned Companies

	Activities	Employees
Public companies		
REK Oslomej	Thermal power plant (incl. coal mines, FORT, and Separator)	1,000
JP Komunalec	Public utilities (incl. Kicevo Pole DOO)	160
JP MAK Sume–Stopanstvo Lopusnik	Forestry	198 (partly seasonal)
ESM (Kicevo outlet)	Electricity distribution	110
JP Makedonia pat (Kicevo outlet)	Regional public utility for roads	80
Post	Post	46
Zeleznica Makedonija	Railways	25
JP za stanovanje	Construction of flats	12
Awaiting privatization		
EMO-Elektromontaza Ohrid AD (Kicevo outlet)	Production of electricity pylons	177
Tane Calevski	Metal working	313
All public companies		2,121

Source: Macedonia (2002: 9).

Ethnic Macedonians and the Failure of the Private Sector

The path out of industrial decline in Kicevo should be the creation of a new private sector—the end goal of the economic transition strategies proposed across the region. What is so striking about Kicevo is the limited knowledge, or even apparent interest, on the part of public institutions in this new sector's development.

According to the State Statistical Office in Skopje, there are 2,357 registered companies in the Kicevo area. Most local businessmen regard this figure as inflated, including many companies which have ceased to operate but have not been formally liquidated. A recent report by the OECD and the EBRD on private-enterprise development at the national level suggests that registered firms "can be categorized as being very active, partly active, and inactive in fairly equal proportions" (OECD, 2001: 16). Among formally registered companies in Kicevo, two thirds are trading companies, in retail or wholesale, or repair shops. Just 9 percent are in hospitality (cafés, restaurants, and hotels) and another 9 percent in transport and communication (in which taxi companies figure prominently). Another 10 percent are registered as manufacturing companies, but many of them are obviously inactive, and it is remarkably difficult to form a picture of their operations from any official source.

Among Kicevo's ethnic Macedonian community, there are only three new private enterprises with more than 30 employees: two construction firms, Bistra Drvo and Bemos, and one textile company, Osogovo. The growth of Bistro Drvo has deep roots in the socialist past. It emerged from a housing cooperative (*stambena zadruga*) established in 1985, which was licensed to sell building material at reduced tax rates to private home builders, mainly Albanians. This evolved into the private company Nas Dom, now employing six workers, and a construction company, Bistra Drvo, which employs 70. Being specialized in civil engineering, Bistra Drvo depends on public contracts from local authorities and special funds for water and sewage infrastructure.

Of companies with more than five employees, there are two bakeries, several firms selling construction material, some wholesale traders in food and beverages, a dozen taxi companies, and a few of the larger bars and restaurants. There is also some employment in furniture and metalworking, two trout farms, a couple of pastry shops, and some pottery manufacturers.

These are precisely the kind of local businesses which could be found in the area prior to the Second World War and which were permitted, to some extent, to operate throughout the socialist era as *mala privreda* (small business). According to official statistics, there were already 494 small businesses in Kicevo's "individual sector" in 1989: 285 tradesmen, 122 working in transport, 49 in trade, and 38 in gastronomy (SGRM, 1991: 503). The OECD/EBRD report points out that many new businesses are "small scale, low risk, and low capital-intensity operations such as petty trading" (OECD, 2001: 17).

Among Kicevo's ethnic Macedonians, it is difficult to see at this moment where the dynamic for substantial new private-sector employment growth might emerge. On the Macedonian end of Aleksandar Makedonski Street, the shops and cafés are often empty of customers, and a number of premises are boarded up. The collapse of household income in Kicevo means that retail trade offers lean pickings for the Macedonian small entrepreneurs. By extension, it serves as a very limited source of capital for new productive businesses.

The difficulty of finding investment capital and the particular skills of the workforce provide further barriers to private-sector development. In the Kicevo municipality, 21 percent of the working age population never completed elementary school, while another 33 percent has gone no further than elementary school. In the rural areas, such as Zajas, the proportion without education beyond the primary level reaches 90 percent (Agri Consulting VIZI, 2002: 5).[10] Until early 2002, the local outlet of the national Stopanska Banka was the only bank in the region. In 2001, it extended 16 commercial credits, totaling only 260,000 euros.[11]

In short, in a place like Kicevo, private-sector growth that could make up for the employment lost in the collapse of Macedonian industrial society is not emerging naturally from the ashes of the socialist economy.

The Politics of Scarce Employment

With little employment to be had in the productive sector of the economy, holding on to jobs in the public administration becomes a key priority for Kicevo's ethnic Macedonian urban middle class. The conditions in public employment are not particularly attractive. A wage freeze has been in place in recent years, and being "on the budget," in other words, being employed by the state, no longer offers either the social status or the standard of living it did under the old regime. However, for an important segment of Kicevo's ethnic Macedonian community, it continues to provide a means to survive, as well as some social benefits.

Those who lose their jobs often have no other form of support available. Of 8,452 registered unemployed in the Kicevo region, only 686 (8 percent) receive regular

10. In Drugovo, 72.6 percent of the population has no secondary education; in Zajas, 87.5 percent; in Vranestica, 77.7 percent; and in Oslomej, 86.3 percent.
11. Information from Stopanska Banka.

unemployment benefits. Another 1,973 of the most difficult social cases receive assistance payments from the Center for Social Work.[12]

The public administration has been the one sector of the economy to experience modest employment growth over the past decade. There are now some 1,481 public-sector employees in the Kicevo region, of which 95 percent work in local outlets of central-level institutions. The five municipal administrations have only 69 employees between them. The largest employer is the schools, with 615 staff members, and is the only public institution offering substantial employment to the nonethnic Macedonians. Outside the education sector, Albanians hold only some 120 of 865 posts, or 14 percent, despite constituting 50 percent of the regional population.

Table 8
Government Employment in the Kicevo Area

Level of government		Employees (estimated)
Central government		1,412
Education	*615*	
Health	375	
Central administration outlets	132	
Police (Ministry of Interior)	230	
Court and prosecutor	60	
Municipal government (Kicevo, Drugovo, Oslomej, Vranestica, Zajas)		69
Total		1,481

Source: Statistical Office of Macedonia (2001); Pension Fund, municipal administrations, and various interviews with central administration employees.

With such a high proportion of employment depending on the state, it is not surprising that the politics of public employment are intense. Scarcity increases the relative value of jobs in the public sector. With public-sector jobs one of the few public goods that local politicians still have at their disposal, their apportionment within the ethnic Macedonian community is often decided along political party lines, and other ethnic groups remain at a significant disadvantage. It is also not surprising to find that pressure from the non-Macedonian communities for better

12. Information from Employment Bureau outlet Kicevo (as of December 31, 2001); Center for Social Work (as of February 2002).

representation in the public sector should be threatening to the Macedonian middle classes, who feel more under siege with each passing year.

In its *Human Development Report 2001*, the UNDP makes certain recommendations to address the growing unemployment problem, including "that the state activates other conventional measures directed toward the creation of new work posts, for example, public posts," and "more intensive support of the companies that are suffering losses but are vital for the state and the population. In that context, especially significant will be the policy for subvention of the salaries of the employed" (UNDP, 2001: 45).

In fact, by one means or another, these are exactly the strategies which the Macedonian state has adopted throughout the 1990s, within the limits of the resources available to it. The preservation of former public companies and the gradual expansion in public-sector employment are the government's response to the social pressures placed on it by its primary constituency. However, at best, such policies can only hope to slow the decline of the public sector. At worst, they crowd out the development of new private employers.

A number of conclusions emerge from this review of employment in Kicevo, with far-reaching implications for understanding the political economy of the area. First, for Kicevo's ethnic Macedonians, the importance of the state as employer and benefactor has continued to grow. The 1,486 jobs in public administration (including education and health care) and 1,631 jobs in public enterprises are, today, more than ever, the last refuge of the urban middle class. Furthermore, they are the last remaining sectors where there is a continuing link between educational qualifications and standard of living. In addition, contracts with the state or its public enterprises are essential to the most important new businesses, particularly in the construction sector.

Second, it seems inevitable that the decline of employment in Kicevo will continue over the next few years. If the government hardens the budget constraints on privatized SOEs, liquidates the companies for which no buyers can be found, and privatizes or restructures the national electricity utility and the Oslomej power station, another third of all jobs across the industrial sector could disappear overnight.

Finally, by necessary implication, the ethnic Macedonian community will bear the lion's share of the costs of transition. In 1990, we estimate that 80 percent of Kicevo's public-sector jobs were held by ethnic Macedonians. It is they who have been hardest hit by job losses over the past decade and who have the most to lose in the coming period. In this environment, it seems inevitable that the struggle for control over diminishing public resources should take on an ethnic color. It is this dynamic which gives the Macedonian political economy its highly combustible nature.

Internal Migration and Development

The migration of ethnic Macedonians from the countryside into the urban centers was the most important demographic shift of the past half century. In 1948, in the mountain areas of Drugovo and Vranestica, most people lived from raising sheep on highland pastures or subsistence agriculture. Over the next 40 years, migration into the town of Kicevo caused a decline in the rural population of 60 percent, while Kicevo nearly quadrupled in size, from 7,000 to 25,000. In the 1980s, a fleet of buses would leave Kicevo every morning, carrying workers from their socially owned apartments to jobs in the power station and the mines.

Table 9
Population Change in 78 Villages in the Kicevo Area from 1948 to 1994

Population change	Macedonian villages	Albanian villages	Mixed villages
Growth of more than 100%	—	6	3
Growth of 33 to 100%	—	10	—
Growth up to 33%	—	2	1
Decline up to 33%	4	3	4
Decline from 33 to 75%	12	2	1
Decline of more than 75%	29	1	—
Total	45	24	9

Source: Census data of 1948 and 1994.

Urbanization was a conscious policy on the part of the communist authorities, part of the process of forging a modern industrial society. It was understood as part of the nation-building process and of catching up with Europe's developed regions. In addition to its new industrial enterprises, Kicevo became host to a court and regional police headquarters, local outlets of various ministries and agencies, the regional office of Macedonia's development bank, two public-utility companies, and a number of schools (including the region's only secondary school). It became the seat of a large hospital and had an important Yugoslav army barracks, housing some 4,000 soldiers.[13]

---

13. At one time, this was under the command of the Bosnian Serb Ratko Mladic.

In addition to providing a regular income, jobs in the socialist public economy were the means to access other state benefits, including highly subsidized apartments, company food allowances, and access to holiday facilities. Many households in Kicevo had two wage-earners, giving them the purchasing power to acquire household appliances and other consumer goods. The birth of an industrial society brought the amenities of a modern life-style—water and sewage systems, asphalt roads, a shopping mall, a cultural center, a cinema, and a football stadium. The inhabitants of Kicevo looked to other southern European countries, which were also catching up with the West during these decades—Greece, southern Italy, and the Iberian Peninsula—and felt that they, too, were arriving at the modern consumer society of postwar Europe.

Today, as ethnic Macedonians grapple with the problem of Kicevo's economic decline, the notion of solving the employment problem through a return to the land is finding its way into the public debate. The most detailed study on economic development and comparative advantage in the Kicevo region in recent times, published in February 2002, came to this conclusion. According to the authors, resettlement of areas with the lowest population density in the region, Drugovo and Vranestica, "should be one of the priorities for future regional development" (Agri Consulting VIZI, 2002: 4.)

The study recognizes the sharp contraction in industrial employment during the 1990s. It quotes official data revealing a dramatic collapse in per capita investment in the Kicevo region, which, by 1999, was a mere 25 percent of the Macedonian average.[14] The authors note that 69 percent of Kicevo's population has no more than primary education. Half of the unemployed, some 4,100 people, have no education at all, severely limiting the potential for developing a more complex service economy. What was therefore required, the study concluded, was a renewed focus on agriculture and natural resources. Economic development should start with greater "utilization of natural wealth through exploitation of ore wealth (marble, coals, and so on), utilization of wood and other forest fruits, utilization of agricultural land and above all pastures, utilization of water and tourism."

One traditional sector in particular is highlighted for its growth potential: sheep breeding. "Thirty to forty years ago this region had 100,000 sheep due to the favorable development conditions. Presently, this number is down to 22,000 sheep, indicating the low usage of the natural conditions of the region" (Agri Consulting VIZI, 2002: 17). The main obstacle to the implementation of such a strategy is that people no longer live in the right places. "In certain parts of the region, where

---

14. The data is taken from the Statistical Review of Investments in Macedonia (1998, 1999, and 2000).

the development of sheep and cattle breeding should be developed, the density of population is very low, as is the size of the labor force." Thus, the study recommends that Kicevo adopt a policy of deurbanization, returning the urban unemployed to the villages their families left a generation ago:

> The development of animal husbandry in those areas should go in parallel with the revitalization of the villages and improvement in living conditions. This should contribute to the return of a part of the unemployed population from the city to the abandoned land in the villages (Agri Consulting VIZI, 2002: 69).

Curiously, this analysis overlooks the situation of the Albanian population, constituting 50 percent of the region, which continues to be concentrated in the villages and indeed owns most of the sheep. Rural depopulation is essentially an ethnic Macedonian phenomenon. Between 1948 and 1994, the population of all 45 ethnic Macedonian villages in the region declined, with 29 of them losing more than three-quarters of their population. At the same time, the population of 18 of the 24 Albanian villages continued to grow, with six of them doubling in size. Of course, employment opportunities in the Albanian areas failed to keep pace with the population growth.

The idea of reversing the trends of half a century and returning the population to the countryside is a curious reflection of this fading dream of modernization. It is not, however, a credible strategy for development. The rural areas hold no appeal at all for an urbanized population: basic infrastructure is lacking, education and health services are underdeveloped, and housing conditions are very poor (UNDP, 2001a: 65–67). In a recent poll, 43 percent of respondents from highland Macedonia stated that they do not have enough money for food, while another 47 percent stated that they could not afford clothing and footwear (UNDP, 2001a: 64). In addition, 40 percent of the agricultural population lives at the subsistence level, earning no cash income from farming (ISPJR in UNDP, 2001a: 63). The economic incentives to pursue agriculture are so low that, in 1996, only 48 percent of all private arable land was actually in use (ISPJR in UNDP, 2001a: 66).

In the entire Kicevo region, there are only 10 households with more than 100 sheep, and only 16 people officially working as shepherds. When Blagoja Gjorgjijoski acquired the assets of the bankrupt agricultural cooperative, he became the region's premier pastoralist, with more than 2,000 head of sheep. He is also president of the only sheep breeders' association in the region, founded in 1998 with mainly Albanian members, and plans to set up a dairy. He notes that at this moment there is neither the know-how to make quality products capable of competing with imports, nor the means to bring them to market. Already, most of the sheep cheese produced in the region cannot be sold.

Most importantly, there is no desire among Kicevo's young urban Macedonians to return to the villages their parents or grandparents abandoned decades ago or to resume an isolated life on the high mountain pastures. Gjorgjijoski has found recruitment of shepherds to be a major problem, despite offering wages which are substantially above the average. No matter how acute the crisis of industry in Kicevo, the habits of life in an industrial society remain very real.

The Globalization of Albanians

In 1998, the municipal administration of Kicevo published a colorful book on the Kicevo region. The chapter on the local economy lists all the former socialist enterprises and their founding directors. It also notes that, "unfortunately, the new transition process, instead of accelerating economic growth, has led to a decrease in social production." Not one private business is mentioned. Albanians, who make up the majority of the population in the region, do not appear at all, except in a section on the Second World War (Municipality of Kicevo, 1998).

This lack of interest on the part of official Macedonia in what is happening on the left side of Liberation Boulevard or in villages like Zajas and Oslomej explains why one of the most dramatic engines of social change in the past decade—the mass migration of Albanians to Western countries—has never figured in official thinking on local development.

The regional development strategy quoted above makes no mention of labor migration. In its 1998 report on Macedonia, entitled *Enhancing Growth*, the World Bank merely notes that "unidentified capital flows accounted for around 70 percent of the financing for the current account deficit during 1994-97. It may be that much, and perhaps all, of the unidentified flows are unrecorded remittances or self-liquidating trade credits" (World Bank, 1998: 5). While the significance of remittances is inescapable in the context of macroeconomic stability, their impact on regional economies is never explored.

Yet in recent European history, labor migration has been recognized as one of the most important exogenous shocks to a stagnant economic system. It is not long ago that the "*calata dei tedeschi*" (the descent of the Germans), the mass return of Italian migrant workers to their villages for Christmas, was the major social event of the year in large parts of southern Italy. As a recent study on economic growth in the past century concluded, there have been periods in recent Italian history when "emigration alone accounted for almost all the growth in real wages and GDP per capita in Italy and explains, as it does in the Irish case as well, much of the catch up with the UK" (Cohen and Federico, 2001: 45).[15] The study continues:

> Emigrant remittances helped to monetize the southern economy: they increased saving among southern families, prompted the use of banks and facilitated greater access to credit. Emigrant remittances stimulated the market in land, while those who returned brought back with them new attitudes and tastes (Cohen and Federico, 2001: 29).

The recent history of socialist Macedonia is a reminder of the fact that economic development and movement of people have always been inextricably linked.

There are no accurate statistics available on Albanian emigration from Kicevo over the years. The common estimate, both by municipal officials and many ethnic Albanian citizens, is that nearly every household in rural areas and every second household in the town has at least one family member working abroad. This gives rise to a conservative estimate of at least 3,300 ethnic Albanians abroad who are supporting their families in the Kicevo area.

In the absence of hard data, one way to capture the significance of the phenomenon is to select at random a first-year class of pupils from Kicevo's gymnasium, Mirko Mileski, and find out where the students have ended up a decade later. The class of 1989–90 was ethnically mixed, consisting of 20 ethnic Macedonians, 7 Albanians, and 4 Turks. Of the 31 students, only 2 were girls (both ethnic Macedonian).

The first thing to note is how few of the Muslims graduated from the school. Four of the Albanians and all four Turks failed in the first year, choosing to leave the school rather than repeat the class. Many assert that language difficulties and a lack of encouragement from the teachers were the cause of their failure. Two were able to complete their high-school education in the neighboring municipality of Gostivar, and others left the country immediately. Only one of the Albanian students ended up graduating in Kicevo.

A decade later, the diverging paths of the two ethnic groups emerge very clearly. Out of seven Albanians, only one remains in Macedonia (although other members of his family are abroad). Of the 20 ethnic Macedonians, all remain in Macedonia, and most are still in the Kicevo region. Four of them work in companies described in this report (the Oslomej power station and Tajmiste), four have regular employment in the private sector, and three do casual work or are unemployed. We were unable to find employment details for the remainder.

---

15. They also note that "although scholars have always paid lip service to the importance of emigration, its causes and consequences have remained until recently largely unexplored" (2001: 43).

Table 10

Current Whereabouts of Albanian, Macedonian, and Turkish Pupils,
Class of 1989/1990, Mirko Mileski Gymnasium, Kicevo

Albanian pupils
Sefer lives in Kicevo. He has his own taxi company (Zajazi), while his father works in Germany
Prparim is in Vienna
Lulzim is in Chicago
Bashkim is in New York
Bashkim works in Alaska
Agron is in a town close to Chicago
Flamur, related to Agron, is in the same town close to Chicago
Turkish pupils
Adnan is in Kicevo and drives a taxi
Enis works in a private company in Kicevo
Samir is a private tradesman in Kicevo
Galip works in Switzerland
Ethnic Macedonian pupils
Robert works in Tajmiste
Vlatko works in Tajmiste
Dusko works in REK Oslomej
Aco works in REK Oslomej
Orce works in a bakery
Zlatko works in a shop for construction material
Goran works in a betting shop
Zoran has a private sector job
Dalibor does occasional work
Maksim does occasional work
Beti (woman) is at home
Nine others live in Macedonia, but information on their whereabouts and employment is unavailable.

Source: The information in this section was generated from interviews in Kicevo, verified by former students who visited the families of former classmates.

This picture is inevitably impressionistic, and it would be valuable to take a broader cross-section of students to see if the pattern holds. But it does provide a snapshot of the dominant social dynamic among Kicevo's Albanians. It also reveals another important feature: the inability of ethnic Macedonians from Kicevo to take the emigration route. Emigration tends to be a cumulative process. Its incidence is a positive function of the number of earlier emigrants who provide money, information, and support for newcomers. If Kicevo's ethnic Macedonians have relatives abroad, they usually emigrated for Australia in the 1950s, and no longer maintain close links with family who remained. There is no equivalent of the dense networks which Albanian have constructed between Kicevo and the outside world over the past two decades.

The diaspora phenomenon explains features of Albanian society in Kicevo which are puzzling to outside observers, particularly the ethnic Macedonians. With its high population growth, the Albanian community has a high proportion of underage dependents, which it manages to support despite an extremely limited employment base. At the same time, the Albanian quarter of Kicevo and the Albanian villages show a remarkable amount of building activity, together with a lively service sector in the center of the town.

There are an estimated 2,000 Albanian households in the municipality of Zajas. There are 135 teachers working in the primary schools, which is the only significant source of public employment. There are seven municipal employees and reportedly 19 police officers, although before the Ohrid Agreement only two were Albanians. There are no individuals employed by outlets of the central government except for two workers in the local registry office (*maticna sluzba*). The largest private company, Perperimi, which sells construction material, has 10–12 employees. According to official statistics, there are 155 registered shops, a restaurant, a motel employing five, and a bakery which employs seven. There are ten employees remaining in the local outlet of the conglomerate Tajmiste, but none are Albanian. In sum, it would be surprising to find that more than one household in five has a family member in formal employment.

The picture in Oslomej is very similar. As mentioned above, the power station and its various associated enterprises employ a thousand people, but only 46 of these are residents of Oslomej. There are eight employees in the municipal administration and two in the utility company, 129 positions in primary schools, 99 registered shops and small traders, a petrol station, two small companies selling construction materials, and two restaurants. Due to problems with the water quality, there is no bakery for Oslomej's 17 villages. The municipality estimates that around 50 people work in sheep and cattle farming. Again, the ratio between workplaces and Oslomej's 1,900 households is hardly favorable.

Officials in the two municipalities estimate that at least 1,500 citizens of Zajas, 1,000 from Oslomej, and 800 from Kicevo town are working abroad and sending home remittances to their families. There is a community of around 250 Kicevo Albanians in Alaska and other communities scattered across the United States from Chicago to the mid-West. Others went to Western Europe, particularly Switzerland and Germany. Kicevo Albanian businessmen own limousine services in Alaska, restaurants in Wisconsin, and hotels in Antalya on the Turkish coast. A significant number draw pensions from Switzerland, Germany, and other European countries. In effect, Albanian Kicevo has become a suburb of Western Europe and the United States.

The diaspora community sends cash transfers, makes personal investments in real estate, and spends a startling amount of money on weddings. The impact on the local economy is highly visible. Based on interviews among the Albanian community, we calculate conservatively that a typical worker abroad sends home or spends in Kicevo more than €5,000 annually, giving total transfers in excess of €16 million. This is equivalent to ten times the consolidated budget of the municipality of Kicevo and about twice the combined annual salaries of the 3,800 ethnic Macedonians employed in the public administration and the former socially owned enterprises.

These financial flows generate a significant amount of real-estate investment. The size of many of the houses in Zajas and Oslomej is quite out of proportion with the state of the local economy. There are also a number of prestigious building projects in the Albanian quarter of Kicevo town, some of them clearly designed to meet the Albanian community's taste for expensive weddings. In the mid-1990s, diaspora money funded the construction of Arabella, a three-story complex hosting shops and offices, the local television station, and a large reception center.

However, despite the aura of prosperity created by these building projects, very little of the capital inflow from the diaspora ends up in productive investment. The environment of the Kicevo region is not seen as conducive to risky capital ventures. There are many stories among Kicevo's Albanians of failed business ventures thwarted by hostile inspectors, problems in obtaining licenses and building approvals, and other bureaucratic hurdles. The lack of public investment is also a significant problem. One Albanian comments, "people get used to a Swiss environment and then encounter only problems: no secure water supply, weak electricity current, roads without asphalt."

The lack of an effective state in the Albanian areas, and the subsequent poor quality of local infrastructure, has meant that the capital flows remain trapped in trade and consumption, generating little in the way of lasting wealth. Albanian shopkeepers in the town therefore remain dependent on the diaspora returning each year to spend their money over the summer months. For the rest of the year, as one carpet seller explains, "our situation is almost as bad as that of the Macedonian shops."

The lack of effective utilization of diaspora capital must rank as the most obvious missed opportunity for lifting Kicevo out of its cycle of economic decline. The one important Albanian private enterprise in Kicevo, the textile company Himara, illustrates the potential. The proprietor, Bajram Selimi, returned from France in 1994, where he had built up his own textile company. Acquiring premises from a trade cooperative that went bankrupt in the early 1990s, he has created a company of 100 employees—the largest new enterprise in Kicevo. Himara produces exclusively for the French market, taking delivery of cloth sent by lorry from France and returning finished products, with Selimi's French company acting as intermediary. Interestingly, apart from the boss himself and the chief accountant, all the employees in the company are ethnic Macedonian, mainly women who once worked for the socially owned textile company Kikoteks.

Given the dire economic circumstances, it is only among the Albanian diaspora that Kicevo is likely to find the right combination of venture capital, entrepreneurial skill, and ready-made business contacts with external markets. The Albanian diaspora is therefore Kicevo's most important economic resource. As the Himara example shows, if ways could be found to mobilize it, the benefits would accrue as much to the ethnic Macedonian community as to the Albanians.

If this resource cannot be utilized, the economic prospects for Kicevo's Albanians are little better than those facing the Macedonian community. At this moment, there are 1,612 students in primary schools in Zajas and another 1,233 in Oslomej. There are no investments underway in either municipality, and no new jobs are being created. Unless a new development strategy emerges, emigration will continue to be the only path available to the new generation of Albanians.

Zajas and the Absent State

There are two rival football clubs in Kicevo. Napredok is the traditional club of the town, founded in the 1950s. Its home is the socialist-era stadium built with compulsory contributions from citizens and recently refurbished with new seats bought with public money. The former IMRO–DPNU mayor, Ilija Kitanoski, is president of the club, which plays in the country's first division.

Vlazrimi is a mainly Albanian football club, although it has two ethnic Macedonian players, and has just been promoted to the second division. It has a brand new stadium built in the late 1990s through donations from Albanians around the world, together with voluntary labor from the local community, and its main sponsor is the wealthiest Kicevo Alaskan businessman. Its impeccably kept turf displays state-of-the-art sports equipment imported from the United States. The stadium was constructed on empty public land, without building permission from the state. As one local businessman puts it, the stadium is the Albanian community's proudest collective achievement. Diaspora money helps substitute for the state itself.

It is not in the Albanian parts of Kicevo town, however, but in the rural Albanian municipalities of the region that the absence of a state is most visible. In the newly established municipality of Zajas, home of Ali Ahmeti, the seven-member municipal administration is housed in a temporary-looking shelter no larger than a family apartment. With a core budget, in 2002, of 54,000 euros for a community of 10,000 people, its capacity to deliver any form of services to its citizens is minimal. The most prominent public institutions in Zajas are the primary schools, which employ 135 staff for 1,600 pupils. The central authorities of the Macedonian state are concentrated in Kicevo town, or in distant Skopje. Only 395 households receive very modest social welfare, and hardly anybody receives unemployment benefits. There are only 24 kilometers of sealed local roads in the municipality. In the former Yugoslav era, there was no important investment in the municipality except the Tajmiste mine, which is now closed, and there has been almost no public investment of any kind since the end of socialism.

The isolation of places like Zajas from the Macedonian state was heightened by local-government reform in 1995–96, which increased the number of municipalities from 34 to 123. Four new rural municipalities composed only of villages were carved out of the Kicevo region, two of which, Zajas and Oslomej, have overwhelmingly Albanian populations. The new municipalities were severed from their traditional administrative center and inherited almost no public institutions or infrastructure.

The new Law on Local Self-Governance left the state highly centralized. The few responsibilities of the municipalities include construction and maintenance of local roads, streets and parks, water supply and street lighting, garbage collection, the administration of markets and graveyards, and a certain degree of urban planning.[16] Formally all five municipalities have the same rights and competencies, exercised by a mayor, municipal assembly, and local administration. However, while Kicevo employs some 45 people, the four rural municipalities have only five to seven each. While Kicevo inherited the old municipal building, the other four municipal administrations are located in barracks or adapted buildings, often no larger than an apartment.

As a result, institutional deficiencies inherited from the socialist period have become even more acute. The health sector is one example. In Kicevo in the 1980s, the health system was scheduled for the most substantial public investment of the

---

16. Law on Local Self-Governance. *Sluzben Vesnik* No. 52/1995, Article 17.

decade, the building of a new hospital in Kicevo town. Construction began in 1986, but it was halted for lack of resources after the walls and roof had been built. In 1992, another brief period of activity saw windows installed, but the project stalled once again, and the interior has never been completed. Outside Kicevo, the resource shortages are even more apparent. The Kicevo hospital operates a series of small, decentralized primary health clinics (*ambulante*), but the standard of care is extremely basic. Part of the problem is that staffing levels (and the geographical distribution of staff) have remained constant even while overall resources have declined, forcing the clinics to cut their operating expenses. As a result, some are open for as little as four hours a day.

Table 11

Consolidated Municipal Revenues of Kicevo, Drugovo, and Oslomej in 2000

Municipal Resources	Kicevo		Oslomej		Drugovo	
	€	% of total revenue	€	% of total revenue	€	% of total revenue
Municipal budget	145,974	9.6	85,000	48.7	70,000	24.6
Fund for local roads	80,172	5.3	65,500	37.5	—	0
Fund for communal services/organization of construction land	559,807	36.8	20,000	11.5	214,947	75.4
Public-utility company	735,400*	48.3	3,900	2.2	—	
Total	1,521,353	100	174,500	99.9	284,947	100.0
From central sources	157,638	10.4	79,557	45.6	226,183	79.4

Source: Local Government Reform Project. Data from municipal budgets and budgets of the respective funds.

* No data is available for Komunalec Kicevo, the public-utility company. This estimate is based on average revenues of Macedonian municipal utility companies on a per capita basis.

With no local production and no urban center, the capacity of the smaller municipalities to generate revenue to build new institutions and infrastructure is severely constrained. In Macedonia's highly centralized fiscal system, municipal revenues depend heavily on local charges and taxes levied on construction and land acquisition, plus the revenues of the public utility companies, both of which are off-budget. As the main urban center, Kicevo town is able to generate most of its revenue from these sources, which is used to fund infrastructure development and municipal services. In Albanian Oslomej, however, there is no commercial construction under-way and very little infrastructure to generate service charges. These two sources amounted to only €24,000, or 14 percent of Oslomej's total revenues.

The lack of financial independence of rural Albanian municipalities makes them dependent on the central government and therefore vulnerable to the unpredictability and inequities of Macedonian public spending. There are very few central resources available for local infrastructure projects. Some water projects are funded by the Ministry of Transport and Communication, there are regular transfers from the Fund for National and Regional Roads to municipal road funds, and certain infrastructure projects are supported by the Bureau for Underdeveloped Regions. These transfers operate in a nontransparent manner, and it is remarkably difficult to find out how they are distributed across the country.

In the area of water supply, there is a clear neglect of the Albanian villages in favor of urban and majority ethnic Macedonian rural areas. Of 27 projects supported by the Ministry of Transport and Communication in the Kicevo region from 1997 to 2001, Zajas received support for only one project, a bare 1.9 percent of the total funds spent in the Kicevo region. At 35 cents per capita, this is less than half the national average. Oslomej fared only slightly better, with five projects. Despite making up 37 percent of the population in the Kicevo region, these two Albanian municipalities received only 14.2 percent of the funding between them. By contrast, the two predominantly ethnic Macedonian rural municipalities, Vranestica and Drugovo, received 47.8 percent of the project funds, despite having only 10 percent of the region's population.[17]

It is apparent that strengthening local autonomy in Macedonia requires appro-priate resources to allow local governments to become effective. The practical effect of the reforms of 1995–96 was that the state as a whole largely disappeared from the smaller municipalities. In effect, the Macedonian state lost control of places like Zajas—not in the sense of security or law and order, but in the sense of being able to maintain an effective administrative presence.

In some Albanian villages, a traditional peace council continues to operate as an informal body unrecognized by the state. It consists of respected village elders who mediate on disputes between community members. While its authority varies from village to village, in some places, it is able to adjudicate and impose compensation payments. Local views differ as to how well these informal structures function. According to some Albanians, they represent a continuation of the *kanun*, the

17. "Odluka za paspredelba na sredstvata za izgradba na vodovodi i fekalni kanalizacii vo Republika Makedonija," 1997–2001. *Sluzben Vesnik* No. 57/1997 No. 41/1998, No. 51/1999, No. 51/2000, and No. 40/2001.

traditional Albanian laws; others say they have lost their social significance. Where they continue to operate, it is in part a sign of lack of confidence in the formal legal system. According to one Albanian villager, "if one calls the police or goes to court, the result is an even greater mess."

Table 12

Funds Allocated from the Water and Canalization Program and the Fund for National and Regional Roads to the Kicevo region, 1997–2001

Municipality	% of region's pop.	Road fund		Water and canaliza-tion		Total	
		€	% of total funds	€	% of total funds	€	% of total funds
Kicevo	53	296,817	31.2	168,333	37.7	465,150	33.3
Drugovo	6.8	176,700	18.6	150,000	33.6	326,700	23.4
Oslomej	17.6	174,283	18.3	56,667	12.7	230,950	16.5
Vranestica	3.2	114,967	12.1	63,333	14.2	178,300	12.8
Zajas	19.3	187,467	19.7	8,333	1.9	195,800	14.0
Total	100.0	950,234		446,667		1,396,900	

Source: Fund for National and Regional Roads. "Odluka za paspredelba na sredstvata za izgradba na vodovodi i fekalni kanalizacii vo Republika Makedonija," *Sluzben Vesnik*. No. 57/1997, No. 41/1998, No. 51/1999, No. 51/2000, No. 40/2001) [60 Denar = 1€].

The high degree of centralization of Macedonia's public institutions ensures that they have only a tenuous connection with these rural areas. The result is a startling lack of information about some of the most important dynamics in Macedonian society. The activities which are most important to a rural community—subsistence agriculture, small-scale trade, labor emigration—are neither subject to state authority nor benefit from public resources. They take place in a realm which is largely invisible to the Macedonian authorities.

The same dynamic holds largely true for the new private sector in Kicevo town. The regional outlet for the Ministry of Economy in Kicevo, for example, was unable to provide a list of private enterprises in Kicevo or even identify the most significant. Its seven or so employees have no computer at their disposal, let alone a database. The Central Registry, one of the successors of the former payments bureau, receives data from every enterprise, but it is sent to Skopje for processing and can only be accessed with a charge of €5 per unit of data, after official permission from the director. No data is ever processed or sent back to the authorities in Kicevo. As a result, there is not even a rudimentary information basis for formulating municipal economic policy.

The legitimacy of any state depends first and foremost on its capacity to deliver practical services to its citizens. It is therefore not surprising to find the Macedonian state entering a crisis of legitimacy, which is of course most acute among the Albanian community. There is a widespread, and to a large extent justified, perception among Albanians that the state is a distant and alien presence, with no real benefits to offer in the areas that matter to Albanians.

Looking at the Kicevo region, it is apparent that this democratic deficit is not an abstract problem, but a very practical question of how public institutions are organized and how public resources are distributed. Reshaping the Macedonian state so it becomes relevant in a place like Zajas, not merely as a police force but as a factor in social and economic development, is the major challenge in overcoming political divisions. It is also a precondition for reversing Kicevo's economic decline.

Perspectives of the Peace Agreement

The story of the political economy of ethnic relations in Kicevo carries important implications for Macedonia as it struggles to implement the Framework Agreement for Peace (Ohrid Agreement).

In Kicevo, there is no war damage to reconstruct, no displaced population to resettle, and no paramilitaries to disarm or disband. The Albanian language is already used in many official contexts, and the education system is bilingual. Implementation of the Ohrid Agreement must surely be easier here than in Tetovo or the northern villages directly affected by the fighting. Yet despite this, even in the Kicevo region, the tools to address the grievances outlined in this report are not yet in place.

This is not a matter of symbolic politics, although symbols have a part to play. It is a matter of engaging with difficult questions about how real power and public resources are distributed in places like Zajas, Drugovo, and Kicevo.

Two developments are coming to a head in the postelection period in Macedonia. The first is the imperative of keeping public expenditure under tight control. As a result of the conflict of 2001, defense- and security-related expenditures have increased significantly over the 2000 level and are likely to remain high for the foreseeable future. According to the IMF, the "security crisis has drastically changed the medium-term fiscal challenges faced by FYROM. Not only have new expenditure demands emerged, but also more are likely to arise over the medium term (IMF, 2002b, 21)."

Macedonia is coming under increasing pressure from the international financial institutions to rein in public expenditure. As the IMF writes: "In the coming years, the budget will face incipient strains on the revenue side and spending pressures in a number of priority areas. The staff encouraged the authorities to introduce from 2003, if not sooner, permanent revenue-enhancing measures. ... Further strengthening of expenditure management and control is also a priority" (IMF, 2002c: 3). Options for local-government reform and fiscal decentralization are constrained by the overall requirement that any changes must be, in the language of the international financial institutions, "revenue neutral" (IMF, 2002a: 11). This means that the creation of new institutions or services by the state must be accompanied by the downsizing of others. Redistributing scarce public resources will necessarily generate winners and losers.

The other development is a potential clash of expectations between the ethnic Albanian and ethnic Macedonian communities and leadership over the pace of Ohrid implementation. In the wake of recent elections fought by Ahmeti's party on the twin themes of Ohrid implementation and employment creation, Macedonia's Albanians expect to feel the impact of the peace agreement on their lives in the near future. Expectations are running high for a restructuring of the basic state architecture, a strengthening of local government, substantial investment in Albanian language education, and an accelerated acceptance of Albanians into public-sector employment. Though reforms of this kind have been on the table throughout the 1990s, ethnic Albanians hope that the process will now move much faster due to the undertakings in the Ohrid Agreement and its promise that outsiders, in particular the European Union, are expected to take an active role in ensuring implementation.[18]

For their part, most ethnic Macedonians have never contested the need for these reforms as a matter of principle. However, against the background of the deepening employment crisis, particularly among the politically influential urban middle class, they are likely to demand that their political representatives protect their existing employment levels in the public sector. The abstract commitment to local-government and public-administration reform may come under severe challenge when it reaches the point of shifting resources (and jobs) away from central institutions in Skopje and other majority Macedonian towns. It is relatively easy to accept a formal requirement that the Albanian language is used in public institutions but much more difficult to accept that ethnic Macedonian employees will have to

---

18. The Ohrid Agreement provides: "The parties invite the international community to assist in the process of strengthening local self-government. The international community should in particular assist in preparing the necessary legal amendments related to financing mechanism for strengthening the financial basis of municipalities and building their financial management capabilities, and in amending the law on the boundaries of municipalities." Annex C, para. 4.

make way for Albanian speakers, or that the extension of secondary education in Albanian areas will come at the expense of cuts in other areas considered essential by the ethnic Macedonian community.

One can anticipate where these strains will emerge by thinking through the politics of Ohrid implementation as they will play out in places like Kicevo. Leaving aside the parts relating to cultural identity—the display of emblems or the protection of cultural diversity—there are three elements of the Ohrid Agreement which will have the most direct impact on life in Kicevo: equitable representation in public administration, the use of the Albanian language in dealings with the state, and strengthening local government. In all three areas, some progress has been made on initial legislative reforms, but the most difficult part is yet to come.

Albanians as Civil Servants

In addition to general provisions on nondiscrimination and equal treatment, the Ohrid Agreement provides that:

> Laws regulating employment in public administration will include measures to assure *equitable representation of communities in all central and local public bodies and at all levels of employment within such bodies,* while respecting the rules concerning competence and integrity that govern public administration.

"Equitable representation" is a somewhat ambiguous term, without the strict mathematical implications of proportional representation, but obviously pointing in the same direction. This vagueness increases the risk of divergent expectations on the part of the different communities. In Kicevo, leaving aside the education sector, which for reasons of language is already ethnically balanced, there are now some 870 state positions. Given their weight of 50 percent in the region's population, Albanians could legitimately lay claim to over 400 of them. This would be more than three times the number they currently hold.

Given the public-finance constraints and the demands of efficient administration, the Kicevo region could not justify achieving equitable representation simply by recruiting additional Albanians. To keep its existing employment levels, which may already be too high, it would need to reduce the number of ethnic Macedonian employees by more than a third to make way for so many Albanians.

There are a number of obvious obstacles likely to arise. The first concerns the number of Albanians in a position to take up posts in the public administration, given the requirement in the Ohrid Agreement of "respecting the rules concerning competence ... that govern public administration" (Para. 4.2). In Zajas and Oslomej, only 3 percent of the population has secondary or university education (some 530 individuals), which is approximately the number of Albanians already employed in the public sector, mostly as teachers. In addition, it is possible that a number of these educated Albanians are working abroad in the diaspora. As the UNDP report noted, if all of the Albanians with higher education were employed in the public administration across Macedonia, "the current structure of employment by ethnic affiliation would not be changed dramatically." Albanian representation would only increase from 10.2 to 10.7 percent (UNDP, 2001a: 39).

Secondly, in the current environment of spiraling unemployment, any rapid dismissal of ethnic Macedonians in favor of Albanians is likely to trigger a serious political backlash. Realistically, correcting the imbalance in representation in the public administration will need to take place through the natural attrition of ethnic Macedonian employees and a program of positive discrimination in favor of Albanians in public-sector recruitment over many years. It will need to go hand in hand with improved access to higher education and professional training for the Albanian community.

Table 13
Estimated Public-Administration Employment in Kicevo, Drugovo,
Oslomej, Vranestica, and Zajas

Institution	Sector	Employees	
		Total	No. of Albanians
Kicevo			
Municipality	Local administration	45	5
Primary schools	Education	198	60
Secondary school	Education	120	50
Center for Social Works	Social assistance	16	3
Fire brigade	(Under Ministry for Internal Affairs)	N/A	N/A
Central administration	Outlets of ministries, central funds, court, prosecutors office, cultural center, library	180	15
Drugovo			
Municipality	Local administration	5	—
Primary schools	Education	24	—

Oslomej			
Municipality	Local administration	8	8
Primary schools	Education	129	129
Vranestica			
Municipality	Local administration	5	—
Primary schools	Education	9	—
Zajas			
Municipality	Local administration	7	7
Primary schools	Education	135	135
Regional			
Medical Center	Hospital in Kicevo, plus small primary health clinics in other municipalities	375	40
Ministry of Interior (police)	Including police stations in smaller municipalities	230	42
Total		1,486	494

Source: ESI estimates based on interviews with mayors, pension fund, and statistical office.

In other words, it is likely to take a generation before the target of equitable representation is achieved. Ethnic Albanian leaders will have to manage the expectations of an impatient electorate, convincing them of the need to pursue their goals through incremental measures over many years, during which the administration will continue to be dominated by ethnic Macedonians. For their part, ethnic Macedonian politicians have an equally challenging job of explaining to future university graduates, in an environment where 48.3 percent of people under 30 have never been employed and the number of educated unemployed is spiraling (UNDP, 2001a: 25), that new recruitment into the public administration in the foreseeable future will strongly favor Albanians.

Albanian as an Official Language

For exactly the same reasons, the provisions on the use of the Albanian language in the public administration will take a long time to implement where they matter most, in the direct interface between citizens and the state across the country. The Ohrid Agreement provides that:

any person living in a unit of local self-government in which at least 20 percent of the population speaks an official language other than Macedonian *may use any official language to communicate with the regional office of the central government* with responsibility for that municipality; such an office will reply in that language in addition to Macedonian (Para. 6.5a).

On the municipal level, any ethnic community which makes up 20 percent of the population may use its own language in dealing with the administration. The agreement also mandates state funding for higher education in Albanian, positive discrimination in favor of the enrollment of minorities in state universities, official translations of documents used in judicial proceedings, and the issuing of personal documents in Albanian.

In Kicevo, Albanian students already attend classes in the secondary school in the Albanian language. There are some measures in place promoting minority enrollment at the universities. In 1995, a law on local self-government stipulated the use of Albanian as an official language in municipalities with more than 20 percent Albanians, including the publication of official documents in both languages.[19] The official gazette in Kicevo is already published in two languages, although translation is notoriously slow.[20]

In practice, however, Albanians in Kicevo can rarely use their language in communications with the municipality or the central state institutions, because very few of the state employees speak Albanian. Regardless of the attitudes of local officials or their legal obligations, this problem will not be resolved until Albanians are represented significantly in these bodies. Thus, the issue of language ultimately equates to the question of Albanian representation in the public administration. Again, the implication is that Albanians will need to be patient in pursuing this goal.

Local Self-Government

If these two targets can be achieved only through incremental measures over many years, the chief weight of expectations will fall on the decentralization of government to produce early, tangible results. The Ohrid Agreement sets out an ambitious legislative program for local-government reform.

19. Law on Local Self-Government, *Official Gazette of the Republic of Macedonia* No. 52/1995.
20. There is, however, no interpretation service in the Kicevo municipal assembly and sessions are conducted exclusively in Macedonian, triggering a recent boycott by the two Albanian delegates.

> A revised Law on Local Self-government shall be adopted that
> reinforces the powers of elected local officials and enlarges substantially
> their competencies. ... Enhanced competencies will relate principally
> to the areas of public services, urban and rural planning, environmen-
> tal protection, local economic development, culture, local finances,
> education, social welfare, and health care.

This will be followed by a law on local finance that will "enable and make responsible units of local self-government for raising a substantial amount of tax revenue" (Annex B, Section 2). A new law on local government was adopted on January 24, 2002, setting out the goals of devolution, including enhanced responsibilities in urban and rural planning, local economic development, communal services, social welfare and child protection, education, and healthcare.[21] The new law is essentially a framework law, laying out the basic principles. Some 70 individual laws will need to be modified in order to fill it with substance.

The Ohrid Agreement foresaw that the next step in the process would be a census, to be carried out under international supervision by the end of 2001; it was sub-sequently rescheduled for November 2002. According to the original agreement, after the census, there would be an agreement on redrawing municipal boundaries, through a consultative process involving local and national authorities "with inter-national participation." Macedonia will have a choice between reducing its current 123 municipalities back to the 34 which existed before 1996, or finding some new configuration.

Smaller municipalities like those in the Kicevo region, with no institutional base and only five to ten employees apiece, are, at present, poorly equipped to assume many of the functions contemplated in the new law on local self-government, parti-cularly education, social welfare, and health care. At present, the regional structure of Macedonia's central institutions is still based around the 34 old municipalities.[22] There are 16 central government institutions with offices in Kicevo town. Basing devolution around the 34 old municipalities would make some of these existing institutional resources available for conversion into locally supervised bodies; any other solution would pose a major additional institution-building challenge.

21. Law on Local Self-Government, January 24, 2002, Article 22.
22. These 16 central government institutions include the Ministry of Finance and the Public Revenue Office, the Ministry of Economy, the Ministry of Urbanism, the Ministry of Agriculture and Forestry, the Ministry of Justice, the Ministry of Interior, the Ministry of Defense, the Ministry of Labor and Social Affairs including the Office for Social Work, the Ministry of Education, the Pension Fund, the Health Fund, the Employment's Bureau, and the successors of the Payments Office such as the Treasury and the Central Registry.

The new municipalities will need adequate resources to fulfill their tasks, as well as an appropriate degree of financial autonomy. Among international organizations, the IMF has expressed most concerns about the implications of fiscal decentralization.

> All stages of the municipal budget process (including budget preparation, execution, monitoring, and audit) are in need of some further improvements. Without additional significant institutional reforms at the municipal level (e.g., establishing comprehensive and timely reporting mechanisms on budget execution, and establishing internal audits) and human capacity building (e.g., training municipal financial officers), fiscal decentralization is bound to fail (IMF, 2002a, 9).

The devolution process is certain to encounter resistance from those with vested interests in the present arrangements. One would expect the central administration in Skopje to fight against losing personnel and resources. In a strategy paper on local-government reform in 1999, the Ministry for Local Self-Government identifies bureaucratic resistance as one of the major potential obstacles to the implementation of the reforms (Ministry of Local Self-Government, 1999: 18–19). At present, the central administration and its social security funds employ 98.5 percent of all government employees, leaving a balance of only 1,441 across the 123 municipalities (Statistical Office, 2001: 341). For the time being, the distribution of power is clearly in favor of the central institutions.

There are a number of essential conditions for effective decentralization of government: the lower levels of government must have sufficient authority over their own affairs; they must have sufficient *financial resources* to fulfill their responsibilities; they must develop *adequate administrative capacity* to exercise their functions; and there must be adequate *accountability mechanisms* in place (Manor, 1999). Most importantly, however, there will need to be a broad political mobilization and sustained pressure from below, both from municipal authorities and from citizens, to accomplish a major shift in resources away from the central government.

As the drafters of the United States constitution well understood, shared powers mean permanent controversy (see, in particular, James Madison in the federalist papers). It is a necessary part of the process that Macedonian municipalities should struggle with the center for resources and influence and that new practical arrangements should emerge out of that struggle. However, it is very important that this conflict not be seen in purely ethnic terms, but that ethnic Macedonian municipalities join actively in the debate. A coalition of different political interests at the local level would be best placed to press for constructive reforms that strengthen the state's capacity at the local level.

To encourage such a coalition to emerge, the new government may need to rethink the current structures. The body established to coordinate the devolution process, established in January 2002, includes 14 members, mostly from central-government institutions. Only one member of the association of municipalities, ZELS, is included in the process as an external member (Ministry of Local Self-Government, 2002). To achieve real results, there should be a much greater voice for local representatives of different ethnic groups.

Both the design and implementation of the devolution process are likely to be difficult and time-consuming. If this process is not pursued energetically, it is likely to fall into the trap of the reforms of 1995–96, creating new municipal structures without transferring real resources and authority, ultimately weakening, rather than strengthening, the state's legitimacy at the local level. The new government must embrace devolution as a tool to help the Macedonian state overcome its present crisis of legitimacy by moving closer to the people in places like Zajas and Oslomej.

Once again, managing expectations as to the pace of change will be critical in this area. The IMF recommends a phased approach to devolution, beginning with the transfer of less complex functions (phase zero), then the transfer of assets (phase 1), the transfer of decision-making powers (phase 2), and, finally, an increase in fiscal responsibilities (phase 3). A recent IMF assessment concludes that: "It would not be surprising if, in many sectors, it were to take five years to complete Phases Zero to II, if not longer" (IMF, 2002a: 16). However, these legitimate practical concerns must not provide an excuse for procrastination. The political imperative is for early action. However long the process might be, it must be seen to begin immediately.

Conclusions: Beyond Zero-sum Politics?

It was an impressive achievement of international conflict management to bring the protagonists from the battlefields of northern and western Macedonia to the negotiating table and arrive at the Ohrid Agreement. The NLA's demobilization, the return of displaced persons, and the adoption of various constitutional and legislative reforms were equally important. The carrying out of elections in September 2002 without major incident has cleared the way for future political change to take place within the constitutional order. In this way, Macedonia has moved away from the nightmare of another Balkan war and out of the headlines of the international media.

It is tempting to think that the most difficult part of achieving sustainable peace has already been achieved. However, the analysis in this report suggests otherwise. Both for the Macedonian political elite and for the international community, many of the most difficult issues must be tackled in the coming period.

Any credible strategy must begin from the recognition that the underlying causes of insecurity—the collapse of Macedonia's industrial society, the weakness of its new private sector, the absence of a responsive state in many parts of the country—remain as acute as ever. When economic collapse becomes coupled with ethnic mobilization, it makes for a uniquely combustible combination.

In 2001, on the eve of the conflict, Freedom House described Macedonia as "a country in transition, but one not entirely decided on its destination" (Freedom House, 2001: 425). The end point of transition in Macedonia may be a situation where the young people of both ethnic groups face a choice between taking the escape route of emigration or remaining behind to struggle for access to the few goods, like public-sector employment, which the state still has at its disposal. The more ethnic Albanians obtain secondary school and university degrees, the more pressure will build. Only significant employment growth in the new private sector or continued large scale labor migration can help to relieve these pressures.

The implications of the story of Kicevo and its many analogues across Macedonia are yet to figure in either domestic or international policy-making circles. So far, economic policy in Macedonia has overlooked the problems generated by the inequitable distribution of public resources and the unique problems (and opportunities) of the Albanian community and its private sector. For their part, throughout the 1990s, international organizations preferred to argue that social and economic transition in Macedonia was going rather well, even if "despite strong policy performance, the recovery of output and employment has been slower to materialize" (World Bank, 1998: vi).

There are a number of preconditions that must be met before the incoming Macedonian government, with international support, can set about developing a credible development strategy. The first is that the Macedonian state needs to overcome its obvious deficit in information about what is going on in the real economy, particularly in the Albanian areas. As the UNDP has noted recently:

> The lack of a precise statistical record (i.e. a record recognized and accepted by everybody) that would reflect the real dimensions of the present situation adds fuel to the existence of insecurity. This especially pertains to the lack of sufficient cross-ethnic data in the areas of health, social welfare, employment and the structure of the state administration, as well as lack of data regarding per capita income by municipalities (UNDP, 2001a: 92).

This kind of knowledge is essential for understanding and addressing the fault-lines in the political economy. Such problems cannot be tackled credibly until they become visible. The census was a key first step toward mapping Macedonian society, but the real challenge lies in reorienting Macedonia's public institutions to be closer and more directly accountable to the people.

Generating an accurate picture of how public resources are distributed throughout Macedonia is the first step toward an open acknowledgement of the history of exclusion of the Albanian community. In a society where the majority of ethnic Macedonians (although only 11 percent of Albanians) believe that "everybody has equal rights," this will take some political courage (UNDP, 2001a: 89). An accurate picture of economic realities and trends would also help to identify new opportunities for generating investment capital and private-sector growth in different parts of the country. The Macedonian government has a vital economic interest in learning more about the diaspora and engaging with it in serious discussions about how to clear the path for economic development. This could take the form of soliciting cofinancing for infrastructure projects in places like Zajas or Oslomej, which would directly improve the conditions for private-sector growth across the entire Kicevo region.

A second precondition is that ethnic Albanian leaders acknowledge the scale and complexity of the challenges ahead. They must accept that the reshaping of the Macedonian state will have to be gradual. There is a danger point not far ahead for Ohrid implementation when the first inevitable disappointments emerge concerning the speed of institutional change. Ethnic Albanian leaders must resist the temptation to pull out of the political game and resort to extraconstitutional means. At the same time, the incoming Macedonian government must ensure that the process of change is seen to begin immediately and to yield concrete results in the field, so as to preserve the momentum which the Ohrid Agreement has achieved. There is a particular danger that the promise of strengthening local government will slip, given the political and technical challenges which lie ahead. Effective interethnic cooperation of local authorities will be crucial to push this process forward.

The third precondition concerns the European Union. For Europe's nascent common foreign and security policy, Macedonia is not just one country among many. Javier Solana, Chris Patten, George Robertson, and the full resources and credibility of the institutions they represent (the High Representative for Foreign and Security Policy, the European Commission, and NATO) were deployed to contain last year's crisis. Macedonia has since become the model for how a European-led multilateral intervention should function in the future.

The EU's flag is now at the center of the Macedonian peace process. At the moment, it is flying high. This means that the stakes for Europe are also extremely high. If European foreign policy cannot make a success of the peace process in Macedonia, on the very border of the European Union, one would hardly expect it to succeed in other areas further away from its interests.

The main risk to Ohrid implementation is its tendency, in an environment of declining public resources, to be reduced to a series of zero-sum games between the ethnic Macedonian and Albanian communities. Only a serious commitment from the European Union can break that dynamic by generating opportunities for both communities to participate equally in a balanced process of development.

For the time being, the tools at the disposal of the international community in Macedonia—diplomacy, reconstruction, and budgetary and balance-of-payments support—are designed for dealing with the disruptions generated by the conflict, rather than its structural causes. If the European flag is planted on the peace agreement and at diplomatic tables in Skopje, why not on construction sites and infrastructure projects in Zajas or on programs of industrial conversion in Kicevo?

The European Union and its member states have a great deal of experience in overcoming precisely the problems of industrial decline and rural underdevelopment which Macedonia faces. Within the EU itself, the goal of economic and social cohesion—the accelerated development of backward areas—is pursued through a massive mobilization of resources in the form of structural and cohesion funds, based on the principles of cofinancing, credible local development strategies (based on sound statistical information), and partnership with local authorities. At present, such tools are not used in the Western Balkans, although they will soon become available to a number of new member states.

Another key area of European engagement is to develop a credible policy on labor migration from Macedonia. For the foreseeable future, the problem of youth unemployment in places like Kicevo will not be soluble without continued migration. Understanding migration not as a problem to be suppressed, but as a means of relieving pressures in local economies and generating new sources of investment capital, must be part of any Europeanization and development strategy in Macedonia.

The EU faces a fundamental strategic choice in southeastern Europe: to continue to fight the fires of underdevelopment that spring up as incipient conflicts that can never be fully resolved; or to make a serious commitment to pulling Macedonia and the Western Balkans out of its development trap, dealing with the causes of instability at their source.

References

Agri Consulting VIZI (2002) *Study for the Economic Development of the Kicevo Region.* Skopje, February, 4–5, 17, 33, 40.

Cohen, Jon and Giovanni Federico (2001) *The Growth of the Italian Economy, 1820–1960.* Cambridge: Cambridge University Press, 28, 43, 45.

European Stability Initiative (2002) *The Other Macedonian Conflict.* Discussion Paper, February.

FIPA (2002) *Bosnia and Herzegovina Textile and Clothing Industries—Profile Report,* Sarajevo, 6.

IMF (2000) "Former Yugoslav Republic of Macedonia—Recent Economic Developments," April 25: 48.

IMF (2002a) "Former Yugoslav Republic of Macedonia: Local Government Financing and the Reform of Intergovernmental Fiscal Relations," May: 9, 11, 16.

IMF (2002b) "Former Yugoslav Republic of Macedonia: Selected Issues and Statistical Appendix," February, 21.

IMF (2002c) "Former Yugoslav Republic of Macedonia: Staff Report for the 2001 Article IV Consultation," February, 3.

Institute for Sociological, Political and Juridical Research (ISPJR) "Strategy, Policy and Management of Development of Rural Areas in Macedonia," Skopje, quoted in UNDP *Human Development Report 2001: Social Exclusion and Human Security in FYR Macedonia.*

ISPPI (2000) Opinion Poll. December.

Law on Local Self-Governance. *Sluzben Vesnik* No. 52/1995.

Law on Local Self-Government, January 24, 2002.

Manor, James (1999) *The Political Economy of Decentralization.* Washington, D.C.: World Bank.

Ministry of Local Self-Government (1999) "Strategy for Reform of the Local Self-Government System in the Republic of Macedonia." November, 18–19.

Ministry of Local Self-Government (2002) "Decision for the Establishment of a Coordinative Body for Planning, Monitoring, Management, and Coordination of the Reform in the Local Self-Government System." Skopje, January 22.

Municipality of Kicevo (1998) *Kicevo i Kicevsko,* Kicevo.

National Bank of the Republic of Macedonia (2002) *Monthly Report 3/2002,* 9.

Odluka za paspredelba na sredstvata za izgradba na vodovodi i fekalni kanalizacii vo Republika Makedonija 1997–2001. *Sluzben Vesnik* No. 57/1997 No. 41/1998, No. 51/1999, No. 51/2000, and No. 40/2001.

OECD and EBRD in cooperation with Macedonian Ministry of Economy (2001) *Entrepreneurship and Enterprise Development in the Former Yugoslav Republic of Macedonia. Country Assessment and Action Plan*, July: 16–17

Statisticki godisnik na Republika Makedonija 1991, Skopje, 503.

Statistical Office of Macedonia (2001a) *Statistical Yearbook of the Republic of Macedonia 2001*, Skopje, 341.

Statistical Office of Macedonia (2001b) "Primary, Lower Secondary, and Upper Secondary schools in the Republic of Macedonia at the Beginning of the School Year 2000/2001," September.

UNDP (2001a) *Human Development Report 2001: Social Exclusion and Human Security in FYR Macedonia*, 25, 29, 39, 45, 63–67, 89, 92, 121.

UNDP (2001b) *Human Development Report Macedonia 2001*, 11.

World Bank (1998) *FYR Macedonia: Country Economic Memorandum—Enhancing Growth*, November 30: 5, 18, 29, 58.

World Bank (1999) "FYROM: Focusing on the Poor." *World Bank Report* No. 19411, vi, 23.

The Benefits of Ethnic War:
Understanding Eurasia's Unrecognized States

Charles King

War is the engine of state building, but it is also good for business. Historically, the three have often amounted to the same thing. The consolidation of national states in Western Europe was in part a function of the interests of royal leaders in securing sufficient revenue for war making. In turn, costly military engagements were highly profitable enterprises for the suppliers of men, ships, and weaponry. The great affairs statecraft, says Shakespeare's Richard II as he seizes his uncle's fortune to finance a war, "do ask some charge." The distinction between freebooter and founding father, privateer and president, has often been far murkier in fact than national mythmaking normally allows.

Only recently, however, have these insights figured into discussions about contemporary ethnic conflict and civil war. Focused studies of the mechanics of warfare, particularly in cases such as Sudan, Liberia, and Sierra Leone, have highlighted the complex economic incentives that can push violence forward, as well as the ways in which the easy labels that analysts use to identify such conflicts—as "ethnic" or "religious," say—always cloud more than they clarify (Keen, 1994; Reno, 1995; Ellis, 1999). Yet how precisely does the chaos of war become transformed into networks of profit, and how in turn can these informal networks harden into the institutions of states? Post-Soviet Eurasia provides an enlightening instance of these processes in train.

In the early 1990s, a half dozen small wars raged across the region, a series of armed conflicts that future historians might term collectively the wars of the Soviet succession: Nagorno-Karabakh, Transnistria, South Ossetia, Abkhazia, Chechnya, and Tajikistan. Each involved a range of players, including the central governments of newly sovereign states, territorial separatists, the armed forces of other countries, and international peacemakers. By the middle of the decade, most of the conflicts had de-crescendoed into relative stability. Numerous rounds of peace negotiations were held

This piece was originally published in World Politics *53(4) July 2001: 524–52. The author would like to thank three anonymous referees for comments on an earlier draft of this article, and Lori Khatchadourian, Nelson Kasfir, Christianne Hardy Wohlforth, and Michael Brown for helpful conversations.*

under the aegis of the United Nations (UN) and the Organization for Security and Cooperation in Europe (OSCE). Little progress was achieved in the talks, but with the exception of the second Chechen war beginning in 1999, none of the post-Soviet disputes returned to the levels of organized violence experienced earlier.

But how can one explain the durability of these disputes, sometimes referred to as "stalled" or "frozen" conflicts, even after the cessation of violence? This article makes two central arguments in this regard. First, the territorial separatists of the early 1990s have become the state builders of the early 2000s, creating de facto countries whose ability to field armed forces, control their own territory, educate their children, and maintain local economies is about as well-developed as that of the recognized states of which they are still notionally a part. The crystallization of independent state-like entities has meant that the resolution of these conflicts is not so much about patching together a torn country as about trying to reintegrate two functionally distinct administrations, militaries, and societies.[1] The products of the wars of the Soviet succession are not frozen conflicts but relatively successful examples of making states by making war.

Second, the disputes have evolved from armed engagements to something close to equilibrium. In many cases, both the separatists and their erstwhile opponents in central governments benefit from the untaxed trade and production flowing through the former war zones. Even in less unsavory ways, individuals inside and outside the conflict areas have an interest in maintaining the status quo—from poets who have built careers extolling their newfound statehood to pensioners worried about how their meager incomes might be further diminished if the country were once again integrated. It is a dark version of Pareto efficiency. The general welfare cannot be improved—by reaching a genuine peace accord allowing for real reintegration—without at the same time making key interest groups in both camps worse off. Even if a settlement is reached, it is unlikely to do more than recognize this basic logic and its attendant benefits.

This article examines the ways in which state-like entities have emerged and thrived in Eurasia since the earliest outbreak of violence in the late 1980s. Section 1 offers a brief overview of current research on civil war endings and the disjuncture between approaches drawn from the international-relations literature and the work of sociologists and development economists on the functions of violence. Section 2

---

1. By "state-like entity," I mean a political unit that has (1) a population and (2) a government exercising sovereign control over some piece of territory—but without the imprimatur of international recognition. In Eurasia, the conceptual bar for statehood cannot be raised too high, for many of the qualities that define relatively well-functioning states in Central Europe do not exist farther east, even among so-called states that have seats at the United Nations.

outlines the course of four Eurasian wars and identifies the de facto states that have arisen after them: the republic of Nagorno-Karabakh (in Azerbaijan); the Dnestr Moldovan republic also known as Transnistria (in Moldova); and the republics of Abkhazia and South Ossetia (in Georgia).[2] There are other areas across Eastern Europe and Eurasia that might be included on this list, such as Montenegro and Kosovo in the former Yugoslavia, Chechnya in the Russian Federation, and Achara in Georgia, not to mention the long-lived Turkish Republic of Northern Cyprus. But the four cases examined here are instances in which local armed forces, often with substantial assistance from outside powers, effectively defeated the armies of recognized governments in open warfare. They are also the cases in which the drive to create independent state structures has raised the most serious questions about whether any real reintegration with the central governments that the international community still recognizes as legitimate can now be reasonably expected. Section 3 analyzes the pillars of state building in each case, including the ways in which the interests of several major groups are satisfied by the limbo status into which these disputes have lapsed. Section 4 describes the equilibrium that the disputes seem to have reached and suggests lessons that the cases might hold for further study of intrastate violence.

Civil War, Negotiations, and State Construction

Scholars have long recognized that civil wars tend to be protracted and that negotiated settlements are rare; even where talks have succeeded, they have produced less stable endstates than outright victory by one side (Pillar, 1983: 25; Stedman, 1991: 9; Licklider, 1995: 686). Given these facts—and the apparent interest of the international community in promoting negotiations, nonetheless—understanding why some belligerents come to the bargaining table while others remain on the battlefield has been of central importance.

Researchers have pointed to two broad categories of explanations. On one view, the qualities of the belligerents themselves may work against compromise. Ethnic groups may feel that a particular piece of real estate is historically theirs and that allowing it to be controlled by an alien group would be tantamount to national be-

---

2. In deeply divided societies, even spelling bees are political events, so place names in each of these instances are controversial. I use Transnistria instead of Pridnestrov'e or Transdnestria because it is more easily pronounceable, and Abkhazia, South Ossetia, and Karabakh because few people will have heard of alternative designations such as Apsny, Iryston, and Azat Artsakh. The same rule of convenience applies to other proper nouns.

trayal (on ethnic war, see Kaufmann, 1996). Committed leaders may sense that they have little choice but to push forward with the fight, lest they fall victim to even more radical comrades in their own camp (De Figueiredo and Weingast, 1999). If groups feel that they can get more by fighting than by negotiating—if they have not reached a "hurting stalemate," in William Zartman's well-known phrase—they are unlikely to seek peace (Zartman, 1985). A second view stresses the structural environment in which decision making takes place. Using insights from neorealist theory, some writers have argued that, in the absence of institutions to ensure credible commitment, even the most well-intentioned leaders would be irrational to seek a negotiated settlement (Posen, 1993; Fearon, 1998; Walter, 1997). Given the host of factors that seem to work against negotiations, other observers have held that seeking peace only after one side has won or accepting the physical separation of warring ethnic groups may be the only truly stable solutions to large-scale communal violence (Kaufman, 1998; Luttwak, 1999).

In all of these debates, however, the benefits of war have been largely neglected. As David Keen (1995, 1998) has observed, a major breakthrough in medicine was the realization that what might be very bad for the organism could be very good for the germ that attacked it; the same can be said for civil wars. There is a political economy to warfare that produces positive externalities for its perpetrators. Seemingly perpetual violence in Sierra Leone, Myanmar, Liberia, and elsewhere has less to do with anarchy—of either the social or the institutional kind—than with the rational calculations of elites about the use of violence as a tool for extracting and redistributing resources. Diamonds in Angola, timber in Cambodia, and coca in Colombia have all become spoils of war that both fuel conflict and discourage settlement. Conflicts, in this sense, may not "burn themselves out," precisely because it is in the interests of their makers, on all sides, to stoke them.[3]

Even after one camp has secured a partial or complete victory in the military contest, the basic networks, relationships, and informal channels that arose during the course of the violence can replicate themselves in new, state-like institutions in the former conflict zones. Belligerents are often able to craft a sophisticated array of formal institutions that function as effective quasi states, from the Jaffna peninsula in Sri Lanka, to the so-called Somaliland republic in Somalia, to the demilitarized zone in south central Colombia. Through these institutions, however, politics in peace

3. These arguments have been central to the study of conflicts in the developing world for some time. They have only recently begun to filter into the study of regional and interethnic violence in other areas. Even more recent is the attempt to see the uses of substate war through a broad, comparative lens. Among the most important works in this field are Reno (1998); Berdal and Malone (2000); Global Witness (1998); and several working papers by Paul Collier and his associates at the Development Research Group of the World Bank, for example, Collier (1999).

time becomes little more than an extension of war. The instruments of violence, sublimated into the institutions of unrecognized regimes, in the long run keep existing states weak, populations poor, and full-scale war a constant possibility, even as they enrich the key players who extol the virtues of peace.

Such has been the case in the Eurasian conflicts of the 1990s. Yet there is also an intriguing twist. Not only have erstwhile separatists become relatively successful state builders, but they have sometimes done so with the collusion of central governments, external actors, and international negotiators ostensibly committed to recreating a stable, reintegrated country.

The Wars of the Soviet Succession

The end of Soviet communism was a relatively peaceful affair. Notwithstanding the range of social grievances and disputed boundaries across the region, few of the potential rivalries actually produced open war (Fearon and Laitin, 1996). But in at least four instances, interethnic disputes, external interests, and elite rivalries interacted to create wars that led to serious loss of life and hundreds of thousands of refugees and internally displaced persons (IDPs). In all four cases discussed here, separatists actually won the armed conflicts, producing recognized states that are only marginally functional and unrecognized ones whose ability to govern themselves is surprisingly strong.

The dispute over Nagorno-Karabakh was not the first instance of open interethnic rivalry within Mikhail Gorbachev's Soviet Union, but it was the first that involved the interests of two Soviet republics, Armenia and Azerbaijan. Although included within the administrative boundaries of the Azerbaijan Soviet republic since the 1920s, Nagorno-Karabakh was populated in the main by ethnic Armenians, constituting around 80 percent by 1989. The region had enjoyed autonomous status since the very beginning of the Soviet Union, but Karabakh Armenians complained of cultural discrimination and economic underdevelopment (on the origins and course of the Karabakh war, see Laitin and Suny, 1999. Increasing openness under Gorbachev allowed these issues to come to the fore. In 1988, Karabakh leaders called for the region's transfer to Armenian jurisdiction. Swift reprisals followed, including an organized pogrom against Armenians in the city of Sumgait in Azerbaijan. Profound grievances were voiced by both sides. From the Armenian perspective, repeated attacks on ethnic Armenian communities were reminiscent of the Ottoman-era genocide, especially given the massive outflow of refugees, over 180,000 by mid-1989 (Zolotarev, 2000: 45). From the Azeri perspective, Armenians were attempting to squelch the Azeri national movement by destroying the republic's integrity.

In 1989, the Armenian Supreme Soviet and the Karabakh local council adopted a joint resolution declaring the unification of Armenia and Karabakh. Local paramilitary groups began to form, with substantial assistance in men and material from Armenia. The Azeris responded by forcibly evacuating villages along the Armenian-Karabakh border and imposing a road and rail blockade on the province and eventually on Armenia as well. Hostilities escalated after the Soviet Union collapsed. Local Armenians in the regional capital, Stepanakert, organized a referendum on independence and declared the creation of a fully separate entity, the Republic of Nagorno-Karabakh. By the middle of 1992, Karabakh forces had opened a land corridor linking Karabakh to Armenia and had driven the Azerbaijani army from Shushi, the last remaining stronghold within Karabakh and a strategic highland from which the military had been able to bombard Stepanakert. A major offensive in 1993 created an Armenian-controlled buffer zone of "liberated" territory around Karabakh. After several unsuccessful mediation attempts throughout the 1990s, in May 1994, the Russian Federation finally managed to secure a cease-fire, which has since remained in place, with some minor violations. But little real progress has been made on deciding Karabakh's final status.

The dispute between Armenians and Azeris might be cast, simplistically, as a reprise of struggles between Armenians and Turks left over from the early twentieth century. But across the Black Sea, in Moldova, no one would have predicted major violence in the 1980s. Rates of ethnic intermarriage were high; there were no religious lines separating ethnic minorities from the majority; and there had been no history of widespread communal violence. Nevertheless, Moldova became embroiled in a small war in the eastern part of the country, the thin Transnistria region east of the Dnestr River on the border with Ukraine.

Transnistrians were not a distinct ethnic population. In fact, ethnic Moldovans were the largest single group in the region. However, the importance of the zone in Soviet steel production and the military sector meant that Transnistria's inhabitants were fundamentally linked—in terms of both livelihood and social identity—to Soviet institutions such as the Communist Party, strategic industries, and the military (King, 2000: chap. 9). The Moldovan national movement of the late 1980s thus hit Transnistrians particularly hard. Prodemocracy groups saw perestroika as an opportunity to reassert the voice of the republic's ethnic Moldovan majority after decades of Russian cultural domination. In 1989, the republican Supreme Soviet adopted a series of language laws that made Moldovan (Romanian) the state language and mandated the use of the Latin alphabet, rather than the Cyrillic.

Industrial managers and military personnel in Transnistria reacted sharply, taking control of governmental and security structures in the districts east of the Dnestr River and in the Russian-majority city of Bender on the river's west bank. In the autumn of 1990, Transnistrian leaders declared a separate republic within the Soviet Union and later opted for full independence when Moldova itself exited the Soviet federation. War accompanied these competing declarations. In 1992, a Moldovan government offensive against the city of Bender sparked the first major intervention by the Russian Fourteenth Army, stationed in Transnistria, on the side of the separatists. With the superior firepower of the Russian troops, the Moldovans were driven out of the city. The uneasy balance of power after the battle produced a formal cease-fire agreement and the deployment of a tripartite Russian-Moldovan-Transnistrian peacekeeping force. Despite numerous rounds of talks, sponsored by the OSCE and regional neighbors, Transnistria's final status has not yet been agreed.

On the surface, the relationship between Georgians and Abkhaz had little in common with that between Moldovans and Transnistrians. The Abkhaz are a distinct ethnic population, speaking a language unrelated to Georgian. During the Soviet period, the Abkhaz were given their own autonomous republic, within which they enjoyed a privileged position in the party and state hierarchy, even though they comprised less than a fifth of the population there. However, the pattern of events in the late 1980s paralleled those in Moldova. A revitalized Georgian national movement emerged in the waning days of Soviet power, eventually leading to a referendum on independence, and Georgia's exit from the Soviet Union.

Abkhaz reacted by demanding greater local autonomy and a say in the politics of independent Georgia. Clashes erupted between the Abkhaz and the local Georgian majority. In early 1992, a new Georgian president, Eduard Shevardnadze, backtracked on the negotiations that had been ongoing with the Abkhaz leadership, and full-scale war followed. Georgian troops marched into Abkhazia in an effort to eject the regional government and succeeded in capturing and holding the regional capital, Sukhumi. But by the end of 1993, Abkhaz militias, assisted by Russian forces, had pushed back the ill-prepared Georgian troops to the Inguri River, the dividing line between Georgia proper and Abkhazia. A Russian-brokered agreement in May 1994 provided for the deployment of a peacekeeping mission of the Commonwealth of Independent States (CIS), although in practice wholly Russian, to monitor the security zone along the river. Negotiations on Abkhazia's final status, brokered by the UN, have continued since then.

Unlike the Abkhaz, the Ossetians were not historically concentrated in Georgia, in the area of present South Ossetia; their cultural center was across the border in North Ossetia, now part of the Russian Federation (Totadze, 1994). By 1989, however, two-thirds of South Ossetia's population was ethnic Ossetian. Despite a history of strong intercultural ties between Georgians and Ossetians, the political climate of the late 1980s encouraged cascading demands for local autonomy and independence. In 1988 and 1989, the Georgian government adopted measures to strengthen

Table 1

Eurasia's Recognized and De Facto States

State	Capital	Independence and recognition	Population	Ethnic composition	Territory [km²]	Armed forces
Azerbaijan	Baku	Declared October 18, 1991 Joined UN March 9, 1992	8,000,000	Azeris—90% Dagestani ethnic groups—3% Russians—3% Armenians—2%	86,600	72,100
Republic of Nagorno-Karabakh (also known as Azat Artsakh in Armenian)	Stepanakert	Declared September 2, 1991	150,000	Armenians—95% Kurds, Greeks, and Assyrians—5%	4,400	15,000–20,000 (incl. 8,000 from Armenia)
Moldova	Chisinau	Declared August 27, 1991 Joined UN March 2, 1992	4,300,000	Moldovans—65% Ukrainians—14% Russians—13% Gagauz—4%	33,700	9,500
Dnestr Moldovan Republic (also known as Pridnestrov'e in Russian and Transnistria in Romanian)	Tiraspol	Declared September 2, 1990	670,000	Moldovans—33% Russians—29% Ukrainians—29%	4,163	5,000–10,000
Georgia	Tbilisi	Declared April 9, 1991 Joined UN July 31, 1992	5,500,000	Georgians—70% Armenians—8% Russians—6% Azeris—6% Ossetians—3% Abkhaz—2%	69,700	26,900

Table 1 (continued)
Eurasia's Recognized and De Facto States

State	Capital	Independence and recognition	Population	Ethnic composition	Territory [km²]	Armed forces
Republic of Abkhazia (also known as Apsny in Abkhaz)	Sukhumi	Declared August 25, 1990	20,000	Mainly Abkhaz but compact Armenian population in north and Georgians (Mingrelians) in south.	7,867	5,000
Republic of South Ossetia (also known as Iryston in Ossetian)	Tskhinvali	Declared September 20, 1990 Recognized by North Ossetia in 1993	70,000–80,000	Mainly Ossetians but some Russians and Georgians.	2,732 minus a few villages still under central government control	2,000

Notes: Figures for the unrecognized states are, at best, imperfect estimates, but they are as close as one can come given the available evidence. Most unrecognized states declared sovereignty first within the context of the Soviet Union, then declared full independence; the first date is the one usually celebrated as the national holiday. Territory and population figures for recognized states also include the unrecognized republics. Military figures do not include reserves, which can quintuple the number of men under arms.

Sources: IISS (2000) *The Military Balance, 2000–2001.* London: IISS; K. G. Dzugaev (ed.) (1997) *Iuzhnaia Osetiia: 10 let respublike* (South Ossetia: On the tenth anniversary of the republic). Vladikavkaz: Iryston; *Sakartvelo/Georgia* (1997) Tbilisi: Military Cartographic Factory; *Atlas of the Dniester Moldavian Republic* (1997) Tiraspol: Dnestr State Cooperative University; www.worldbank.org; author's interviews.

the use of the Georgian language in public life and, shortly thereafter, rejected demands by regional leaders for an increase in South Ossetia's status from autonomous region to autonomous republic, the same as Abkhazia's. As in Transnistria, Ossetian leaders argued that language reforms would unfairly disadvantage them. The spark for violence, however, came in 1990, when the South Ossetian regional administration declared a separate South Ossetian republic within the Soviet Union, moved to unite with North Ossetia, and shortly thereafter held elections for a separate South Ossetian parliament—a variation on the Karabakh theme. In response, the Georgian parliament voted to revoke South Ossetia's existing autonomous status. President Shevardnadze ordered troops to the region, but their entry met with the fierce resistance of Ossetian irregulars and their supporters from North Ossetia and other parts of the Russian Federation. In July 1992, a cease-fire agreement provided for the cessation of hostilities and final-status negotiations under the auspices of the OSCE.

The Politics of Surreptitious State Building

Today, the political elites that made these wars, both in the national capitals and in the separatist regions, are in large part the same. Most continue to refer to the events of the late perestroika period as explanations for why the violence erupted and why a stable settlement has been so elusive. Karabakh leaders talk of the revocation of their local autonomy and the massacre of ethnic Armenians in Sumgait. Transnistrians speak of the threat of cultural Romanianization and the unwelcome possibility of Moldovan unification with Romania. Abkhaz and Ossetians list Georgia's oppressive cultural policies and the dilution of the local autonomy that both regions had during the Soviet years.

These putative root causes, however, are slippery explanations for the absence of a final settlement. Most central governments and international organizations have in fact done everything that the conventional wisdom on conflict resolution would suggest in order to reach an equitable solution. Generally stable cease-fires, monitored by outside parties, have been put in place. Regular negotiations have continued under the aegis of the UN and the OSCE, with the support of the United States and the Russian Federation. Governments have, to varying degrees, amended their constitutions, citizenship laws, educational statutes, and local administrative structures to provide for civil-rights guarantees and local autonomy, all of which have allowed all three recognized states—Azerbaijan, Moldova, and Georgia—to join the Council of Europe.

The real block on a final settlement has been the fact that, beneath the façade of unresolved grievances and international negotiations, political elites in each region have gone about the process of building states that now function about as well as the recognized countries of which they are still formally constituents. These unrecognized entities, moreover, are shielded by independent militaries: 15,000 to 20,000 men in Karabakh, 5,000 to 10,000 in Transnistria, 2,000 in South Ossetia, 5,000 in Abkhazia, all with substantial supplies of armor and equipment (IISS, 2000: 100). At the same time, interest groups outside the conflict zones have learned to live with the effective division of their countries, finding ways to profit from a state apparatus that is chronically weak—and, in the process, ensuring that it remains so. The mechanisms of surreptitious state building have become increasingly clear in each case: the economic benefits of state weakness, the support of key external actors, the legitimization of statehood through cultural and educational policies, the complicity of central governments, and in some instances, the unwitting assistance of international negotiators.

The Political Economy of Weak States

By any measure, Azerbaijan, Georgia, and Moldova are exceptionally weak states. Per capita GNP in 1999 was under $650 in all three countries. In the first two, public revenues (including foreign grants) account for 20 percent or less of GDP, a figure too low to support even the most basic state functions.[4] Significant portions of each country's territory, population, and wealth-producing potential—the separatist regions—remain wholly outside central-government control. Karabakh and the occupied buffer areas constitute around 20 percent of Azerbaijan's territory; Abkhazia and South Ossetia together are 17 percent of Georgia's; Transnistria is 12 percent of Moldova's. Even outside the separatist republics, there are many parts of the country where the central government's power is virtually nil, areas where banditry is common, local notables run their own affairs, and the institutions of the central state are conspicuous by their absence. The lives of average Azerbaijanis, Georgians, and Moldovans rarely intersect with the state, and where they do, it is often in the form of a policeman demanding payment for an imagined traffic offense.

State weakness is of obvious benefit to the unrecognized regimes. Business can be carried on with neighboring states without paying production taxes or tariffs. Luxury goods, especially cigarettes and alcohol, can be brought in for resale or export. The republics differ, though, in terms of their relative economic success. The lowest on the development scale is probably Karabakh. Situated in a mountainous area where

4. Economic figures are based on World Bank reports at www.worldbank.org.

most roads are barely passable, and with little indigenous industry and a collapsed agricultural system, Karabakh is a largely poverty-stricken region. Its total population, estimated at 150,000, survives mainly on the basis of subsistence farming or the resale of goods imported from Iran and Armenia.[5] Important urban centers, such as the city of Shushi, have yet to rebuild apartment buildings and offices gutted during the war. Although demining of fields and villages has progressed since the cease-fire, with the assistance of international relief agencies, agricultural production has remained stunted by the fear of unexploded ordnance.[6] Nevertheless, local authorities have been able to construct something resembling a state, with its own foreign ministry (which charges visitors $25 for visas), armed forces, police, and court system. Even in Karabakh's dire straits, citizens have been able to find economic potential. The export of wood to Armenia and farther afield has become a booming enterprise, but it has also caused serious worries about deforestation and the long-term effects on Karabakh's eroding agricultural land, a situation that also obtains in Abkhazia.[7]

Abkhazia and South Ossetia are only marginally better off than Karabakh. During the Soviet period, both were reasonably important regions. Abkhazia supported a booming tourist trade along its Black Sea coast, as well as a substantial hazelnut industry. In South Ossetia, lead and zinc mines, and factories producing enamel fittings, wood products, and beer and fruit juices were important parts of the Georgian economy. Now, however, few of these enterprises function, since the outflow of refugees and IDPs more than halved the populations of both regions, which stand at under 200,000 in Abkhazia and 70,000 to 80,000 in South Ossetia.

Local inhabitants have turned to other pursuits. In Abkhazia, tangerines and hazelnuts remain an important source of revenue, particularly since there are no taxes to pay to the central Georgian government; local gang activity, in fact, tends to be seasonal, centered around the attempts by bandits to steal hazelnut shipments in the late summer and early autumn. Trade in scrap metal, both from dysfunctional industries as well as from power lines, is also important. South Ossetia has little in the way of functioning industry or export-oriented agriculture, but the region's geographical position has been its chief asset. Just outside the entrance to the regional capital, Tskhinvali, the South Ossetian highway police maintain a customs checkpoint to monitor the vigorous trade along the highway to Vladikavkaz, the capital of the Russian republic of North Ossetia. The police, however, have become more

5. Author's interviews in Stepanakert, September 27–28, 2000.

6. Author's interview with Edgar Sargsian, field officer, International Committee of the Red Cross, Stepanakert, September 28, 2000.

7. Author's interview with Tevfik Yaprak, World Bank head of mission, Tbilisi, October 11, 2000; *Svobodnaia Gruziia*, September 27, 2000, 4.

facilitators of this commerce than its invigilators. A massive market in petrol and wheat flour flourishes along the roadside, with hundreds of trucks laden with goods from the Russian Federation.[8] Controlling this trade, the road link to Vladikavkaz, and especially the passage through the mountain tunnel linking North and South Ossetia, provides a major source of revenue for the South Ossetian administration. OSCE officials estimate that some $60–70 million in goods pass through the tunnel each year, compared to an official South Ossetian budget of roughly $1 million.[9] In both Abkhazia and South Ossetia, drugs, especially heroin, have also joined the list of transit goods.

Of all four unrecognized republics, Transnistria's economic position is probably the best. During the Soviet period, Transnistria was the mainstay of Moldovan industry. While areas west of the Dnestr River were largely agricultural, most heavy machine industries and power-generating plants were located to the east (IMF, 1993: 46). Many still operate on the basis of barter trade, but some have even managed to secure contracts with firms abroad. The Ribnita mill, in northern Transnistria, was one of the Soviet Union's most important producers of high-quality rolled steel, especially for munitions. Originally built in 1984 using German technology, the plant remains one of the best in the former Soviet Union, and firms from Western Europe continue to sign contracts with the plant—so many, in fact, that by the late 1990s the firm employed a bevy of translators to process foreign orders.[10] The plant's profits provide roughly half the revenue for Transnistria's state budget.[11] It is indicative of Transnistria's international links that the Dnestr Moldovan Republic ruble, introduced as the region's official currency in 1994, was printed in Germany. In addition to steel, small arms—an important local industry during the Soviet period—are also manufactured, and Transnistria's president, Igor Smirnov, has hailed their export as a sign of his republic's importance on the world stage and its links with other embattled peoples in Kosovo, Chechnya, Abkhazia, and elsewhere.[12] Given the dire state of Moldova's own economy, Transnistria looks rather better in some areas. Average household income is higher, and in every major field except consumer goods, the separatist region is a net exporter to the rest of Moldova, delivering more construction materials, chemicals, ferrous metals, and electrical energy than it receives (World Bank, 1998: 27).

8. Author's interviews in Tskhinvali, October 13, 2000.

9. Author's interview with Hans-Gjorg Heinrich, advisor to OSCE mission, Tbilisi, October 23, 2000.

10. Author's interviews with Transnistrian steel workers, Ribnita, August 1, 1997.

11. *Oxford Analytica East Europe Daily Brief*, January 11, 1999.

12. Author's interview with Valeriu Prudnicov, Moldovan police commissioner, Bender, August 1, 1997.

From the earliest days, these conflicts were never simple confrontations between an embattled ethnic minority and a nationalizing central government. The relationships involved were even more complex than Rogers Brubaker's "triadic nexus"—ethnic minority, central government, external homeland—would suggest (1996: chap. 3). Indeed, many interested players have been crucial in assisting the separatist republics not only in winning the wars but also in consolidating statehood afterward.

By far the most significant has been the Russian Federation. The Russian official history of the post-Soviet wars argues for Moscow's pacifying role in each of the conflicts (Zolotarev, 2000: chap. 8). It is clear, though, that Russian assistance was a crucial component in the early stages of state building. Whether prompted by the whim of brigade commanders or by a policy directive from Moscow, Soviet armed forces, later to become Russian Federation troops, were the main supplier of weaponry (and often soldiers) to separatist groups. Throughout 1991 and 1992, the Moldovans issued numerous notes to the Soviet and Russian governments protesting the involvement of the Soviet Fourteenth Army on the side of the Transnistrians.[13] In December 1991, the army's commander left his post to become head of the Dnestr Guards, the newly created army of the Dnestr Moldovan republic; he was followed by his former chief of staff, who became the republic's defense minister (Bowers, 92: 484). Azerbaijan was able to secure the complete withdrawal of Russian troops from its territory by mid-1993, but the forces that remained in Armenia—the Russian Seventh Army—are known to have aided both Armenian government troops as well as Karabakh irregulars during the war. Russian newspapers published the names of soldiers who participated in the fighting, and, in 1992, Russia's Defense Ministry promoted the commanders of both the Fourteenth and Seventh Armies for their leadership in the Transnistrian and Karabakh campaigns.[14] Leakage of weapons and soldiers from the Russian 345th airborne regiment, based in Abkhazia, as well as the influx of freelance fighters from Russia's north Caucasus, contributed to the Abkhaz defeat of Georgian forces (Gribincea, 1999: 42–43).

Russian foreign and security policy since the wars has been complex in each of these cases, but it has centered around three main elements, all of which have turned out to be crucial resources for the unrecognized republics. First, Russian

---

13. *Moldova suverana*, June 11, 1991, p. 1; *Curierul national*, April 4, 1992, pp. 1, 7; *Romania libera*, April 4–5, 1992, p. 8.

14. *Den'*, August 9–15, 1992, and Radio Maiak, September 18, 1992, both cited in Gribincea (1999: 15). Gribincea's book is the most thorough study of the Russian military's role in Moldova and Georgia. See also Gribincea (1998).

economic support has been essential. The Russian gas monopoly Gazprom, while pressuring Azerbaijan, Moldova, and Georgia to pay their massive energy debts, has continued to supply subsidized gas to the separatist areas. Russian officials have even staffed positions within key economic institutions. Until late 1996, the head of the Transnistrian central bank was reportedly a member of the Russian intelligence service; even after that, bank officials continued to receive training in Moscow and Saint Petersburg.[15]

Second, negotiations with Moldova and Georgia regarding the withdrawal of Russian troops have been linked with the resolution of the separatist disputes. In 1999, both Moldova and Georgia managed to secure Russian agreement to an eventual full-scale withdrawal, but in both cases the devil has been in the details. The Moldovan government, under both Russian and OSCE pressure, signed an agreement in 1994 mandating that the withdrawal of the Fourteenth Army be "synchronized" with Transnistria's final status. That agreement has effectively blocked real progress in withdrawal negotiations, since it is unclear whether withdrawal should precede resolution or vice versa. Russian troop strength is much lower now than in the past—in 2000, around 2,600 men plus local contract hires, reorganized as an "operational group" rather than an army (IISS, 2000: 125)—but the military presence continues to be a boon to the Transnistrians, providing civilian and military employment for local citizens and a sense of security for the unrecognized regime.[16]

In Georgia, the Russian military began downsizing in 2000. However, much of the materiel was moved to Armenia, with which Russia has a long-term basing agreement; that, in turn, raised Azerbaijani fears that some of the equipment would eventually find its way into both Armenian and Karabakh hands.[17] The Russian military base in Abkhazia serves much the same function as the troop presence in Transnistria, providing employment and security for an effectively separate regime. The Russian and Georgian governments have carried out negotiations regarding the transformation of the base into a convalescence station for Russian peacekeepers, but that change of label would not substantially alter the strong role that the facility

---

15. Author's interview with Elena Niculina, World Bank representative, Chisinau, July 29, 1997. The same point, however, could be made even about the recognized states. Russia continues to provide what amounts to subsidized gas deliveries, since outstanding debts from the former Soviet republics are often paid in government-issued bonds, which are, as Gazprom must realize, virtually worthless.

16. A referendum, in March 1995, organized by the Transnistrian administration indicated that 93 percent of voters wanted a permanent Russian base in the region.

17. Azerbaijani officials have suggested that the deployment of Turkish troops into Nakhichevan, the Azerbaijani enclave bordering Armenia, Turkey, and Iran might be considered as a response to the increase in Russian forces in Armenia. *Svobodnaia Gruziia*, October 25, 2000, p. 4.

plays in Abkhaz political and economic life.[18] In both Moldova and Georgia, even the salaries of Russian soldiers and peacekeepers, paid in rubles, have ensured that Transnistria, Abkhazia, and South Ossetia remain economically tied to Russia rather than to their recognized central governments because local goods and services are purchased using rubles rather than national currencies.[19] For these reasons, both the Transnistrians and the Abkhaz have insisted that the bases remain in place or, if they are closed, that the Russian military equipment be transferred to Transnistrian and Abkhaz control.[20]

Third, Russian citizenship and visa policy has encouraged the separatist regions to see themselves as effectively independent states. Azerbaijan, Moldova, and Georgia have all been wary of allowing dual citizenship for fear that inhabitants of the unrecognized republics would secure foreign citizenship and therefore become further disconnected from the center.[21] Plenty have taken Russian citizenship nevertheless. According to the Transnistrian administration, as many as 65,000 people (about 10 percent of the population) now have Russian citizenship.[22] Georgian officials worry that Abkhaz and South Ossetians have done likewise, especially since much of their livelihood depends on the ability to travel easily to the Russian Federation. The citizenship option is another reason that contract work in Russian Federation forces in Abkhazia and Transnistria has been an attractive option for many locals, since it often leads to a passport and citizenship. Even for those who are not citizens, changes in Russian visa policy have also widened the gap between the separatist zones and the central governments. Under a previous visa regime, citizens of former Soviet republics could travel visa-free to Russia. But as part of a move to tighten border security in the wake of the Chechen wars, Russia announced that it would pull out of the agreement and begin requiring visas for citizens of particular post-Soviet states. From late 2000, regular Russian visas were required of citizens of Georgia—but not inhabitants of South Ossetia and Abkhazia.

18. *Georgia Today*, October 6–12, 2000, p. 4.

19. Russian peacekeeping forces, although under a separate command from regular army personnel, have had a similar influence on the local economy. By early 2000, there were around 1,500 Russian peacekeepers in Abkhazia (formally a CIS peacekeeping mission), 500 in South Ossetia, and 500 in Transnistria.

20. *Svobodnaia Gruziia*, October 24, 2000, p. 3, and October 25, 2000, p. 1.

21. In August 2000, Moldova adopted a new citizenship law that provides for dual citizenship based on bilateral agreements. Currently, however, Moldova does not have any such agreements with foreign countries.

22. *Oxford Analytica East Europe Daily Brief*, June 29, 2000.

While overwhelmingly significant, Russia is not the only external dimension to state building. Diaspora politics has also played a role. Armenia and the Armenian diaspora have been the sine qua non of Karabakh's existence. For all practical purposes, Karabakh is now more an autonomous district of Armenia than a part of Azerbaijan. The Armenian *dram*, not the Azerbaijani *manat*, is legal tender. Substantial numbers of Karabakh inhabitants enjoy Armenian citizenship and travel abroad with Armenian passports; some have even risen to political office in Armenia—including Robert Kocharian, who has the distinction of having been president of both Karabakh and, now, Armenia. The highway connecting the Armenian city of Goris to Stepanakert, the so-called Lachin corridor carved out during the war, may now be the finest road in the entire south Caucasus. Built to European standards, it was financed in part by Armenians abroad, which accounts for the bizarre sign outside Stepanakert, in Spanish, acknowledging contributions from Argentina in its construction. Military convoys regularly journey back and forth along the highway, taking fuel to Karabakh and returning with timber to Armenia, and there is nothing more than a small police checkpoint at the putative international frontier. Foreign investment from abroad, usually from Armenian communities, has begun to pick up. Swiss-Armenian businessmen have invested some $900,000 in a watch-manufacturing facility; others have spent $2 million to renovate Stepanakert's central Hotel Karabakh; and still other investors have pledged some $17 million to build tourist facilities near Karabakh's striking medieval monasteries.[23]

The four unrecognized states also act in the international arena as if they were independent entities and, to a great degree, cooperate with one another. They have officially recognized one another's existence. The four presidents exchange visits during each republic's national day celebrations. Official delegations sign trade agreements, and firms execute import and export deals. Security services share information on possible threats. For example, in the autumn of 2000, a delegation of leaders of Moldovan nongovernmental organizations arrived in Georgia for a brief tour. The Moldovans asked, via the local OSCE office, if they could arrange a trip to South Ossetia as part of their program. After approaching the South Ossetian leadership, the OSCE came back with a categorically negative response. As it turned out, the deputy speaker of the Transnistrian parliament had been in South Ossetia only weeks earlier, to attend the celebrations surrounding the tenth anniversary of

---

23. Author's interviews in Stepanakert, September 27–28, 2000; *Russia Journal*, October 7, 2000 (electronic version at www.russiajournal.com/weekly); *Radio Free Europe/Radio Liberty Armenia Report*, May 1, 2000. Diaspora support, however, has not been as enthusiastic as Karabakh leaders would like. A tour through the United States by Karabakh premier Anushavan Danielian in 2000 produced pledges of around $5 million. The campaign had hoped to raise four times that amount.

South Ossetian independence, and he had strongly advised the Ossetian interior and foreign ministries against approving the Moldovan visit.[24] Networks such as these were formalized in November 2000, when the four republics' foreign ministers held an official conference in the Transnistrian capital, Tiraspol, and pledged to coordinate their bargaining positions in talks with the three central governments.

Making Denizens Into Citizens

From early in all four conflicts, local authorities moved to take over educational and cultural institutions within the conflict zones. Polytechnics were upgraded to universities, academies of science established, and new national festivals inaugurated. History curricula were redesigned to highlight the citizens of the separatist regions as the indigenous inhabitants of their territory and to strengthen the connection between previous forms of statehood and the current, unrecognized states. The new Ministry of Information and press of the South Ossetian republic began to reproduce works of nineteenth-century travelers who described the customs of the Ossetians, in order "to bring to the masses the most interesting pages in the history of Ossetia and the Ossetians" (Ianovskii, 1993: 3, preface). The Ossetians located the origins of their modern statehood in ancient Iryston, the lands of settlement of the Iranian-speaking Alans. They were thus considered, as a new Ossetian encyclopedia argued, the true "autochthonous population" in their republic (Dzadziev, 1994: 64).

Local intellectuals also worked, as far as possible, to discover cultural or historical heroes around which semiofficial cults could be built. In Transnistria, Alexander Suvorov, the eighteenth-century field marshal who conquered Transnistria for the Russian empire, became a symbol of the Dnestr Moldovan republic, his visage appearing on the newly minted Transnistrian ruble. In South Ossetia, the statue of Kosta Khetagurov, a nineteenth-century poet, became one of the focal points of the annual republic day in September. Previous instances of statehood, no matter how tenuous, were marshaled to serve the cause. Armenians in Karabakh pointed to their own briefly independent republic which existed before Karabakh's absorption into Soviet Azerbaijan in the 1920s. Abkhaz writers lauded their 1925 constitution, which established an autonomous regime. Transnistrians identified the Moldovan autonomous republic, which existed inside Soviet Ukraine between the two world wars, as the basis of their modern statehood.[25]

24. Author's interview with Igor Munteanu, director, Viitorul Foundation, Tbilisi, October 12, 2000.
25. Author's interview with Vladimir Atamaniuk, first deputy speaker of Supreme Soviet of the Dnestr Moldovan Republic, Tiraspol, August 1, 1997.

The armed conflicts themselves also became sanctified as a struggle against external aggression. Children who were not even born when the conflicts began are now almost teenagers, schooled in the view that the republics they inhabit not only represent ancient nations, but have also been forged in the crucible of war and sacrifice. A special textbook, published to celebrate South Ossetia's first decade of independence in 2000, proclaimed (Dzugaev, 2000: 4):

> Ten years ago ... at the height of the Georgian-Ossetian confrontation, the Republic of South Ossetia was declared, a republic that has proved to be durable. The war killed and maimed thousands of our citizens; left tens of thousands of innocent people without shelter, work, and means of survival; razed our infrastructure; robbed the people of kindergartens and schools; and made peaceful citizens into refugees. Nevertheless, these years have a special historical significance for us, because we not only managed to defeat the aggressor but also to build our own statehood.

Transnistrian textbooks put forward a similar point of view, especially with regard to the decisive battle of Bender in 1992 (Babilunga, 1997: 98):

> The traitorous, barbaric, and unprovoked invasion of Bender had a single goal: to frighten and bring to their knees the inhabitants of the Dnestr republic ... However, the people's bravery, steadfastness, and love of liberty saved the Dnestr republic. The defense of Bender against the overwhelming forces of the enemy closed a heroic page in the history of our young republic. The best sons and daughters of the people sacrificed their lives for peace and liberty in our land.

As strange as they may sound, these arguments are little different from the equally tendentious views often used to justify the existence of Azerbaijan, Moldova, Georgia, and other new Eurasian states. As in those instances, there were rational reasons for the strategies that intellectuals and academics at the heart of these nation-building efforts pursued. In Karabakh, the opportunity for greater connections with educational and research institutions in Armenia was at the center of the early movement for transferring the region to Armenian jurisdiction. Many Karabakh writers and educators eventually moved to Russia or Armenia, but others found themselves catapulted into new jobs as professors and administrators of the new Artsakh State University in Stepanakert. In Moldova, the effective purge of Soviet-era scholars in the late 1980s created a class of disgruntled researchers and writers who looked on the Transnistrian cause as their own. Although not native to the region, many moved to Transnistria, where they could continue to thrive by writing the same Soviet-style versions of history and socialist internationalism that had made their careers—and become the shapers of Transnistrian national identity in the process (see, for example, Babilunga, 1993; Shornikov, 1997). In South Ossetia, professors at the local polytechnic found that increasing ties with institutions in Vladikavkaz, Moscow, and Saint Petersburg was more appealing than continued existence as a backwater in an increasingly Georgianized educational system. While the new ideologies of nationalism and statehood at times did violence to historical fact, most grew as much from the professional backgrounds and interests of their makers as from a romantic commitment to nationalist ideals.

The Complicity of Central Governments

Central authorities frequently point to the modalities of state building outlined above, complaining that the separatists and their external supporters are indeed constructing states that have come to depend less and less on the recognized governments. But that is only part of the story. In Georgia and Moldova, policy elites at the central level have also played a role in prolonging the disputes. The benefits of state weakness accrue not only to the separatists but also to the institutions and individuals who are ostensibly responsible for remedying it. Both countries are arguably among the most corrupt in the former Soviet Union, indeed, the most corrupt in the world.[26] The links between corrupt central governments and the separatist regions have further imperiled already weak state structures while enriching those who claim to be looking after the states' interests.

In South Ossetia, the illegal trade with Russia benefits all sides. The South Ossetian government receives money from resale and haphazardly applied "transit taxes," while Georgian authorities, especially the Interior Ministry, are able to take a cut by exacting fines from truck drivers on the outskirts of Tbilisi. The expansion of international humanitarian aid to the region has also provided another cover under which goods can be traded. Organizations are set up in Tbilisi to receive assistance destined for South Ossetia, and the goods are then sold in local markets.[27] It is partly for these reasons that relations between Tskhinvali and Tbilisi have generally been cordial, notwithstanding the lack of a final settlement. The South Ossetian president, in fact, openly supported Eduard Shevardnadze in his campaign for Georgian president in early 2000 (RFE/RL, 2000b).

26. See the *Corruption Perceptions Index* at www.transparency.org.
27. Author's confidential interview with senior United Nations official, Tbilisi, October 30, 2000.

In Abkhazia, similar formulas apply. Police officials in Zugdidi and Tsalenjikha, the two districts on the Georgian side of the border with Abkhazia, carry out periodic crackdowns on illegal transborder commerce, but local observers are convinced that these efforts are designed less to enforce the law than to root out small-time smugglers who might disrupt the police monopoly on transborder trade.[28] None of this is lost on local Georgians, who express deep skepticism about their own state institutions. A full two thirds report having no faith in parliament or the president, and some 80 percent have no faith in tax and customs officials (UNDP, 2000: 74).

These connections are even easier to document in Transnistria. In accords signed in 1996 and 1997, the Moldovan government, encouraged by the OSCE, agreed to establish joint customs posts with the Transnistrian administration, providing official customs stamps and export licenses to the separatists. Transnistria was also given the right to import and export goods, directly or via other parts of Moldova, without paying duties at the point where the goods entered Moldovan-controlled territory. The agreement was intended as a measure to build confidence between the two sides, but, in practice, it has represented little more than a conduit for illegal commerce under the cover of law. The scale of this trade is easily traceable, since customs duties are duly registered with the Moldovan central government, even if the money never makes it into state coffers. For example, in 1998, Moldova imported around $125 million in goods subject to import taxes. At the same time, another $500 million was registered with Moldovan customs officials as entering the country for transit on to Transnistria.[29]

The figures are as instructive as they are incredible. A piece of territory that holds around 17 percent of Moldova's total population imported four times as much merchandise as the country as a whole, including around 6,000 times as many cigarettes—all with the full knowledge of the central tax inspector's office. While some of the imports no doubt do reach Transnistria, the majority find their way onto the Moldovan market. Moldova's senior presidential advisor on Transnistria, Oazu Nantoi, resigned in protest when he discovered these figures and later put together a series of broadcasts on public television that brought this illegal trade to light. But in late 2000, the director of Moldovan National Television ordered the broadcasts stopped, reportedly on the order of senior government officials.[30] Throughout these conflict zones, the weak state is not a condition that has somehow simply happened.

28. Author's interview with Hans-Gjorg Heinrich, advisor to OSCE mission, Tbilisi, October 23, 2000; Naira Gelashvili, director, Caucasus House, Tbilisi, October 3 and 23, 2000; *Ekho-Daidzhest*, August 1–15, 2000, p. 7.

29. *Buletinul Social-democrat* (2000); author's conversations with Oazu Nantoi.

30. *Foreign Broadcast Information Service—Soviet Union*, October 24, 2000.

Continued weakness is in the interests of those in power, whether in the separatist regions or in central governments.

Even in less unpalatable ways, there are powerful disincentives for central governments to change the status quo. Even politicians who may be committed, in good faith, to resolving the dispute must deal with radical domestic forces pushing in the opposite direction. In Georgia, the Apkhazeti faction in parliament, the remnants of the former Georgian administration in Abkhazia that fled to Tbilisi during the war, has proved to be a brake on genuine compromise. The Apkhazeti, who enjoy set-aside seats in parliament, function as a regional government-in-exile. Although they do not control enough parliamentary votes to challenge the strong government majority, they are vocal opponents of any move that might seem to compromise their own interests in returning to power in Abkhazia.[31] For example, they have long blocked legislation that would provide for resettlement and integration of the 250,000 people displaced during the Abkhaz war; people who have spent much of the past decade living in so-called temporary accommodation in run-down hotels and resorts. Resettling the IDPs in Georgia proper, the faction leaders fear, would reduce their own political and economic power since they control state budgetary disbursements to the IDPs and the provision of social services.[32] The Apkhazeti group has, in turn, proved a useful foil for the most independence-minded Abkhaz. The failure of negotiation can always be blamed on the militaristic language of the Apkhazeti and on their supporters on the ground, the ethnic Georgian guerrilla movements that harass Abkhaz troops. The Abkhaz, the Apkhazeti, and the Georgian government—although radically distinct groups—have a common interest in blocking real change.[33]

International Intervention as a Resource

In each of these conflicts, international involvement has been frequent if not frequently successful. In Azerbaijan, the OSCE-sponsored Minsk Group has provided good offices and a mechanism for negotiations since 1992. In Moldova, an OSCE mission has been active since 1993 and has sponsored numerous rounds of negotiations. In Georgia, a UN observer mission was deployed in 1993 to provide a basis for negotiations on Abkhazia's future and to monitor the peacekeeping

---

31. *Georgia Today*, August 11–17, 2000, p. 3.

32. Author's confidential interview with senior official, United Nations, Tbilisi, October 30, 2000.

33. Similar situations exist in Moldova (where pro-Romanian intellectuals have opposed concessions on Transnistria) and Armenia (where militants assassinated the prime minister in 1999 when he seemed to be moving toward a compromise with Azerbaijan).

operation conducted by the CIS forces in the Georgian-Abkhaz security zone. In South Ossetia, Russian peacekeepers have been in place since the end of the war, and negotiations on South Ossetia's final status have continued apace, involving Russia, North Ossetia, and the OSCE as mediators.

Despite this active engagement, little of significance has been achieved. There are three broad reasons for the lack of real progress. First, in all cases, the incumbent governments are arguing from positions of weakness. They were the military losers in the conflict and therefore have little to offer the separatist regimes. That basic dynamic is compounded by the parlous state of their own economies, which makes reintegration of little interest either to separatist elites or to their constituent populations. In all four disputes, the separatists have insisted that full recognition of their independence should come first, after which they might be willing to negotiate some form of loose confederation with the incumbent governments. Central governments, on the other hand, want precisely the opposite: an acceptance of state unity first, followed by discussions about devolution of power.

Second, because of the beneficial economies of conflict, no key elites on either side have a major incentive to implement the agreements that have been signed. The belligerents have been favorably disposed to negotiate, even if scheduled sessions are routinely canceled or postponed, but rarely have the talks produced more than an agreement to maintain dialogue—an outcome that both sides seem to see as acceptable. And so long as the sides maintain "dialogue," they receive the political support and financial assistance of the international community. The major players have been willing to talk to each other precisely because the stakes are so low. Few people on either side believe that what happens at the bargaining table will ever be implemented on the ground.[34]

Third, at times the policies of international negotiators have actually strengthened the statehood of the separatist regions. International intervention can itself be a useful resource for the builders of unrecognized states. Even accepting the separatist delegation as a negotiating partner confers some degree of legitimacy on that side's demands, but in more important and subtle ways, otherwise neutral facilitators have bolstered the separatists' hands. In Karabakh, the difficulty of crossing the trenches between Karabakh and Azerbaijani forces—not to mention the excellent road link from Armenia—has meant that humanitarian and development programs, including those sponsored by the United States government, are managed from Armenia, not

34. Author's confidential interviews with senior officials, OSCE and United Nations, Tbilisi, October 23 and 26, 2000.

from Azerbaijan.[35] In Transnistria, the local OSCE delegation strongly encouraged the Moldovan government to sign the agreements that provided customs stamps to the Transnistrians, thereby facilitating illegal commerce through the region. Later, the OSCE pressured the Moldovans to sign another accord that committed both sides to existence within a "common state," a form of language that the Transnistrians now interpret as Moldovan acquiescence to no more than a loose confederation.[36] In Abkhazia, humanitarian relief agencies have become a pillar of the local economy, injecting as much as four to five million dollars into the economy each year through rents, services, and payment of local staff.[37] Even the most dedicated peacemakers thus find themselves in a no-win position: pushing an agreement with separatists who have no incentive to negotiate in good faith, central leaders who benefit from the status quo, and an impatient international community looking for any symbol of progress, regardless of whether it actually contributes to resolution.

Peace as a Public Good

Eurasia's de facto countries are informational black holes. Traveling there is difficult and often dangerous. Elections have been held but never under the eyes of international observers. Economic and demographic data are not included in statistics compiled by national and international agencies. Books and newspapers barely circulate within the separatist regions themselves, much less to national capitals or abroad.

For all that, they may seem instances of what Freud called the narcissism of small differences. In most instances, the leaders of these republics and their counterparts in central governments speak a common language—Russian—during negotiating sessions. Many had similar professional backgrounds during the Soviet period. The territory that separates them is in some cases miniscule. Tiraspol is 50 kilometers from the Moldovan capital, Chisinau; Tskhinvali is under two hours' drive from the Georgian capital, Tbilisi. Yet the problems they have spawned are immense. They are the central political problem for the recognized states whose territory they inhabit,

35. Author's confidential interview with senior manager, United States assistance program, Stepanakert, September 28, 2000. Even the OSCE Minsk Group, the main negotiating forum, is based in Tbilisi, since basing the mission in either Baku or Yerevan would have been unacceptable to one of the sides.

36. "Memorandum ob osnovakh normalizatsii otnoshenii mezhdu Respublikoi Moldova i Pridnestrov'em," signed May 8, 1997, Moscow.

37. Author's confidential interview with senior official, United Nations Office for the Coordination of Humanitarian Assistance, Tbilisi, August 29, 2000.

and they have become conduits for trafficking in drugs, arms, and even people across Eurasia into Europe and beyond.

The strict security dimension of each of these conflicts—the threats posed by massive refugee flows or renewed fighting, say—is no longer a major concern. Since the end of the wars, separatist elites have got on with the process of building states, and even central elites and average citizens have learned to accommodate themselves to that process. But the cessation of the armed conflict has perversely made a final political settlement even more difficult to achieve. Peace has now become something like a public good, an outcome from which all groups might potentially benefit, but which entails some sacrifice from all interested parties. Just as the political economy of war can perpetuate violence, so too the institutions of Eurasia's unrecognized states have ensured that the benefits born of conflict continue to accrue to belligerents on both sides, the erstwhile losers as well as the winners.

To a certain degree, the energetic institution building in the separatist regions is a legacy of Soviet socialism. Three of the conflict zones had some of the basic institutions of statehood already (through their status as autonomous areas), and, even in Transnistria, local party organs and city councils provided the germ for what would later become a parliament, presidency, and security structure. The Soviet system provided a convenient template for how national issues ought to be channeled, a template that placed a premium on having and controlling state-like institutions drawn along national lines. It is indicative of the power of the Soviet model that among the first official acts of separatist elites was to set up a parliament and to adopt legislation on a national flag, anthem, and seal—long before they were even able to secure the territory they claimed as theirs. The supply of stateness in the Soviet system was there even before the demand.

Still, once the accoutrements of statehood have been put into place, they are extremely difficult to deconstruct. Why be mayor of a small city if you can be president of a country? Why be a lieutenant in someone else's army if you can be a general in your own? Of course, those calculations might be different if Azerbaijan, Moldova, and Georgia were strong, wealthy or even marginally functional states, in which individuals in the separatist regions could see some advantage to reintegration. So far, however, life inside a recognized state (especially beyond the capital cities) is little different from life in one of the unrecognized ones.

There is an obvious solution to this conundrum. Central governments could simply recognize the power of the separatist regions and opt for the maximum devolution of authority to them, in exchange for commitment to the existence of a single state. That has been the recommendation repeatedly put forward by the Russian Federation and generally supported by other external mediators, the idea of a final peace settlement based around the concept of a "common state" (*obshchee gosudarstvo*). As the Russian Defense Ministry's official history of these conflicts argues, the only possible course now is "the preservation of the existing de facto independent status of Abkhazia, Nagorno-Karabakh, and South Ossetia as juridically legitimate entities, as something like associated parts of internationally recognized states" (Zolotarev, 2000: 395).

But even though this course might provide some diplomatic cover—a document that would allow the international community to claim that the conflicts had been solved—it would do little to alter the basic structure of power. In fact, it would simply legitimize the continued division of these states into areas controlled by central governments and areas where their writ does not run. That may have been a workable solution in empires, where rebellious peripheral elites were granted tax-farming powers in exchange for loyalty to the center. It is not, however, a viable option for new, fragile, and allegedly democratizing states.

These dynamics call into question the academic lenses through which researchers have addressed the problems of intrastate war. Given the Western policy interest in the Balkans and the Caucasus in the 1990s, the study of conflict in these regions became of serious interest to security studies and, by extension, to international relations as a whole. Research has normally focused on the dimensions of conflict derived largely from confrontations between states, such as the security dilemma. But seeing ethnoterritorial confrontations as mainly a security problem can blind researchers to the deep political and economic incentives that sustain disputes and fossilize networks of war into institutions of de facto states. The lesson of Eurasia's unrecognized countries is that these mechanisms are precisely where one should look to explain the conflicts' intractability. In civil wars, as in politics, asking *cui bono* can be illuminating.

References

Babilunga, N. (ed.) (1993) *Bessarabskii vopros i obrazovanie Pridnestrovskoi Moldavskoi Respubliki* (The Bessarabian question and the formation of the Dnestr Moldovan Republic). Tiraspol: Dnestr State Cooperative University.

Babilunga, N.V. and V.G. Bomeshko (1997) *Pagini din istoria plaiului natal* (Pages from the history of the fatherland). Tiraspol: Transnistrian Institute of Continuing Education, 98.

Berdal, Mats and David M. Malone (eds.) (2000) *Greed and Grievance: Economic Agendas in Civil Wars.* Boulder: Lynne Reinner.

Bowers, Stephen (1992) "The Crisis in Moldova." *Jane's Intelligence Review,* November: 484.

Brubaker, Rogers (1996) *Nationalism Reframed: Nationhood and the National Question in the New Europe.* Cambridge: Cambridge University Press, especially chap. 3.

Collier, Paul (1999) "On the Economic Consequences of Civil War." *Oxford Economic Papers* 51, January.

De Figueiredo, Rui J., Jr. and Barry R. Weingast (1999) "The Rationality of Fear: Political Opportunism and Ethnic Conflict." In Barbara F. Walter and Jack Snyder (eds.) *Civil Wars, Insecurity, and Intervention.* New York: Columbia University Press.

Dzadziev, A.B., Kh.V. Dzutsev and S.M. Karaev (1994) *Etnografiia i mifologiia osetin* (Ethnography and mythology of the Ossetians). Vladikavkaz: n. p., 64.

Dzugaev, K.G. (ed.) (2000) *Iuzhnaia Osetiia: 10 let respublike* (South Ossetia: on the tenth anniversary of the republic). Vladikavkaz: Iryston, 4.

Ellis, Stephen (1999) *The Mask of Anarchy: The Roots of Liberia's War.* New York: New York University Press.

Fearon, James D. and David D. Laitin (1996) "Explaining Interethnic Cooperation." *American Political Science Review* 90 (December).

Fearon, James D. (1998) "Commitment Problems and the Spread of Ethnic Conflict." In David A. Lake and Donald Rothchild (eds.) *The International Spread of Ethnic Conflict: Fear, Diffusion, and Escalation.* Princeton: Princeton University Press.

Global Witness (1998) *A Rough Trade: The Role of Companies and Governments in the Angola Conflict.* London: Global Witness.

Gribincea, Mihai (1998) *Trupele ruse in Republica Moldova: factor stabilizator sau sursa de pericol?* (Russian troops in the Republic of Moldova: Stabilizing factor or source of danger?) Chisinau: Civitas.

—— (1999) *Politica rusa a bazelor militare: Moldova si Georgia* (Russian policy on military bases: Moldova and Georgia). Chisinau: Civitas, 15.

International Monetary Fund (1993) *IMF Economic Reviews: Moldova, 1993.* Washington: International Monetary Fund.

International Institute for Strategic Studies (2000) *The Military Balance, 2000–2001.* London: International Institute for Strategic Studies.

Ianovskii, Aleksandr (1993) *Osetiia* (Ossetia). Tskhinvali: Ministry of Information and Press of the Republic of South Ossetia, 3. editor's preface.

Kaufmann, Chaim (1996) "Possible and Impossible Solutions to Ethnic Civil Wars." *International Security* 20 (Spring).

—— (1998) "When All Else Fails: Ethnic Population Transfers and Partitions in the Twentieth Century." *International Security* 23 (Fall).

Keen, David (1994) *The Benefits of Famine: A Political Economy of Famine Relief in Southwestern Sudan, 1983–1989.* Princeton: Princeton University Press.

—— (1995) "When War Itself Is Privatized." *Times Literary Supplement*, December 29.

—— (1998) *The Economic Functions of Violence in Civil Wars*. Adelphi Paper 320. Oxford: Oxford University Press and International Institute for Strategic Studies.

King, Charles (2000) *The Moldovans: Romania, Russia, and the Politics of Culture*. Stanford: Hoover Institution Press, chap. 9.

Laitin, David D. and Ronald Grigor Suny (1999) "Armenia and Azerbaijan: Thinking a Way Out of Karabakh." *Middle East Policy* 7 (October).

Licklider, Roy (1995) "The Consequences of Negotiated Settlements in Civil Wars, 1945–1993." *American Political Science Review* 89 (September): 686.

Luttwak, Edward N. (1999) "Give War a Chance." *Foreign Affairs* 78 (July/August).

Pillar, Paul R. (1983) *Negotiating Peace: War Termination as a Bargaining Process*. Princeton: Princeton University Press, 25.

Posen, Barry R. (1993) "The Security Dilemma and Ethnic Conflict." In Michael E. Brown (ed.) *Ethnic Conflict and International Security*. Princeton: Princeton University Press.

Reno, William (1995) *Corruption and State Politics in Sierra Leone*. Cambridge: Cambridge University Press.

—— (1998) *Warlord Politics and African States*. Boulder: Lynne Reinner.

Shornikov, M. (1997) *Pokushenie na status* (Striving for status). Chisinau: Chisinau Society of Russians.

Stedman, Stephen John (1991) *Peacemaking in Civil War: International Mediation in Zimbabwe, 1974–1980*. Boulder: Lynne Reinner, 9.

Totadze, Anzor [Georgian deputy minister of labor, health, and social affairs] (1994) *The Ossets in Georgia*. Tbilisi: Samshoblo.

United Nations Development Program (2000) *Human Development Report, Georgia 2000*. Tbilisi: United Nations Development Program, 74.

Walter, Barbara F. (1997) "The Critical Barrier to Civil War Settlement." *International Organization* 51 (Summer).

World Bank (1998) *Republic of Moldova: Economic Review of the Transnistria Region, June 1998*. Washington: World Bank.

Zartman, I. William (1985) *Ripe for Resolution: Conflict and Intervention in Africa*. Oxford: Oxford University Press.

Zolotarev, V.A. (ed.) (2000) *Rossiia (SSSR) v lokal'nykh voinakh i voennykh konfliktakh vtoroi poloviny XX veka* (Russia [USSR] in local wars and armed conflicts in the second half of the twentieth century). Moscow: Institute of Military History, Russian Ministry of Defense.

Buletinul Social-democrat 2, 2000

Curierul national, April 4, 1992, pp.1, 7.

Den', August 9–15, 1992.

Ekho-Daidzhest, August 1–15, 2000, p.7.

Foreign Broadcast Information Service—Soviet Union, October 24, 2000.

Georgia Today, August 11–17, 2000, p.3.

Georgia Today, October 6–12, 2000, p.4.

"Memorandum ob osnovakh normalizatsii otnoshenii mezhdu Respublikoi Moldova
   i Pridnestrov'em," signed May 8, 1997, Moscow.

Moldova suverana, June 11, 1991, p.1.

Oxford Analytica East Europe Daily Brief, January 11, 1999.

Oxford Analytica East Europe Daily Brief, June 29, 2000.

Radio Free Europe/Radio Liberty Armenia Report, May 1, 2000a.

Radio Free Europe/Radio Liberty Caucasus Report, April 7, 2000b.

Radio Maiak, September 18, 1992,

Romania libera, April 4–5, 1992, p.8.

Russia Journal, October 7, 2000 (electronic version at www.russiajournal.com/
   weekly);

Svobodnaia Gruziia, October 24, 2000, p.3, and October 25, 2000, p.1.

Svobodnaia Gruziia, October 25, 2000, p.4.

Author's Interviews

Elena Niculina, representative, World Bank, Chisinau, July 29, 1997.

Transnistrian steel workers, Ribnita, August 1, 1997.

Valeriu Prudnicov, Moldovan police commissioner, Bender, August 1, 1997.

Senior official, United Nations Office for the Coordination of Humanitarian
   Assistance (confidential), Tbilisi, August 29, 2000.

Edgar Sargsian, field officer, International Committee of the Red Cross, Stepanakert,
   September 28, 2000.

Senior manager, United States assistance program (confidential), Stepanakert,
   September 28, 2000.

Naira Gelashvili, director, Caucasus House, Tbilisi, October 3 and 23, 2000.

Tevfik Yaprak, head of mission, World Bank, Tbilisi, October 11, 2000.

Igor Munteanu, director, Viitorul Foundation, Tbilisi, October 12, 2000.

Igor Munteanu, director, Viitorul Foundation, Tbilisi, October 12, 2000. Tskhinvali,
   October 13, 2000.

Hans-Gjorg Heinrich, advisor, OSCE mission, Tbilisi, October 23, 2000.

Senior officials, OSCE and United Nations (confidential), Tbilisi, October 23 and 26, 2000.

Senior official, United Nations (confidential), in Tbilisi, October 30, 2000.

IV.
Assessing the Institutional Tools

Is Ethnofederalism the Solution or the Problem?

Valerie Bunce

Introduction

The literature on multinational states suggests that conflicts between majorities and minorities are more likely to occur under four conditions: (1) when minorities are spatially concentrated; (2) when economic and social interactions between majorities and minorities are limited; (3) when there is a history of such conflicts; and (4) when regimes are in transition from dictatorship to democracy (see especially, Horowitz, 1985; Gurr, 2000; Kaufman, 2001; Bunce, 1999b; Varshney, 2001). These factors help explain, for example, cross-national patterns in interethnic conflict and changes over time in such conflicts—for example, the rise of such conflicts in Eastern Europe and the Soviet Union during the first half of the 1990s following the collapse of communism.

There is a fifth factor that has also received a great deal of attention: the design of political institutions. While analysts concur that institutional choice has powerful effects on interethnic relations, they disagree about the *consequences* of particular choices. A case in point is the debate over ethnofederalism—a common approach to the management of interethnic relations in multinational states. Like all federal systems, ethnofederalism features: (1) territorially defined subunits; (2) dual sovereignty, where the center and the subunits each have their own political and economic spheres of responsibility (see, especially, Dent, 1995 on this point); and (3) a relationship between the center and the subunits that combines autonomy and coordination, rather than the subordination typical of unitary states (see Stepan, 1999; 2000; MacPherson, 1994). What is distinctive about ethnofederalism is that some—and sometimes all—of the subunits are composed of (and are deemed to represent) geographically concentrated minority communities (see Verney, 1995; Stepan, 1999, 2000; Simeon and Conway, 2000; Mastny, 2000). To provide some examples, Canada, Spain, Belgium, India, Nigeria, Russia, Bosnia and Herzegovina, and Serbia and Montenegro are all ethnofederal states, as were the states of the Soviet Union, Yugoslavia, and Czechoslovakia during the communist period.

The Debate Over Ethnofederalism

Some scholars argue that ethnofederalism (and other forms of power sharing) invests in interethnic peace, stable borders, and sustainable democratic governance (see, especially, Lijphart, 1977, 1990, 1996; Gagnon and Laforest, 1994; Corbridge, 1995; Guibernau, 1995; Bajpai, 1997; Stepan, 1999; King, 2000). In their view, ethnofederalism has three key benefits. It legitimates difference, empowers minority communities, and prevents, as a result, domination by the majority.

Ethnofederalism, therefore, is thought to generate trust and provide minorities a stake in both democracy and the state, easing the security dilemma, which is so common in multiethnic systems (see Posen, 1993; Fearon, 1998). At the same time, ethnofederalism is understood to provide a reasonable solution to a common problem characteristic of federalist systems: a center bent on expanding its powers, thereby compromising the federalist project. In multiethnic contexts, therefore, ethnofederalism may counter two temptations—of minorities to defect and majorities to dominate (see Lijphart, 1990; Bednar et al., 1999; Sisk, 1996). For precisely these reasons, scholars have written in relatively favorable terms about ethnofederalism in India, South Africa, and Canada. They have also highlighted the advantages, especially in the longer-term, of ethnofederalism for countries such as Moldova and Spain and now identify some ethnofederal features in those two countries, which were previously viewed as purely unitary states (see, especially, Gagnon and Laforest, 1994; Corbridge, 1995; Guibernau, 1995; Lijphart, 1996; Bajpai, 1997; Stepan, 1999; King, 2000).

However, there are equally persuasive arguments against ethnofederalism. The key insight here is that there may be a fine line between legitimating difference and undermining commonality (see, especially, MacPherson, 1994; Bunce, 1999b; Roeder, 2000, 2001a, 2001b; Karklins, 2000). It is now the received wisdom that nations are constructed, and identities are fluid. By drawing tight linkages among the nation, territory, and political power, ethnofederalism can lock in differences and freeze identities. This can, conceivably, have three consequences. One is to limit interaction and prevent cooperation among communities, given the absence of common identities, political projects, and economic activities (Varshney, 2001). Another is to give minorities the institutional resources and leadership they need to press for independence. This second argument against ethnofederalism is all the easier to embrace, given the plausible relationship between ethnofederalism and group isolation, intergroup distrust, and increasing competition among local elites who are unable to build careers outside their region and, as a result, are in search of local issues that can mobilize support among voters and outflank competitors (see Horowitz, 1985; Roeder, 2001b).

Finally, the center can weaken, which exacerbates the other dynamics—a cost that serves as the point of departure for the Federalist Papers, especially number ten (see King, 1982). A weak center often encourages local leaders to engage in ethnic outbidding to expand their power. In addition, with a weak center, central-level leaders, who represent the majority nation and are increasingly resentful of the gap between large numbers, but limited political power may use violence against minorities and suspend the democratic experiment to close this gap (see, especially, Bunce, 1999b on the Yugoslav case). For these reasons, rather than supporting the state, democracy, and interethnic peace, according to many scholars, ethnofederalism can undermine all three (see Martiniello, 1995, 1998; Murphy, 1995; Williams, 1995; Simeon and Conway, 2001; Bunce, 1999b, 2002; Treisman, 1997; Roeder, 2000). To reverse the argument above: an ethnofederal approach to state design can push minorities out, and encourage majorities to be aggressive, thereby deconstructing both democracy and the state.

Who is Right?

The purpose of this paper is to use the communist and the postcommunist experience in East Central Europe and the former Soviet Union to evaluate these competing perspectives on ethnofederalism.[1] The analysis will proceed in two stages. In the first stage, I will focus on the decline of state socialism—or the developments that transpired in this region from the mid-1980s to the end of 1992. Of interest here is how, during a time of authoritarian decline, the design of communist states—or the contrast between the ethnofederations of Yugoslavia, the Soviet Union, and Czechoslovakia and the unitary states of Poland, Hungary, Bulgaria, Romania, and Albania—affected interethnic relations, state borders, and bargaining between the communists and opposition forces.

The second part of the chapter turns to political developments after the disintegration of communist regimes and states—the period from 1993 to the present. Here, I will focus on political dynamics in the new states with sizeable minority populations. Of interest here is how the design of these new states has affected interethnic cooperation and conflict, state capacity, and the course of democratic politics. In this part of the study, three types of states will be compared: ethnofederal republics that maintained that structure after independence, states that inherited and maintained

---

1. As I have argued elsewhere (Bunce, 1999a, 1999b, 2003c), the postcommunist region is ideal for comparative study, given significant variation in dependent variables and, because of the communist past, constrained variation in causal factors.

a unitary structure, and, finally, unitary republics that added some ethnofederal features after independence. It is interesting to note, in passing, that none of the postcommunist states fall into a fourth category, that is, republics that were ethnofederal in form but shifted to a unitary structure following independence. Indeed, this 'missing cell' seems to represent a more general pattern. Once adopted, ethnofederalism seems to be unusually sticky.

State Socialism and Ethnofederalism

There is a substantial body of work in the social sciences supporting the claim that, by shaping preferences and allocating resources and incentives, the design of political institutions has enormous influence on both the identities and behavior of mass publics and political leaders. It would be wrong, however, to assume that those elites powerful enough to design political institutions can analyze the consequences of their institutional choices. This is because of two factors. The first is that the context of institutions matters a great deal. This is because most social settings are dense with institutions, which may operate at cross-purposes with each other. Indeed, contextual considerations can shape both the forms and the supply of incentives and resources. Thus, the same institutions can be placed in different settings and have very different results—as Pauline Jones Luong (2002) has argued, for example, with respect to the role of pacts in transitions from dictatorship to democracy. From a longer-term perspective, moreover, institutions serving one purpose—the consolidation of an empire for example—can have quite different effects over time, such as deregulating centralized political control (see Bunce, 1999b). Institutional design, in short, has powerful, but often unpredictable effects, especially over the long run.

This was certainly the case with respect to the design of state socialism—a distinctive form of dictatorship, combining state ownership of the means of production, central planning, governance by a Leninist party, isolation from the global economy, and an ideology committed to rapid socioeconomic transformation. On the face of it, the concentration of economic and political resources in the Party's hands—or a centralized and fused political and economic monopoly—would seem to have been ideally suited to reproduce state socialism. However, it was precisely this monopoly that, over time, proved to be the undoing of these economic and political regimes—given, for example, growing intra-Party conflict; the Party's declining capacity to control its lower reaches and, more generally, society; the periphery's growing capacity to stake out autonomy from the core; and, finally, declining economic performance, which had necessarily politically destabilizing consequences in these systems. Because of this institutional design, therefore, and precisely in opposition to the goals of the elites, state-socialist systems deregulated themselves. Absent the monopoly that defined and defended them, these systems eventually collapsed (Bunce, 1999b; Solnick, 1998).

The question before us, however, is whether this process played out differently in ethnofederal and unitary state contexts. Here, several generalizations can be drawn. First, the deconstruction of communist party rule was accompanied in three cases by the state's deconstruction. Each of these cases—the Soviet Union, Yugoslavia, and Czechoslovakia—was an ethnofederal state. By contrast, every state that survived the demise of communist party hegemony with its borders intact was a unitary state. What this seems to suggest is that ethnofederalism invites considerable contestation over state borders when authoritarian regimes are in decline.

However, this conclusion would be more persuasive if two factors were not conflated, that is, the state's design and population diversity. Put simply, Yugoslavia, the Soviet Union, and Czechoslovakia were the most heterogeneous countries within communist Eurasia. Thus, their unraveling, it could be countered, may reflect not so much the state's design as the diversity of the constituent populations. Having said that, however, several other considerations return us to the importance of ethnofederalism. One is that diversity in and of itself does not explain patterns of nationalist mobilization within these states—or, for that matter, within the unitary states that were also part of this region. The fact is that the best predictor of nationalist mobilization against the state at the end of the communist era—and, indeed, even earlier in the communist era as well as in the postcommunist context—is whether the minority mobilizing against the state was the titular nation in a political unit within the federation. When it was, the probability of protest rose considerably (Treisman, 1997; Beissinger, 2002; Barany, 2001). Thus, those minorities that lacked their own institutions, even when they had other characteristics that encourage mobilization (for example, territorial concentration, a history of conflict with the majority, experiences of discrimination, and majority status in a neighboring state), were far less likely to mobilize in practice and, if they did mobilize, less likely to embrace a secessionist political agenda.

Moreover, the borders of the new states formed as a consequence of the break-up of these three ethnofederations were precisely the boundaries that had demarcated the republics constituting these states before their break-up. This was the case despite, for example, the low correlation between the geographical distribution of minority populations and the administrative boundaries of the republics.[2] Despite a host of

2. Serbia and Montenegro provide somewhat of an exception, because in this case the state combines two republics, along with two autonomous regions (to use the language of the communist era). However, even here, what matters is the absence of any violation of prior administrative boundaries.

difficulties, moreover, each of these new states has survived. All this seems to suggest, at the very least, that by joining territory, ethnicity, and institutional resources, ethnofederalism undermines the state when authoritarian rule is breaking down.

A second generalization is that in only one case—Yugoslavia—was the state's disintegration a violent process (although there were instances of violence in the Soviet case, but largely within republics, rather than between them or between republics and the center). While ethnofederalism seems to have contributed in important ways to these states' dissolution along republican lines, it did not guarantee by any means that this process would be violent—or, for that matter, that it would be peaceful, as Rogers Brubaker (1996: chap. 2) argued at one time with respect to the advantages of ethnofederalism for the Soviet Union's peaceful break-up. There have been a number of arguments seeking to explain why Yugoslavia's break-up was violent. Most of these arguments emphasize cultural, economic, historical, or geopolitical factors. Yet, in my view, institutional considerations are still critical—in particular, some of the details of ethnofederalism, such as whether the structure was symmetrical or asymmetrical, how decentralized it was prior to the weakening of communist party rule, and whether republics had access to their own militaries. In addition, a key factor was whether the military had been a key player in politics during the communist era.

In Yugoslavia, and in direct contrast to both the Soviet and Czechoslovak cases, the federation was symmetrical. This was important because it gave the communist party of Serbia—the republic representing the dominant although not majoritarian nation—the institutional resources to preserve its powers while inviting party leaders to capitalize on Serbian concerns about being underrepresented within Yugoslav political and economic life. Second, and also in contrast to the Soviet and Czechoslovak cases, the Yugoslav Federation was far more decentralized, especially after the adoption of the 1974 Constitution and the decentralization of decision making after Tito's death. Because of this, the republics were quite different with respect to party politics, civil-society development, and the like. In addition, this decentralization generated a dynamic of inter-republican conflict, weakening the center and, thus, its capacity to respond effectively to the breakdown of communist party hegemony. Finally, it was only in Yugoslavia that the military had been long-engaged in domestic politics and that republics had their own military units. As I have argued elsewhere in detail (Bunce, 1999b; also see Vujacic, 1996), as a result, the Serbian leadership contested the state's dissolution (while also encouraging this to happen and while using the dissolution as a pretext for building a "Greater Serbia"), whereas the leaders of the dominant republics in the Soviet Union and Czechoslovakia did not. Indeed, leaders in both of the latter two countries saw the state's break-up as helpful to the accumulation of their own power and to the realization of their agenda of economic and political liberalization. Thus, the particular form of ethnofederalism, together with civil-military relations, were critical in producing either a peaceful or a violent dismemberment of the state.

The final generalization addresses the relationship between the state's design and the rise of democratic politics. Here, the story is complex. On the one hand, unitary states on the whole clearly had stronger political oppositions. In some cases, such as Hungary and Poland, the opposition quickly filled the political vacuum (with the communists cooperating with them), whereas in other cases, such as Bulgaria, Romania, and Albania, the opposition had to share the political stage with the communists, thereby producing a more contested and prolonged transition from dictatorship to democracy. However, in all of these countries, important elements of democratic politics were introduced quickly and the opposition, even when overtly nationalist (as in Poland), invariably supported a democratic transition. Voices in support of redrawing state borders or an illiberal nationalist agenda were virtually absent in all of these transitions—despite the pressure on the communists to embrace nationalism as a means to stay in power (as was the case in Bulgaria and Romania in the last years of communism) and despite the presence of geographically compact minority populations (again, as in Bulgaria and Romania). All of this points to the benefits, within the communist context, of a unitary state for the development of a large and liberal opposition, a marriage between nationalist and liberal ideologies, and a communist party that either cooperated with the opposition or lost substantial political support by clinging to the authoritarian past. However, it is also true that in none of the unitary cases was the minority larger than 15 percent of the population—a situation that provides a less than an ideal test of the relationship between state structure and democratic transitions.

By contrast, within the ethnofederations, there was enormous variation between the republics in three factors: (1) the relative power of the opposition vis à vis the communists; (2) whether the communists and the opposition were allies or competitors; and (3) whether the communists and the opposition supported democracy and supported an independent state. Ethnofederalism, therefore, created multiple struggles—by expanding the political issues on the bargaining table, by creating variable combinations of positions on nationalism, secession, and democracy, and by creating both spatially and nationally divergent political dramas. These dramas reflected, of course, differences in republican politics during the communist era—variations that were made possible by the segmentation of the polity and the economy brought by the ethnofederal arrangements. These dramas, in turn, contributed to these states' break-up—testimony far more to the irreconcilability of their political struggles than to differences in culture. The end of state socialism in an ethnofederal context is better understood, then, as a process of competing republic-level struggles over the form and future of both the regime and the state.

However, if ethnofederalism contributed to the multiplication of both regimes and states within the state when communist party hegemony began to unravel, it also had a more positive effect. It is hard to imagine that states such as Slovenia, Macedonia, the Baltics, Russia, or the Czech Republic would have become democratic orders if they had remained within their federations. In this sense, the break-up of these states invested in democratic politics by giving those republics with the dynamics most supportive of a democratic outcome the possibility of becoming democratic orders. The parallel between the postcommunist experience in this regard and, after World War II, the impact of the substraction of East Germany on postwar West German democratization cannot be lost (see Bernhard, 2001). However, at the same time, it is clear that those republican leaders that resisted liberalization within these ethnofederal states were also more free, as a consequence of state dissolution, to solidify their political control and pursue their authoritarian and often illiberal nationalist political agenda. This was certainly the case, for example, in Serbia, Slovakia, and Belarus.

During the breakdown of authoritarian rule, therefore, ethnofederalism seems to have largely negative consequences on interethnic relations, continuity of state borders, and the introduction of democratic politics. In particular, ethnofederalism—at least in the context of the decline of communist party rule—is far more likely than its unitary counterpart to generate violent conflicts between the majority and minority communities. Moreover, only in the ethnofederal context was regime change inextricably linked to state dismemberment and to the rise of exclusivist nationalism—which became highly problematic in multinational republican contexts. In addition, ethnofederalism was distinctive in creating incentives for communists and, when the communists had been compromised by past nationalist protests, the opposition, to embrace an exclusivist nationalist agenda as a means of maintaining power in the first instance and acquiring power in the second. While Serbia exemplifies the first case, Croatia, Georgia, Moldova, and Slovakia exemplify the second. In either case, the opposition found it extraordinarily difficult to reconcile democracy with nationalism (though this was done in some republican contexts, such as Slovenia, the Czech Republic, Russia, and Ukraine). Finally, as a result, ethnofederalism created islands of authoritarian resurgence—which either solidified authoritarian rule after communism or, as in Croatia, Slovakia, and Serbia, prolonged the transition to democratic politics. However, at the same time, it can be argued that by facilitating the state's dissolution, ethnofederalism also ensured that some of the new states, such as Slovenia, Russia, and Ukraine, would have a far easier time becoming democratic polities. In this sense, ethnofederalism generated multiple political pathways after communism, with those pathways testifying to the costs—and a few benefits—of marrying nation, territory, and public administration.

After Communism and the State

By January 1, 1993, 22 new states had been formed in the postcommunist region. Four of these states had been ethnofederated republics during the communist era and, with independence, had become ethnofederal states: the Russian Federation, Georgia, Azerbaijan, and Serbia and Montenegro. A full 15 of these states were unitary republics, which became unitary states. Finally, three unitary republics that became states—Bosnia and Herzegovina, Moldova, and Ukraine—added ethnofederal features in reaction to conflicts between minority communities and the majority. The question, then, is how these differences in state design relate to the course of democratic politics, interethnic relations, and the state's viability.

To answer these questions and to provide a controlled setting for systematic comparison, I have limited the assessment to those countries that meet three criteria. The first is that their political arrangements and political dynamics be a function of domestic actors and their interactions, not a function of international interventions. The case of Bosnia and Herzegovina is an instance of power-sharing imposed after a war rather than power-sharing reflecting historical institutional legacies and domestic political dynamics. Thus, I will ignore Bosnia and Herzegovina in this analysis because of the distinctive origins of that country's political institutions. Second, I will focus only on new states, and, within that set, the new states with reasonably large minority populations (15 percent of the total population) that are geographically concentrated. Finally, because of our interest in democratic politics, I will focus only on those countries that, since the transition from socialism, have averaged a score of at least "partly free"by Freedom House. This leaves 13 cases: four ethnofederations (Azerbaijan, Georgia, Russia, and Serbia and Montenegro); seven unitary states (Croatia, Estonia, Kyrgyzstan, Latvia, Lithuania, Macedonia, and Slovakia); and two states that have elements of both types (Moldova and Ukraine) (see Bunce and Watts, 2002 for documentation). The question, therefore, is whether these cases illustrate patterns that are associated with differences in state design.

There are, indeed, several patterns that emerge in this comparison. First, the ethnofederal states are far more likely to feature a dynamic of exclusivist majority nationalism and minority mobilization that begins with modest goals (often in reaction to discriminatory citizenship laws and reductions in local autonomy) but ultimately pushes for secession, resulting in considerable tensions between the majority and minority regions Indeed, each of the ethnofederal states—Russia, Serbia and Montenegro, Georgia, and Azerbaijan—feature such a dynamic, which began when the larger state was dissolving into its component parts and continued into the era of independence (see, for example, Derluguian, 1998; Garb, 1998; Goltz, 2001; Gorenburg, 1999; Jones, 1997; King, 2001b; Lapidus, 1998; Lieven, 1998, 2001;

187

Pula, 2001; Stoner-Weiss, 1999). However, a small number of the unitary states have featured similar dynamics—in particular, Croatia, the former unitary state of Moldova, and, most recently, Macedonia. Nonetheless, what is striking is that every ethnofederal state features this pattern.

Even more striking is another pattern—violent conflicts that resist resolution and limit the state's capacity to control its borders, establish a single economic space, and extract popular compliance. Such conflicts are the clear exception in the unitary state context and, indeed, seem to end when such states grant autonomy, thereby taking on some ethnofederal features. This was the case, for example, in both Moldova and Ukraine, and such an approach may very well materialize in Macedonia as well. Thus, unitary states seem to have two advantages. They are unlikely to experience violent conflicts, but, if they do, they are strikingly successful in mediating them. By contrast, violent and continuing conflicts between the center and the regions is the norm in the ethnofederations. Here, I refer, for example, to the ongoing war in Chechnya within the Russian Federation; the continuing struggle in Kosovo, which has only been interrupted by international interventions; and the periodic breakout of conflict in Georgia, involving Abkhazia and, to a lesser degree, Southern Ossetia.

However, this does not mean that all of the regions within these new ethnofederal states are secessionist or that the center always responds with force to minority mobilization. In practice, three kinds of interactions occur in these contexts (Bunce, 2003a; 2003b). The first is minimal regional mobilization and full cooperation with the center (for example, until very recently, in Vojvodina in Serbia and Montenegro, and Dagestan in Russia). The second is regional mobilization demanding autonomy, which then produces a compromise between the center and the region establishing significant regional autonomy (as with Montenegro after 1997 within Serbia and Montenegro, Adjaria within Georgia, and Tatarstan within Russia). The final variation is the one already discussed at length—violent conflict that either continues, as in Chechnya, or that abates only when leaders at the center and in the secessioned region agree to keep the state week and extract rents (King, 2001). Dynamics within Georgia best typify this latter process.

These contrasts in nationalist mobilization, interethnic relations, and violent conflict between unitary and ethnofederal states have led, not surprisingly, to differences in democratic performance. These can be summarized in numerical form. Freedom House has a scale for political rights and civil liberties that runs from 1 (fully free) to 7 (fully dictatorial). The average Freedom House scores for the unitary states in our group from the beginning of the transition to 2001 is 2.9, whereas the average score for the ethnofederations is 5.2. The mixed systems of Moldova and Ukraine fall in the middle, averaging 3.7. These numbers, moreover, correspond to more finely tuned analyses of these cases. For example, a survey of minority rights would lead to a clear distinction between the ethnofederal states—excepting the Russian Federation, which is the only state in the region to define citizenship in fully civic terms in its constitution—and the unitary states. However, this does not mean either that the unitary states have enviable records in this regard, or that a unitary state design is a sufficient condition for the provision of minority rights. For example, just as the international community has pressed the Macedonian leadership to be more inclusive with respect to rights and representation of the Albanian minority, so pressures by the European Union have been critical in expanding minority access to citizenship and other rights in Latvia and Estonia. What this seems to suggest is that, while ethnofederalism is surely a problem, it does not follow that a unitary state approach is a solution.

Conclusions and Amendments

The experiences of the new ethnofederations resemble in many ways, therefore, the experiences of the larger ethnofederal states within which they were once embedded. Ethnofederalism emerges in either case as a highly problematic approach to the management of majority–minority relations. Ethnofederalism seems to undermine the state's territorial integrity. Ethnofederal states seem more prone to violence and continuing violence at that; and such a structure appears to complicate and sometimes derail the transition from dictatorship to democracy. What is striking about this story, moreover, is that the new ethnofederal states put to rest one problem with generalizing about the break-up of Yugoslavia, the Soviet Union, and Czechoslovakia—that is, the conflation of state design with national diversity. One can compare the diversity of the new unitary and ethnofederal states, and, for that matter, their levels of economic development, the state's age, the institutional design of their regimes, and even the forms of diversity represented by national communities (for example, differences in ethnicity, religion, and language). Once matched, one factor emerges as critical—whether the state was ethnofederal or unitary in form.

The postcommunist region, therefore, like the communist region before it, argues against the advisability of ethnofederalism in contexts that are multinational and that feature a transition from dictatorship to democracy. The arguments against ethnofederalism elaborated in this chapter's introduction have considerable empirical support.

Yet this leaves us with several issues to be resolved. One is the fact that regions within the ethnofederations behave in fact in diverse ways. Until we can explain these variations (or what could be termed the alternatives of cooperation, compromise, or conflict), we cannot be as precise as would be desirable about *how* the design of the state affects relations between majorities and minorities, centers and regions.

What is clear at this point is that a number of plausible factors do not explain this variation—for example, the size of the titular minority, the region's socioeconomic development, or differences in religion, ethnicity, and language. Second, we need to expand our comparative horizons before we can be more certain that ethnofederalism is a costly approach to managing interethnic relations. However, it is interesting to note that this chapter's insights—that ethnofederalism is a problem particularly when it is in place when authoritarian rule begins to falter and when transitions to democracy commence, but that ethnofederalism is less costly when unitary states use some of these principles to assuage angry minorities—are supported by two other cases—India and Spain. It is commonly argued that ethnofederalism contributed to the success of India's dual transition to democracy and independent statehood and the Spanish transition from dictatorship to democracy. However, what is important to realize is that, in both cases, the transitions began with unitary states in place, and that the leaders of these two new democracies later introduced ethnofederalism as a means of tying their heterogeneous societies to the democratic order.

Moreover, the Indian and Spanish cases remind us of why ethnofederalism at the point of departure for regime and state transition proves to be so costly. In both countries, the opposition forces were united, nationalism was relatively inclusive, and there was a consensus—at the elite and public level—in support of democratic governance. Moreover, leadership in both contexts was not contested. All of these characteristics were helpful for democracy's consolidation. However, it was precisely these characteristics that cannot materialize when an ethnofederal institutional legacy is in place at the point of departure for the transition to democracy and statehood. This is because ethnofederalism generates a divided opposition, competitive and exclusivist nationalisms, and spatially and nationally defined contestation involving the nation, the state, and democracy. Moreover, ethnofederalism generates competing political pathways within the state and elites with competing visions about the nation, the state, and democracy. It multiplies political struggles rather than uniting them. Thus, the key issue seems to be *when* ethnofederalism is introduced. In this sense, there are two faces to ethnofederation, and it is these two faces that can help account for the competing views in the literature about its costs and benefits.

References

Bajpai, Kanti (1997) "Diversity, Democracy and Devolution in India." In Michael E. Brown and Sumit Ganguly (eds.) *Government Policies and Ethnic Relations in Asia and the Pacific*. Cambridge: MIT Press, 33–81.

Barany, Zoltan (2001) *The Eastern European Gypsies: Regime Change, Marginality and Ethnopolitics*. Cambridge: Cambridge University Press.

Barbarosie, Arcadie (2001) "Understanding the Communist Electoral Victory in Moldova." *Transition: Newsletter about Reforming Economies*, Feb.–March: 9–10.

Bednar, Jenna, William N. Eskridge, Jr. and John Ferejohn (1999) "A Political Theory of Federalism." Unpublished manuscript. Stanford University.

Beissinger, Mark (2002) *Nationalist Mobilization and the Collapse of the Soviet State*. Cambridge: Cambridge University Press.

Bernhard, Michael (2001) "Democratization in Germany: A Reappraisal." *Comparative Politics* 33.

United States Institute of Peace (2000) "Bosnia's Next Five Years: Dayton and Beyond." (2000). United States Institute of Peace Special Report No. 62. Nov. 3: 1–12.

Brass, Paul R. (1991) "Ethnic Conflict in Multiethnic Societies: The Consociational Solution and its Critics." In Paul Brass (ed.) *Ethnicity and Nationalism: Theory and Comparison*. London: Sage, 333–48.

Brubaker, Rogers (1996) *Nationalism Reframed: Nationhood and the National Question in the New Europe*. Cambridge: Cambridge University Press.

Bunce, Valerie (2003a) "Conflict, Compromise and Cooperation: Explaining Center-Regional Bargaining in Multi-Ethnic Ethnofederations." Paper presented at the annual meeting of the International Studies Association, Portland, Oregon, Feb. 27.

—— (2003b) "Federalism, Nationalism and Secession." Chapter forthcoming in Ugo Amoretti, Nancy Bermeo and Larry Diamond (eds.) *Does Federalism Matter?* Baltimore: Johns Hopkins University Press.

—— (2003c). "Rethinking Recent Democratization: Lessons from the Post-communist Experience." *World Politics* 55(2).

—— (1999a) "The Political Economy of Postsocialism." *Slavic Review* 58 (Winter): 756–93.

—— (1999b) *Subversive Institutions: The Design and the Destruction of Socialism and the State*. Cambridge: Cambridge University Press.

Bunce, Valerie and Stephen Watts (2002) "Managing Diversity and Sustaining Democracy: Ethnofederal Versus Unitary States in the Postsocialist World." In Philip Roeder and Donald Rothchild (eds.) *Power-Sharing and Peace-Making*. Manuscript under review.

Cerovic, Stojan (2001) "Serbia, Montenegro: Reintegration, Divorce or Something Else?" U.S. Institute of Peace Special Report No. 68, April 2.

Cichock, Mark A. (1999) "Interdependence and Manipulation in the Russian-Baltic Relationship: 1993–97." *Journal of Baltic Studies* 30(2): 89–116.

Corbridge, Stuart (1995) "Federalism, Hindu Nationalism and Mythologies of Governance in Modern India." In Graham Smith (ed.) *Federalism: The Multiethnic Challenge.* London: Longman: 101–27.

Crowther, William (1997a) "Moldova: Caught between Nation and Empire." In Ian Bremer and Ray Taras (eds.) *New States, New Politics: Building the Post-Soviet Nations.* Cambridge: Cambridge University Press: 316–52.

—— (1997b) "The Politics of Democratization in Postcommunist Moldova." In Karen Dawisha and Bruce Parrott (eds.) *Democratic Changes and Authoritarian Reactions in Russia, Ukraine, Belarus and Moldova.* Vol. 3 of *Democratization and Authoritarianism in Postcommunist Societies.* Cambridge: Cambridge University Press.

Csergo, Zsuzsa (2000) "Language and Democracy: A Comparative Study of Contestations over Language Use in Romania and Slovakia." Unpublished doctoral dissertation. George Washington University.

D'Anieri, Paul (1997) "Nationalism and International Politics: Identity and Sovereignty in the Russian-Ukrainian Conflict." *Nationalism and Ethnic Politics* 3(2): 1–28.

Dent, Martin (1995). "Ethnicity and Territorial Politics in Nigeria." In Graham Smith (ed.) *Federalism: The Multiethnic Challenge.* London: Longman, 128–54.

Derluguian, Georgi M. (2001a) "The Forgotten Abkhazia." Program on New Approaches to Russian Security, Council on Foreign Relations, Working Paper Series No. 18. January.

—— (2001b) "How Adjaria Did Not Become Another Bosnia: Structure, Agency and Congency in Chaotic Transitions." Forthcoming in George Katsiaficas (ed.) *After the Fall: 1989 and the Future of Freedom.* New York: Routledge.

—— (1998) "The Tale of Two Resorts: Abkhazia and Ajaria Before and Since the Soviet Collapse." In Beverly Crawford and Ronnie D. Lipschutz (eds.) *The Myth of 'Ethnic Conflict': Politics, Economics and Cultural Violence.* Research Series No. 98. Berkeley: University of California International and Area Studies.

Fearon, James (1998) "Commitment Problems and the Spread of Ethnic Conflict." In David Lake and Donald Rothchild (eds.) *The International Spread of Ethnic Conflict.* Princeton: Princeton University Press, 107–26.

Friedman, Victor A. (1996) "Observing the Observers: Language, Ethnicity, and Power in the 1994 Macedonian Census and Beyond." Appendix in Barnett R. Rubin (ed.) *Toward Comprehensive Peace in Southeast Europe: Conflict Prevention in the South Balkans.* New York: The Twentieth Century Fund Press.

Gagnon, Alain G. and Guy Laforest (1994) "The Future of Federalism: Lessons from Canada and Quebec." In Stephen J. Randall and Roger Gibbins (eds.) *Federalism and the New World Order*. Calgary: University of Calgary Press, 113–31.

Gagnon, V.P., Jr. (2001) "Liberalism and 'Minorities': Serbs as Agents and Victims of Liberal Conceptions of Space." Paper presented at the workshop, "Citizenship in Multicultural States: Comparing Former Yugoslavia and Israel." Austrian Institute for International Affairs, Vienna, April 20–21.

Ganguly, Rajat (1997) "The Move Towards Disintegration: Explaining Ethnic Mobilization in South Asia." *Nationalism and Ethnic Politics* 3(2): 1–28.

Garb, Paul (1998) "Ethnicity, Alliance-Building, and the Limited Spread of Ethnic Conflict in the Caucasus." In David Lake and Donald Rothchild (eds.) *The International Spread of Ethnic Conflict*. Princeton: Princeton University Press, 185–200.

Goltz, Thomas (2001) "Georgia on the Brink." *Perspectives* 11(3): 1–8.

Gorenburg, Dmitry (1999) "Regional Separatism in Russia: Ethnic Mobilization or Power Grab?" *Europe-Asia Studies* 51(2): 245–74.

Guibernau, Montserrat (1995) "Spain: A Federation in the Making?" In Graham Smith (ed.) *Federalism: The Multiethnic Challenge*. London: Longman, 239–54.

Gurr, Ted Robert (2000) *Peoples Versus States: Minorities at Risk in the New Century*. Washington, D.C.: U.S. Institute of Peace.

Horowitz, Donald (1985) *Ethnic Groups in Conflict*. Berkeley: University of California Press.

Hurlburt, Heather F. (2000) "Preventive Diplomacy: Success in the Baltics." In Bruce W. Jentleson (ed.) *Opportunities Missed, Opportunities Seized: Preventive Diplomacy in the Post-Cold War World*. New York: Carnegie Commission on Preventing Deadly Conflict. Lanham: Rowman and Littlefield Publishers, Inc.

International Crisis Group (2001) "Macedonia: The Last Chance for Peace." ICG Balkans Report No. 113. Skopje/Brussels.

Jones, Stephen (1997) "Georgia: The Trauma of Statehood." In Ian Bremer and Ray Taras (eds.) *New States, New Politics: Building the Post-Soviet Nations*. Cambridge: Cambridge University Press, 505–46.

Kaplan, Cynthia (1998) "Ethnicity and Sovereignty: Insights from Russian Negotiations with Estonia and Tatarstan." In David Lake and Donald Rothchild (eds.) *The International Spread of Ethnic Conflict*. Princeton: Princeton University Press, 251–74.

Karklins, Rasma (2000) "Ethnopluralism: Panacea for East Central Europe." *Nationalities Papers* 28(2): 219–41.

Kaufman, Stuart (2001) *Modern Hatreds: The Symbolic Politics of Ethnic Wars*. Ithaca: Cornell University Press.

King, Charles (2001a) "The Benefits of Ethnic War: Understanding Eurasia's Unrecognized States." *World Politics* 53(4): 524–52.

—— (2001b) "Misreading or Misleading? Four Myths about Democratization in Post-Soviet Georgia." Unpublished manuscript, Georgetown University.

—— (2000) *The Moldovans: Romania, Russia and the Politics of Culture*. Stanford: Hoover Institution Press.

King, Preston (1982) *Federalism and Federation*. Baltimore: Johns Hopkins University Press.

Lapidus, Gail (1998) "Contested Sovereignty: The Tragedy of Chechnya." *International Security* 23(1): 5–49.

Lieven, Anatol (2001) "Georgia: A Failing State?" *Eurasia Insight*, Jan. 30. From Johnson's Russia List No. 5077, February 7.

Lieven, Anatol (1998) *Chechnya: Tombstone of Russian Power*. New Haven: Yale University Press.

Lijphart, Arend (1996) "The Puzzle of Indian Democracy: A Consociational Interpretation." *American Political Science Review* 90 (June): 258–68.

—— (1990) "The Power-Sharing Approach." In Joseph V. Montville (ed.) *Conflict and Peacemaking in Multiethnic Societies*. Lexington: D.C. Heath, 491–510.

—— (1977) *Democracy in Plural Societies: A Comparative Exploration*. New Haven: Yale University Press.

Luong, Pauline Jones (2002) *Institutional Change and Political Continuity in Post-Soviet Central Asia: Power, Perceptions and Pacts*. Cambridge: Cambridge University Press.

Lustick, Ian (1979) "Stability in Deeply Divided Society: Consociationalism Versus Control." *World Politics* 31(3): 225–44.

MacPherson, James C. (1994) "The Future of Federalism." In Stephen J. Randall and Roger Gibbins (eds.) *Federalism and the New World Order*. Calgary: University of Calgary Press, 1994, 9–16.

Martiniello, Marco (1998) "The Use of Images of Cultural Differences in Belgian Political Life." Paper presented at the Conference on Federalism, Nationalism and Secession at Cornell University, Ithaca, NY, May 1–2.

—— (1995) "The National Question and Political Construction of Ethnic Communities in Belgium." In Alec G. Hargreaves and Jeremy Leaman (eds.) *Racism, Ethnicity and Politics in Contemporary Europe*. London: Edward Elgar, 131–44.

Mastny, Vojtech (2000) "The Historical Experience of Federalism in East Central Europe." *East European Politics and Societies* 14(1): 64–96.

Melvin, Neil J. (2000) "Post-Imperial Ethnocracy and the Russophone Minorities of Estonia and Latvia." In Jonathan P. Stein (ed.) *The Politics of National Minority Participation in Post-Communist Europe*. East-West Institute. Armonk: M.E. Sharpe.

Murphy, Alexander (1995) "Belgium's Regional Divergence: Along the Road to Federation." In Graham Smith (ed.) *Federalism: The Multiethnic Challenge*. London: Longman, 73–100.

Park, Andrus (1994) "Ethnicity and Independence: The Case of Estonia in Comparative Perspective." *Europe-Asia Studies* 46(1): 69–87.

Posen, Barry R. (1993) "The Security Dilemma and Ethnic Conflict." *Survival* 35(1): 27–47.

Pula, Besnik (2001) "Contested Sovereignty and State Disintegration: The Rise of the Albanian Secessionist Movement in Kosova." Master's Thesis, Georgetown University, Department of Political Science, March 10.

Raun, Toivo U. (1997) "Democratization and Political Development in Estonia, 1987–96." In Karen Dawisha and Bruce Parrott (eds.) *The Consolidation of Democracy in East-Central Europe*. Cambridge: Cambridge University Press.

Raun, Toivo (1996) "Estonia: Independence Redefined." In Ian Bremmer and Ray Taras (eds.) *New States, New Politics: Building the Post-Soviet Nations*. Cambridge: Cambridge University Press.

Roeder, Philip (2001a) "The Rejection of Authoritarianism." In Richard Anderson, Jr., M. Steven Fish, Stephen E. Hanson and Philip G. Roeder (eds.) *Postcommunism and the Theory of Democracy*. Princeton: Princeton University Press, 11–53.

—— (2001b) "The Triumph of Nation-States: Lessons from the Collapse of the Soviet Union." Unpublished manuscript, University of California, San Diego.

—— (2000) "The Robustness of Institutions in Ethnically Plural Societies." Paper presented at the Annual Meeting of the American Political Science Association, Washington, D.C., August 31–September 2.

Sisk, Timothy D. (1996) *Power Sharing and International Mediation in Ethnic Conflicts*. Washington, DC: United States Institute of Peace.

Skvortsova, Alla (1998) "The Russians in Moldova: Political Orientations." In Ray Taras (ed.) *National Identities and Ethnic Minorities in Eastern Europe*. London: Macmillan Press, 159–78.

Simeon, Richard and Daniel-Patrick Conway (2001) "Federalism and the Management of Conflict in Multinational Societies." In Alain Gagnon and James Tully (eds.) *Multinational Democracy*. Cambridge: Cambridge University Press.

Slezkine, Yuri (1994) "The USSR as a Communal Apartment, or How a Socialist State Promoted Ethnic Particularism." *Slavic Review* 53 (Summer): 414–52.

Smith, Graham, Vivien Law, Andrew Wilson, Annette Bohr and Edward Allworth (1998) *Nation-building in the Post-Soviet Borderlands: The Politics of National Identities*. Cambridge: Cambridge University Press.

Smith, Graham (1998) "Russia, Multiculturalism and Federal Justice." *Europe-Asia Studies* 50(8): 1393–411.

Smith, Graham and Andrew Wilson (1997) "Rethinking Russia's Post-Soviet Diaspora: The Potential for Political Mobilisation in Eastern Ukraine and North-east Estonia." *Europe-Asia Studies* 49(5): 845–64.

Smith, Graham (1995) "Mapping the Federal Condition: Ideology, Political Practice and Social Justice." In Graham Smith (ed.) *Federalism: The Multiethnic Challenge.* London: Longman, 1–28.

Snyder, Tim and Milada Vachudova (1997) "Are Transitions Transitory? Two Types of Political Change in Eastern Europe Since 1989." *East European Politics and Societies* 11(Winter): 1–35.

Solchanyk, Roman (1994) "The Politics of State-building: Centre-Periphery Relations in Post-Soviet Ukraine." *Europe-Asia Studies* 46(1): 47–68.

Solnick, Steven (1998) *Stealing the State: Control and Collapse in Soviet Institutions.* Cambridge: Harvard University Press.

—— (1996) "The Breakdown of Hierarchies in the Soviet Union and China: A Neoinstitutional Perspective." *World Politics* 48(2): 209–38.

Steen, Anton (2000) "Ethnic Relations, Elites, and Democracy in the Baltic States." *Journal of Communist Studies and Transition Politics* 16(4): 68–87.

Stepan, Alfred (2000) "Russian Federalism in Comparative Perspective." *Post-Soviet Affairs* 16(2): 133–70.

—— (1999) "Federalism and Democracy: Beyond the U.S. Model." *Journal of Democracy* 10(4): 19–34.

Stoner-Weiss, Kathryn (1999) "Central Weakness and Provincial Autonomy: Observations on the Devolution Process in Russia." *Post-Soviet Affairs* 15(1).

Suny, Ronald Grigor (1994) *The Making of the Georgian Nation*, ed. II. Bloomington: Indiana University Press.

Suberu, Rotimi T. (2001) *Federalism and Ethnic Conflict in Nigeria.* Washington, D.C.: The U.S. Institute of Peace.

Treisman, Daniel (1997) "Russia's 'Ethnic Revival': The Separatist Activism of Regional Leaders in a Postcommunist Order." *World Politics* 49(2): 212–49.

United States Institute of Peace (2001) "The Future of Macedonia: A Balkan Survivor Now Needs Reform." United States Institute of Peace Special Report No. 67.

Varshney, Ashutosh (2001) "Ethnic Conflict and Civil Society: India and Beyond." *World Politics* 53(3): 362–98.

Verney, Douglas V. (1995) "Federalism, Federative Systems and Federations: The U.S., Canada and India." *Publius* 25(2): 81–98.

Vujacic, Veljko (1996) "Historical Legacies, Nationalist Mobilization and Political Outcomes in Russia and Serbia: A Weberian View." *Theory and Society* 25(6): 763–801.

Walker, Edward (2001) "Dagestan and the Stability of Instability in the North Caucasus." In Victoria E. Bonnell and George W. Breslauer (eds.) *Russia in the New Century: Stability or Disorder*. Boulder: Westview, 326–57.

Ware, Bruce Robert and Enver Kisriev (2001) "Russian Recentralization has Arrived in the Republic of Dagestan: Implications for Institutional Integrity and Political Stability." *East European Constitutional Review* 10(1): 68–75.

Weingast, Barry (1998) "Constructing Trust: The Political and Economic Roots of Ethnic and Regional Conflict." In Karol Soltan, Eric M. Uslaner and Virginia Haufler (eds.) *Institutions and Social Order*. Ann Arbor: University of Michigan Press, 163–200.

Williams, Colin H. (1995) "A Requiem for Canada?" In Graham Smith (ed.) *Federalism: The Multiethnic Challenge*. London: Longman, 31–72.

National Self-Determination and Postcommunist Popular Sovereignty

Philip G. Roeder

As communism was collapsing, both the discipline of political science and American foreign policy were becoming captivated by two concepts—the third wave of democratization and the democratic peace. The third wave of democratization is the worldwide movement to democracy that occurred in more than thirty countries during the decade and a half that began with the Portuguese coup of 1974 (Huntington, 1991: 3–4). The democratic peace is the special peace that develops among liberal states "because they exercise democratic caution and are capable of appreciating the international rights of foreign republics" (Doyle, 1986: 1161). Developments in the postcommunist states since 1989 appear to be in accord with both of these concepts: the replacement of totalitarianism by democracy and the incorporation of these democracies in the Western alliance conform to both expectations.

Yet, developments in the postcommunist states also highlight the importance of a missing third element in the liberal equation. Without the right of national self-determination, neither democracy nor democratic peace is likely to flourish in this part of the world. That is, the successful introduction of democracy inevitably poses the national question.[1] Popular sovereignty and implementation of the democratic ideal of self-government demand prior agreement on the boundary issues—in both the tangible and figurative senses of boundaries—that define who belongs to the political community, who gets a vote in its decision-making processes, and who does not. Paraphrasing Sir Ivor Jennings's (1958: 56) now famous quote, the people cannot govern until they agree on who are the people—and who are not.

The tripartite formula that links national self-determination, popular sovereignty, and peace was central to the original Kantian-Wilsonian idealism from which the modern variants descend. Inis Claude (1962: 48) clearly summarized the original equation: "The realization of the ideals of democracy and self-determination was regarded as the essential means for minimizing the element of conflict in international

---

1. Parts of this manuscript originally appeared in "Peoples and States after 1989: The Political Costs of Incomplete National Revolutions." *Slavic Review* 58 (Winter 1999): 854–82. All data has been updated in this version.

relations. Given the proper division of the world into political units based upon considerations of nationality, those units would tend to develop along democratic lines" (also see Cobban, 1951: 20).[2] Nowhere is the importance of this tripartite formula more obvious than in southeastern Europe. Throughout the twentieth century and particularly during its last decade, disagreements over who belongs together within a common state and who should have states of their own—the core of the national question—have spawned wars and throttled democracy.

Although the Kantian-Wilsonian claim is often treated as normative in inspiration, it is also rooted in a substantial body of empirical evidence. For example, scores of scholars have tested and attempted to disprove the democratic-peace hypothesis, but they have yet to find evidence of war between modern democracies (Russett, 1993; Ray, 1997). In this chapter, I discuss only two elements of the tripartite formula—national self-determination and democracy—and only the empirical evidence, not the normative debates. I will argue the following two points. First, the evidence from postcommunist states tells us that democracy is less likely to survive in societies divided by competing national projects. Second, this evidence also reveals that many of the institutions recommended by political scientists for such deeply divided societies actually aggravate the problems of political stability, thus undermining democracy.

These lessons speak to the social sciences. Among the earliest questions asked by the field of comparative politics within the discipline of political science are two that seem very contemporary. Can democracy survive in plural societies? Can we design democratic institutions so that they are better able to contain the conflicts often brought on by this diversity? For example, in his *Considerations on Representative Government*, frequently cited as the seminal work in the institutionalist debates over electoral rules, John Stuart Mill asked whether representative government could survive in a society deeply divided by ethnic and regional loyalties. He concluded that even the proportional representation that he saw as a solution to so many other problems of representative government could not make democracy work under these conditions (Mill, 1962: 82–91). The decades of rich, but cacophonous, debate that followed on these seminal insights have left behind competing prescriptions for new states faced with fragmented societies. The experience of the postcommunist states offers strong evidence to suggest that there is a measure of truth in John Stuart Mill's original democratic-impossibility hypothesis.

2. See, for example, Woodrow Wilson's last public speech, delivered in Pueblo, Colorado on September 25, 1919, prior to his stroke; reprinted in Cronon (1965: 514–31).

National Revolutions and Democratization

The postcommunist experience reminds us that successful democratic transitions are improbable when national revolutions are incomplete (cf. Vachudova and Snyder, 1997). Three decades ago, this had figured prominently in theories that sought to explain democracy's failure in so many new states of Africa and Asia. It is perhaps natural that during the latter part of the Third Wave, the experience of Latin America and southern Europe should partially blind us to this higher-order constraint on the processes of reform; most of our models of redemocratization are now drawn from old states based on relatively well defined nations (Linz and Stepan, 1996: 16–17). Yet, earlier theories, reflecting on the first and second waves of democratization (1826–1926 and 1943–63, respectively), often treated national integration as a necessary prior condition. For example, Dankwart Rustow (1967: 120–32) observes that the first states that successfully democratized had to resolve three problems—unify the people, establish stable political authority, and expand political participation to the population at large. He concludes that the "political ingredients of the modern nation-state are more effectively assembled one by one than all at once, and that political participation and equality should be the last, crowning achievement in the total process." The best sequence is unity-authority-equality as in Japan. The alternative sequence of authority-unity-equality, as in Turkey, is a close second. In either case, however, national integration (unity) must precede democratization (equality) (also see Verba, 1971: 311).

Much early social science argued not only that democracy cannot survive in plural societies, but that political stability in such societies requires some form of undemocratic political domination over society. According to J. S. Furnivall (1944: 446–69), plural societies are inherently unstable and require some external force—a colonial power in the case he knew best—in order to hold them together. Michael Smith (1965: 86) subsequently modified this to argue that domination by one ethnic group over others could maintain stability in plural societies; indeed, the "monopoly of power by one cultural section is the essential precondition for the maintenance of the total society in its current form." John Stuart Mill (1962: 82–91) advocates for such societies a "constitutionally unlimited, or at least a practically preponderant, authority in the chief ruler."

At least five factors—none is determining, but all affect the likelihood of democratic outcomes—explain why national unity is essential to a successful transition to democracy and to democracy's survival. Two of these concern the willingness of authoritarian rulers to open the political process. First, and most directly, the claim that some peoples are not legitimately part of the nation becomes a primary premise for excluding them from citizenship rights and, in particular, for restricting the franchise

(Roeder, 2001). Second, authoritarian rulers are more likely to consider the costs of tolerating an opposition prohibitively high where they suspect that division *within the titular nationality* will create an opening for other nationalities to take power (Dahl, 1971: 14–16). For example—to use a stylized scenario—in a divided society where the dominant nationality constitutes less than two-thirds of the population and an alternative nationality constitutes the remaining third, competition within the majority nationality that led to an even split between this nationality's competing parties would permit a unified minority to become the senior partner in the government. Fearing such an outcome, authoritarian leaders are more likely to resist democracy that could open up competition within the titular nationality.

Third, during negotiations to initiate a transition to democracy or during the initial stages of an actual transition, democratic experiments in states divided among nationalities are less likely to survive. National disunity increases the chances for democratic deadlock, crisis, and failure—particularly in these early stages. The original logic behind the democratic-impossibility hypothesis argues that democracy, as a set of rules for conducting conflict and aggregating conflicting preferences in decisions binding on all, is ill equipped to manage these types of most intense conflicts. Because nationality often involves the most fundamental preferences that grow from individuals' conception of self, conflicts among nationalities are likely to engender conflicts that democracy cannot moderate and resolve (Dahl, 1971: 105–21). Alvin Rabushka and Kenneth Shepsle (1971: 217) extend this logic and conclude with the rhetorical flourish: "We ask, is the resolution of intense but conflicting preferences in the plural society manageable in a democratic framework? We think not."

The fourth and fifth reasons concern the indirect effect of national disunity on democracy through its direct effect on political instability and economic prosperity—major direct constraints on democratic success. National disunity increases the likelihood of political instability that can prevent the emergence of democracy or bring down a new democracy (Roeder, 2003). Less obviously, national disunity undermines the foundations of economic prosperity, which has been shown to be a primary constraint—and possibly *the* primary constraint—on the survival of democracy (Przeworski, 1996). Political economists have argued that more homogeneous nation-states promise greater economic efficiency because they can more easily identify policies to be applied uniformly throughout society. Unified nation-states have less need for either costly schemes to compensate different national communities or wasteful administrative duplication of bureaucracies for distinct cultural communities (Tilly, 1975: 79; Alesina and Spolaore, 1997). Unified nation-states are more likely to nurture the trust and solidarity that early sociologists like Émile Durkheim and J.S. Furnivall (1944) (Miller, 1994) claimed is necessary for the contracting and exchange of the modern market and that contemporary political economists (Alesina, Baqir, and Easterly, 1999; Alesina, Spolaore, and Wacziarg, 1997; Friedman, 1977; Wittman, 1991) claim leads to greater willingness to invest in public goods like education, roads, and other infrastructure essential to economic growth. In short, heterogeneity and, in particular, national disunity undermine the most important foundations for democratic success.

Transitology has recently discovered the inconvenient fact of the nation-state, yet transitologists have chosen to construe this as a problem of state-ness rather than the problem of nation-ness. Following closely the argument made by Robert Dahl (1971: 105–23) two decades earlier, Juan Linz and Alfred Stepan (1996: 33–37) see the answer to this inconvenient fact in state-building measures. Yet, the evidence from the postcommunist transitions suggests that until the nation-ness problem is addressed, state building cannot contain the damaging pressures of a multinational society. Moreover, as a later part of this article will argue, attempting to address the nation-ness problem with the state-building measures recommended by the transitologists aggravates, rather than ameliorates, political instability.

New States and Incomplete National Revolutions

For the fate of democracy and the democratic peace in the postcommunist world, the single most important confounding constraint has been the incompleteness of the national transformation. The revolutions of 1989 created new states that correspond more closely to the ethnographic map of the region but also left behind many multinational states populated by minorities who seek statehood for themselves. This does not mean that *ethnic* diversity is democracy's enemy. The claims of ethnicity tend to be backward-looking and reflect an attempt by individuals and groups to explain their origins (Schermerhorn, 1970: 12–14). It is *national* diversity that is the enemy of democracy. The claims of nationalism tend to be forward-looking, asserting that a specific people should have a state of their own for the future (Weber, 1958: 171–79). Of course, ethnic groups and nations can become hopelessly intertwined as intellectuals and politicians ethnify nations, embellishing their histories with myths of common origins, and nationalize ethnic groups, claiming that their common past demands a common future in statehood.

The national revolutions created many entirely new states that are ill-equipped to cope with the problems of the remaining national diversity. Only six countries— Poland, Hungary, Albania, Romania, Bulgaria, and Mongolia—can be considered old states; meaning they have been nation-states continuously since World War I (although some were occupied and divided during World War II).[3] An additional six—the Czech Republic, Estonia, Latvia, Lithuania, Russia, and Yugoslavia (now known as Serbia and Montenegro)—might be classified as renewed states. Three of these were independent for more than a decade after World War I, and the other three were the leading core of a multinational state that soon shed many of its minority homelands. The remaining 16 regimes are entirely new states in this century.

The revolutions of 1989 changed the way states construe themselves. It swept away workers' states built on transnational appeals of proletarian and socialist internationalism and left behind nation-states that proclaim themselves the expression of the titular nationality's sovereign rights to self-determination and statehood. This can be seen in the justifications given in their founding documents. For example, Slovenia's constitution, adopted in 1991, proclaims that the Republic of Slovenia is predicated on the "basic and permanent right of the Slovene nation to self-determination." The preamble describes the nation's history in light of this claim—"after many centuries of struggle for national liberation the Slovenes have formed their own national identity and established their own statehood." Similarly, most Soviet successor states have jettisoned the mythology that an ethnically indifferent working class founded the state, and in their declarations of sovereignty, declarations of independence, and constitutions, most proclaim their state to be the realization of their respective nation's will to statehood. For example, following the logic expressed in the republic's declaration of sovereignty in 1988, the authors of Estonia's constitution, adopted in 1992, proclaim in its preamble that the document is the act of the Estonian people—the state "is established on the inextinguishable right of the Estonian people to national self-determination ... [and] shall guarantee the preservation of the Estonian nation and its culture throughout the ages." Some temper these nationalist claims with a commitment to the rights of all nationalities living within the new nation-state, and some even claim that the state represents the sovereign prerogative of all its peoples. Yet, in even the most heterogeneous states, such as Kazakhstan, the core of the state is officially a nation (Kaiser and Chinn, 1995; Liebich, 1996). One of the few exceptions to this is the Russian Federation—Article 3 of the constitution, from 1993, defines the people (a nation in the strict sense used here) comprising multiple nationalities as the sole source of sovereignty (Tolz, 1998; Breslauer and Dale, 1997).

---

3. Even some of these are very newly constructed nations; see, for example, Draper (1997).

Table 1
The Largest Nationality as a Proportion of Total Population

State	Last communist census/estimate		Postcommunist census/estimate	Year(s)*
	Ratio of largest to second largest**	Percent of total	Percent of total	
Hungary	197.0	98.5	—	1990c/—
Poland	109.1	98.2	—	1985e/—
Albania	54.4	97.9	—	1989c/—
Armenia	36.3	93.3	—	1989c/—
Slovenia	31.4	87.8	—	1991c
Czech Republic	[25.5]	—	81.2	1991c
Russia	21.7	81.3	—	1989c/—
Azerbaijan	14.8	82.5	—	1989c/—
Mongolia	13.4	78.8	—	1989c/—
Romania	11.7	88.6	89.5	1985e/1992c
Bulgaria	[9.1]	[no data]	85.7	1992c
Georgia	8.7	69.6	—	1989c/—
Uzbekistan	8.6	71.0	—	1989c/—
Lithuania	8.5	79.6	81.4	1989c/1996e
Slovakia	[7.8]	—	85.6	1999e
Turkmenistan	7.6	72.0	73.3	1989c/1993e
Croatia	6.4	78.1	—	1991c/—
Belarus	5.9	77.5	81.2	1989c/1999c
Moldova	4.7	64.4	—	1989c/—
Serbia-Montenegro	3.8	62.6	—	1991c/—
USSR	3.3	50.8		1989c
Ukraine	3.3	72.4	—	1989c/—
Macedonia	3.1	64.6	66.6	1991c/1994c
Tajikistan	2.6	62.1	—	1989c/—
Kyrgyzstan	2.4	52.0	64.9	1989c/1999c
Czechoslovakia	2.2	63.5		1983e
Estonia	2.0	61.5	65.3	1989c/2000e
Yugoslavia	1.8	36.3		1985e
Latvia	1.5	52.0	57.7	1989c/2000c
Bosnia	1.4	43.7	—	1991c/—
Kazakhstan	1.0	39.5	53.4	1989c/1999c

*   c indicates census; e indicates estimate;

** Bracketed ratios are derived from postcommunist censuses but are adjusted for communist-period definitions of nationalities.

Source: The census data and official estimates are from the annual editions of *The Europa World Yearbook* (1990–2001); the unofficial communist-period estimates are from Iu. V. Bromlei (ed.) *Narody mira: istoriko-etnograficheskii spravochnik* (1988).

As a consequence of the division of states, upon the collapse of communism, the postcommunist countries were almost immediately more homogeneous than their predecessors had been. Most importantly, the division of the multinational federations—Czechoslovakia, the Soviet Union, and Yugoslavia—left behind 22 successor states. With the sole exception of Kazakhstan, at the moment of independence, each of these was more homogeneous than the earlier federation (see the second and third columns of figures in table 1). Due to assimilation, expulsion, and migration, the process of homogenization continued even after the break-ups so that a decade later, all but Bosnia now have a titular nationality that constitutes a majority of the population. (Compare the fourth column of numbers in table 1 with the second and third columns.)

Nevertheless, even after this momentous change, a majority of the postcommunist states remain more diverse than the stable democracies in the West. Among the 13 stable European democracies that were originally established during the first and second waves of democratization, the largest nationality constituted, on average, 89 percent of the country's respective population in 1960 and 85 percent in 1985.[4] The largest group constituted at least 90 percent of the population in nine of these countries in 1960 and in eight in 1985. In only two did the largest group form less than 80 percent of the population. By contrast, even today, in only five postcommunist states, does the major nationality apparently constitute over 90 percent of the population and, in less than half, does it constitute at least 80 percent. At the other extreme, in eight postcommunist states, the largest group constitutes less than two-thirds of the population.

The Toll of Diversity on Democratization

In the postcommunist world, stable democracy has triumphed only in countries that have solved their nation-ness problem. That is, democratization has been most successful in states that are both older and more homogeneous. No states that are both new and diverse are full democracies. Close examination shows that this pattern is due more to the continuing problems of nation-ness than to the newness of the states.

A common minimalist definition of democracy draws on Joseph Schumpeter's insight that democracy is a decision-making arrangement "in which individuals acquire power to decide by means of a competitive struggle for the people's vote." Robert Dahl has elaborated this definition by noting that democracy implies both

4.   Included are countries with populations that exceed one million. The data on ethnic proportions are from Bromlei (1988).

(1) that the political arena is liberalized so that opposition, public contestation, and organized political competition are allowed and (2) that entry into this political arena is open to all adults under the state's decision-making authority. In a century that has seen the "virtual disappearance of an outright denial of the legitimacy of popular participation in government," the major distinction among regimes has become their liberalization. For Dahl (1971: 1–9), Soviet-style systems represented the model of inclusive hegemonies—illiberal regimes in which the population was mobilized into the political arena.

Over a quarter of the postcommunist polities have consistently met the simplest standards of democracy by maintaining liberalized and inclusive polities since 1990 (or since independence). In figure 1, all 28 states are arrayed along these two dimensions. The measure of liberalization (public contestation) is the average of Freedom House's political-liberties scores from 1990 to 2002 (or since independence for the Czechoslovak, Soviet, and Yugoslav successor states). This ranges from 1 (most liberal) to 7 (most restrictive). The measure of inclusiveness (participation) is the average proportion of the adult population registered to vote in elections from 1990 (or since independence) through 2002. This ranges from the most inclusive polities, on the one hand, which grant citizenship and voting rights to virtually 100 percent of all adults, to the more restrictive polities, on the other, which exclude over 20 percent of adults from the right of citizenship. Of 28 postcommunist states, eight (29 percent) have maintained competitive political processes granting full citizenship rights to almost all adults. Another nine postcommunist states fall short in either liberalization or inclusion; these might be called illiberal democracies and exclusive republics, respectively. Eleven regimes fall far short of the standard of liberalization necessary to be considered democracies.

Where the national revolution had succeeded and a nation-state had been established prior to communist rule, the revolutions of 1989 were more likely to culminate in democracy. Indeed, as table 2 shows, two-thirds of the old states have been fully democratic since the fall of communism and all are at least illiberal democracies. Alternatively, where a national revolution had not succeeded prior to communist rule and the 1989 revolution assaulted the country with national, political, and economic transformations simultaneously, democracy was seldom the result. Indeed, politics have been inclusive and liberal throughout this decade in only one-eighth of the new states; over three-fifths of the new states are nondemocracies. The pattern among the renewed states falls between these two extremes.

Figure 1
Political Liberalization and Political Inclusion, 1990 to 2002

1.0 **Most Liberal** (1.0-1.9)	Estonia Latvia **Exclusive Republics**	**Democracies**	Czech Republic Hungary Lithuania Poland Slovakia Slovenia
(2.0-2.9)		Mongolia	Bulgaria
(3.0-3.9)		Moldova **Illiberal Democracies**	Albania Croatia Macedonia Romania Russia Ukraine
(4.0-4.9)	**Nondemocracies**	Armenia Georgia Kyrgyzstan	
(5.0-5.9)	Kazakhstan	Bosnia	Azerbaijan Belarus
Most Restrictive (6.0-7.0) 7.0		Tajikistan	Serbia and Montenegro Turkmenistan Uzbekistan

More Exclusionary Under 80.0%	80.0–89.9%	Most Inclusive 90.0–100.0%

Source: The data are from the Freedom House (available online at www.freedomhouse.org/ratings/index.htm) and International Institute for Democracy and Electoral Assistance (available online at www.idea.int/vt/index.cfm).

Table 2
Newer States, Older States, and Democracy [%]

	Democracies	Illiberal democracies	Other regimes
New States (n=16)	12.5	25.0	62.5
Renewed States (n=6)	33.3	16.7	50.0
Old States (n=6)	67.0	33.3	0.0

Far more important for the success of democratic transitions has been the incompleteness of many national revolutions. The probability of stable democracy falls off with greater national diversity. As table 3 shows, among the most diverse countries (that is, those that began the transition with a titular nationality that constituted less than two-thirds of the country's population), none maintained inclusive, competitive polities throughout the decade. Even among the moderately diverse postcommunist states, fully 75 percent failed to maintain liberal, inclusive democracy. Conversely, among the more homogeneous states, over half have been fully democratic. In short, the probability of successful democratic transitions corresponds closely to the homogeneity of these societies.

Table 3
National Diversity and Democracy [%]

	Democracies	Illiberal democracies	Other regimes
Greatest Diversity (Largest <.67) (n=9)	0.0	22.2	77.8
Moderate Diversity (.67<Largest<.80) (n=8)	25.0	25.0	50.0
Homogeneity (Largest>.80) (n=11)	54.5	27.3	18.2

Even more important to the stability of polities and the willingness of authoritarian leaders from dominant nationalities to extend the franchise to minorities and to tolerate political competition within their own nationalities' ranks is the *relative* size of the majority and large minorities. In the postcommunist transitions, the closer in size the next (second) largest nationality to the largest nationality, the greater was the threat to stability and to democracy. The first column of figures in table 1 shows this ratio; thus, for example, according to communist-era estimates, ethnic Hungarians outnumbered the next largest nationality within Hungary by almost 200 times. At the other extreme, in 13 unlucky states, this ratio of largest to second largest nationality was below five to one. Among these latter, nine faced significant secessionist threats; in four states these threats succeeded (Czechoslovakia, Moldova, the Soviet Union, and Socialist Yugoslavia), and in six, secessionist attempts led to civil wars (Bosnia and Herzegovina, Macedonia, Moldova, Serbia and Montenegro, Tajikistan, and Socialist Yugoslavia). Only five of these unlucky 13 (Estonia, Kazakhstan, Kyrgyzstan, Latvia, and Ukraine) escaped secession and civil war. Yet, none established a fully inclusive liberal democracy.

Bringing together these two dimensions of nation-states underscores the importance of the continuing nation-ness problem. Table 4 shows the frequencies of successful democratization and of partial democratization (illiberal democracies) under the joint effects of a state's newness and the national diversity of its population. There is a stark difference between the frequencies among the 15 states that are newer *and* more diverse (the three cells in the upper-left corner), on the one hand, and the frequencies among the nine states that are older *and* more homogeneous (the three cells in the lower-right corner), on the other. None of the newer, more diverse states maintained fully democratic regimes and only one-fifth even maintained illiberal democratic regimes. By contrast, over three-fifths of the older, more homogeneous states maintained full democracy, and all have been either illiberal democracies (inclusive politics with some restrictions on contestation) or full democracies. Yet, the relative importance of these two dimensions of the nation-state is revealed by the off-diagonal cases—diverse old states and homogeneous new states. (As one might expect, there are no instances of the former.) Comparing the variation across columns in table 4 with the variation across rows reveals that a consolidated nation as the core of the state is a more important precondition than the state's age—as well as being a parsimonious predictor—of successful democratization in the first decade of post-communist politics.

The pattern of restrictions on political participation and contestation reveal the importance of the incomplete national revolutions and continuing national diversity in the failure of democratization. For example, in Kazakhstan, continuing fears over the loyalty of Russians has led Nursultan Nazarbaev's government to restrict contestation. As Ian Bremmer and Cory Welt (1995: 140) note, the government has sought "to manipulate elections and abrogate the rights to speak, publish, and associate freely when it thought that to do so served the goal of creating a stable multinational state in which the Kazakh nation is first among equals." In Estonia and Latvia, electoral exclusion took place through restrictive definitions of citizenship, which was granted only to those who were residents or descendants of residents in the republics prior to their incorporation in the Soviet Union in 1940 (Barrington, 1995; Park,

1994; Kolsto and Tsilevich, 1997; Roeder, 2001). These laws had the predictable effect of reshaping the electorate's ethnic composition. In Estonia, the new law initially disfranchised about 45 percent of the electorate, which declined from 1.14 million to about 625,000. In Latvia, the disfranchised accounted for about one-third of the adult population. During the first parliamentary elections held shortly after the new citizenship laws were in place, more than 90 percent of those permitted to vote in Estonia were ethnic Estonians, and more than 90 percent of the disfranchised were non-Estonians. In Latvia's first postindependence election, although ethnic Latvians constituted barely half of the population, they represented about 70 percent of the eligible voters. The incompleteness of the national revolutions and the attempt to remedy this have been the enemies of democracy in postcommunist states.

Table 4
Probability of Democracy.
Effect of New and National Consolidation[*]

	Most diverse	Moderately diverse	Homogeneous
New States	0.0% 33.3% (n=6)	0.0% 33.3% (n=6)	50.0% 50.0% (n=4)
Renewed States	0.0% 0.0% (n=3)	100.0% 100.0% (n=1)	50.0% 100.0% (n=2)
Old States	— — (n=0)	100.0% 100.0% (n=1)	60.0% 100.0% (n=5)

[*] Top figure in each cell is proportion of states that are fully inclusive democracies; second figure in each cell is proportion that are either fully inclusive or illiberal democracies.

Institutions for Managing National Conflicts

The nation-ness problem and the democratic-impossibility hypothesis have inspired various attempts to identify democratic institutions that might be more stable in the face of national diversity. Indeed, it is fairly common in comparative studies of democratization to overlook the inconvenient fact of the nation-ness problem and to proceed with discussions of the institutional options for state builders. These options have become policy prescriptions. Indeed, advocates of these various options have descended on the postcommunist world with the intention of schooling new democracies in the ways to manage national conflict. Foreign governments have imposed these arrangements on some postcommunist states in southeastern Europe—despite the objections of many of their leaders. Yet, the postcommunist states should also be the teachers, for their experience speaks loudly to the issues of the viability of these institutions in deeply divided societies.

The Case for Power Sharing

For countries confronting incomplete national revolutions and continuing national diversity, political scientists typically argue that some form of power sharing is necessary for the survival of democracy in these societies. Advocates of power sharing argue that in plural societies, stability and democracy can be achieved together only through practices and institutions that compromise majority rule and mandate broad-based coalitions that include all major national groups in the governance of the state. The case for power sharing in societies divided by nationality was originally made by Eric Nordlinger (1972), Arend Lijphart (1977), and Donald Horowitz (1985). They argue that designers of state institutions seeking stability in these plural societies must either accommodate national diversity by power-sharing arrangements or establish the domination of one nationality over another (Lustick, 1979). For example, according to Lijphart, if the designers of democracies in plural societies reject consociationalism, majoritarian democracy threatens to bring about a tyranny of the majority (Lijphart, 1984: 23).

Although there are important debates among individual authors about specific institutions, these power-sharing proposals have two *constitutional* features in common—inclusive decision making and partitioned decision making.[5] First, in realms where decisions are binding on all members of society, power-sharing institutions guarantee participation of representatives of all major nationalities in the central government. Voting rules are frequently consensual, either requiring concurrent support in the separate nationalities or granting representatives of nationalities a veto over decisions of the central government. The advocates of power sharing divide on the precise combination of central governmental institutions, such as a collective presidency or grand coalition, and electoral rules, such as proportional representation or the alternative vote. Lijphart (1995: 856) argues for collective executives such as the coalition governments found in parliamentarism with a proportional representa-

---

5.   In addition to the constitutional prescriptions, which describe distributions of decision-making powers, these authors often prescribe various policies such a proportional allocation of expenditures. In this chapter I address only the constitutional issues.

tion electoral system, which he opposes to the majoritarian domination found in presidential systems and in elections using single-member districts. Horowitz (1985: 628–51) has argued for proportional representation, but he increasingly favors an electoral system that permits voters to register their first, second, and lower preferences among candidates and requires a victor to command an absolute majority consisting of first and lower-ranked votes (also see the debate between Barkan, 1998 and Reynolds, 1998).

Second, in some policy realms, the issues that divide nationalities are especially important to their members, but policy need not be standardized for the country as a whole. In these realms, power sharing prescribes partitioned decision making so that state agencies representing nationalities, such as local homeland administrations in an ethnofederation, make policy (Lijphart, 1995: 856; Horowitz, 1985: 613–22). Rather than bringing representatives of the nationalities into the central government, this power-sharing arrangement divides the state's decision-making powers in these policy realms and allocates these powers among independent decision-making agencies in which specific national groups have greater voice.

The themes of power sharing have been adopted as an agenda for action by a number of governmental, international, and nongovernmental organizations advising new states on institutional design. For example, scholars associated with the United States Institute of Peace, the Institute for Democracy and Electoral Assistance, and the East Europe Constitutional Design Forum have issued studies that explain alternative power-sharing arrangements to solve national conflicts (Sisk, 1996; Lapidoth, 1996; Harris and Reilly, 1998; Reilly and Reynolds, 1999; Chapman, 1999; also see Varady, 1997). For international and governmental policy practitioners, these power-sharing institutions have become the preferred response to reconstructing civil authority after a civil war in ethnically divided societies. At this moment, the international community maintains three power-sharing settlements in southeastern Europe. Seeking immediate payoffs in the form of an end to civil war, the international community seized on power sharing as a foundation for Bosnia's Dayton Accords of November 21, 1995, Kosovo's Constitutional Framework inaugurated on May 15, 2001, and Macedonia's Ohrid Agreement signed on August 13, 2001.

The experience of countries that have made the transition from communism suggests that these states should not simply be a tabula rasa on which to inscribe lessons drawn from elsewhere. Instead we can learn from the experience of postcommunism and improve those theories. In particular, we might ask, have any institutional arrangements in the states making transitions from communism managed national conflicts better? Have any prevented the normal conflict found in politics from escalating to the level of constitutional crises?

The experience of the postcommunist states suggests that the influence of institutions can be profound, but where the nation-ness problem is severe, the most important institutional choice is still the state's boundary, while other constitutional choices are far less important. First, under unfavorable demographic conditions—particularly where the population is deeply divided—other institutions had little effect on the stability of democracy. By deeply divided demography, I mean the objective conditions of nearly equal numbers of core (titular or majority) group and largest minority and great cultural distance between these two groups. This increased the likelihood of deeply divided politics in which each group constituted a nation—that is, a group that believed it should have a state of its own. In these circumstances, the only hope for democracy appears to have been national self-determination and re-drawing of the state boundaries. Second, in less deeply divided societies—where the largest minority constituted a smaller part of the population and was culturally similar to the core population—other institutions had some significant effect. Yet, under these more favorable demographic conditions, the power-sharing institutions usually recommended by political scientists to manage the problems of national diversity in democratizing states actually made matters worse.

After 1989, the break-up of the multinational federations, the consolidation of nation-states, and the incompleteness of many national revolutions fostered national conflicts (Brubaker, 1996). In particular, these fostered a series of what I have called ethnoconstitutional crises—conflicts between central governmental leaders and politicians making claims on behalf of one or the other nationality over the constitutive rules concerning the allocation of decision-making powers.[6] On the eve of the 1989 revolutions, the territory of the nine countries contained 69 major nationalities—that is, each nationality constituted 1 percent or more of the population of at least one of the nine states (or comprised at least 100,000 members in one of the largest states). Over the next six years, more than three-quarters of these nationalities (a total of 54) were engaged in ethnoconstitutional crises with at least one of the governments in this region over issues of civil rights, greater participation in the decision-making process of the central government, communal autonomy, or independence. Fully 98 percent of these crises entailed claims to some form of statehood—either territorial autonomy within an existing state or complete independence. A fifth of all these nationalities engaged in violence against at least one of the governments. By the

---

6. The concept of ethnoconstitutional crisis is both narrower and broader than the various definitions of nationalist conflict. Its virtue is its precision. Moreover, it forces us to focus on the core issue of nationalism.

end of the decade, this violence had developed into severe armed conflict for seven nationalities—the Abkhazians in Georgia, the Albanians in Serbia, the Armenians in Azerbaijan, the Bosniacs in Bosnia, the Chechens in Russia, the Croats in Bosnia, and the Serbs in both Bosnia and Croatia.

The transitions from communism cast considerable doubt on the claim that democratic institutions can be crafted to contain major national conflicts. Moreover, evidence from these transitions suggests that power-sharing institutions increased the likelihood that minor ethnic conflicts would become severe national conflicts. The combination of inclusive and partitioned decision making was particularly destabilizing. Under their Soviet-style constitutions, these states maintained unity in the face of national diversity by an extreme form of control. Yet, a number of these regimes adopted institutions that power-sharing advocates identified as "consociational" (Goldman, 1985; Van den Berghe, 1981). These provided for autonomous homeland administrations and cooptation of some of these leaders into central government organs. Yet, the three states that attempted to make the transition from communism with these power-sharing institutions in place—Czechoslovakia, the Soviet Union, and Yugoslavia—are the only three states that failed and split apart. Moreover, among the 22 successor states spawned by the break-up of these three countries, six inherited some form of power-sharing institutions—Azerbaijan, Georgia, Russia, Tajikistan, Uzbekistan, and Serbia and Montenegro. Four of these six—all but Tajikistan and Uzbekistan—have been plagued by civil wars between the new central governments and secessionist republics.[7]

This empirical pattern could be dismissed as containing no lesson at all because it might be simply a coincidence or because the problems of transition from communism were unique. Yet, the postcommunist experience points to problems within these institutions themselves that are in no way unique to postcommunist transitions. Crisis and instability inhere in the structure of power-sharing arrangements because inclusive and partitioned decision making gives rise to three problems. It privileges nationality as a basis for solidarity and conflict. It fosters divergence of preferences among nationalities. It creates institutional weapons that can be used against other politicians and to tear apart the state.

Privileging nationalistic claims. Power sharing institutionalizes differences among nationalities, increasing the likelihood that these differences will become the primary points of cleavage in all subsequent disputes (Suny, 1993; Verdery, 1996: 79–83; Denitch, 1990: 78). First, inclusive and partitioned decision making guarantees the politicians who lead formal institutions of nationality

7. Of course, Tajikistan has suffered through a severe civil war, but the ethnic claims of the Pamiris and Gorno-Badakhshan autonomous oblast have played only a minor role in this.

self-governance, such as the leaders of union republics, a place at the bargaining table of politics—particularly the bargaining over constitutional redesign—from which they can press their agendas. So, the bargaining among leaders of republics in Yugoslavia, the Soviet Union, and Czechoslovakia that sought to create new federations became dominated by disputes over the powers of the autonomous homeland administrations and made it difficult to identify common institutions and policy concerns. Second, in order to gain access to these seats at the table, politicians are likely to find that they must outbid one another in their appeals to their respective nationality groups, making ever more extreme claims about what they will win at the central bargaining table (Hislope, 1997). Nationalistic out-bidding or flanking is not inevitable in diverse societies. Often the logic of politics in multiethnic societies dictates competition for the median voter, but power-sharing institutions segment political competition by nationality and increase the likelihood of outbidding within each community. Thus, in the last year of the Soviet Union, democratization of politics in some homelands led to victories of politicians who claimed they would make their republic's sovereignty a reality. Even in some republics that failed to democratize, leaders of Communist Party machines had to promise they would wrench more power from Moscow. Third, politicians with other agendas that might cut across national issues—such as class or profession—find they must frame their demands as national issues in order to gain access to the privileged centers of decision making. As Sharon L. Wolchik (1994: 163) observes about Czechoslovakia, the federal system "institutionalized ethnicity as a factor that had to be considered in all policy-making areas." In this institutional environment, all politics become nationalistic politics; all politics come to involve more extreme issues of national rights.

Polarization of preferences. Inclusive and divided decision making increases the likelihood that policies in the different nationalities will diverge, the communities will consequently develop in different directions, their resulting needs and preferences will also diverge, and common policies for the country as a whole will become more difficult to find and increasingly irrelevant. In the transition from communism, both democracy and economic liberalization in postcommunist federations frequently progressed at different rates in the separate national homelands within the same state. In the postcommunist federations this led to what Valerie Bunce (1999: 87–88) aptly calls the "diversification of interrepublic dynamics, as regional party elites fought for their survival by distancing themselves and their republics from the center through particular and varying but usually self-serving combinations of nationalism and reform." Carol Skalnik Leff (1999: 212–13) argues compellingly that the powers of the separate homelands to control education, media, and culture led to separate frames of discourse and to what Susan Woodward labels "segregated intellectual universes" and Leff calls the "segmentation of public opinion." This made the subsequent problem of agreeing on common policies for the federation all the more difficult. This disappearance of a bargaining range that encompassed the preferences of the different nationalities became apparent and most damaging in the attempt to renegotiate the constitutional structure of the three major federations (Wolchik, 1994: 153–8; Butora and Butorova, 1993: 709; Hill, 1993). The central governments allowed more decisions to devolve onto the regions, but at some point the central state simply withered away. Indeed, this is what was ratified by the Belovezhskaia Agreements signed by Russia, Ukraine, and Belarus. These agreements did not dissolve the Soviet Union; they simply confirmed that it had, for all intents and purposes, already disappeared.

Proliferation of institutional weapons. Every power assigned to a nationality is also a potential weapon to be used against another nationality and the state at the bargaining table of ethnoconstitutional politics. According to Philip Selznick (1960: 2) such weapons are powers that "are used by a power-seeking elite in a manner unrestrained by the constitutional order of the arena within which the contest takes place," and they are used to change that constitutional order. This is an obvious problem when designing the armies and police forces of the multinational state. Federalization of the armed forces gives national-homeland administrations the power to challenge the central government, secede, and bring down the state. In addition, however, control over critical revenue sources is the power to starve other nationalities and the central government into submission. Veto power in inclusive decision making gives the leaders of national homeland administrations, like republics in a union, the ability to paralyze the government, and thus threaten mutual disaster, in order to induce the central government or other politicians to give in (Bebler, 1993; Roeder, 1998).[8]

The lesson of the transition from communism is that, taken together, by privileging particularistic nationalisms, fostering divergence of preferences, and proliferating institutional weapons, power-sharing institutions increase the probability that the leaders of nationalities will challenge the central government in order to transform and possibly dissolve the state. The institutional environment of power sharing changes the process of liberalization and democratization. Transitions from communism and, specifically, liberalization entail devolution of power from the state to society. Democratization entails devolution of power to individuals who seek to

---

8. An instructive comparison is the opposite extreme in which ethnopoliticians have no institutionally based leverage over the central government; see, for example, Barany (1998).

replace the government. In the context of power-sharing institutions, however, these processes take on a very different quality, because they entail devolution not just to groups that may constitute alternative governments but to groups that can demand alternative states. Moreover, power-sharing institutions empower the leaders of these nationalities with alternative national projects to press these demands by inflicting costly damage on the politicians across the bargaining table of constitutional politics (Roeder, 1991).

Were the Consequences of Communist Power Sharing Unique?

This argument inevitably begs two questions. One concerns whether these consequences of power sharing were unique to communism and will not recur now that communism is dead. The second concerns the endogeneity of power sharing itself—that is, whether the observed relationship between power sharing and nationalist challenges to the state may be simply spurious and the real cause is the demographic, cultural, or historical factors that give rise to both power sharing and nationalist challenges. Ethnic groups that are more likely to make nationalist challenges for demographic, cultural, or historical reasons may also, for these same reasons, be more likely to be recognized in power-sharing institutions. If these deeper causes are the real reason for ethnonational challenges, and power-sharing institutions contribute nothing to the likelihood of such challenges, we may have simply mistaken a symptom for a cause. Can we estimate the contribution that power-sharing institutions make to the likelihood of ethnonational crises while controlling for the effect of demographic, cultural, and historical factors?

As a first attempt to answer these questions, I turn to a statistical procedure called logit analysis. The cases to be analyzed and compared (that is, the observations) include 658 ethnic groups around the globe within 153 independent states between 1955 and 1999. This is a sufficiently large population to test whether the observed consequences of power sharing in the transition from communism can be generalized. The ethnic groups include all that constituted at least 1 percent of the country's total population or, in the largest countries with a population over 20 million, that consisted of at least 200,000 members. The observations cover five-year periods beginning with January 1, 1955, although periods are omitted if the country was not independent on its first day. (An example of an observation is Spain's Basques from 1960 to 1964.) The total number of observations in this analysis is 8,074.

The logit analysis permits us to estimate the likelihood of an event such as an outbreak of an ethnonational crisis within a five-year period under various conditions. The first probability we want to estimate is the likelihood of an ethnonational crisis—a public dispute between the central government and members of an ethnic group over the latter's claim to expanded rights of self-governance (statehood) either for greater autonomy within the existing state or for independence outside it.[9] The second probability that we want to estimate is the likelihood of the use of violence between forces of the central government and the ethnic group in one of these crises. This involves instances of what Ted Robert Gurr classifies as rebellion or the Stockholm International Peace Research Institute classifies as an armed conflict—but only those instances in which one of the issues was the ethnic group's right to self-governance.

The three dichotomous indicators of power sharing are limited to the most important form of this—territorial autonomy with either a first-order or second-order homeland (such as either a union republic or an autonomous republic in the Soviet Union or either a republic or an autonomous province in Yugoslavia) or disfranchisement of the ethnic group by denying it a homeland within a state that grants other ethnic groups such autonomy. To control for the demographic, cultural, economic, political, and historical factors that may be the true deeper causes, the equations include eight other independent variables: (1) whether the ethnic group was a cultural minority—indicated by religious or linguistic difference between the ethnic group and the majority of the country's population;[10] (2) whether the ethnic group had enjoyed statehood in the form of an independent state (for example, Lithuanians in the Soviet Union), wartime puppet state (for example, Slovakians in Czechoslovakia), a protectorate (for example, Tuvinians in the Soviet Union), a semistate during a civil war (for example, Ukrainians in the Soviet Union), or a protostate (for example, Ashanti in Ghana) immediately *prior* to their incorporation or reincorporation within the current state; (3–5) whether the state was a democracy, autocracy, or in political turmoil/transition at the beginning of the period;[11] (6) the ethnic group's

9. These data are drawn from *Facts on File* (1955–99); Ted Robert Gurr's Minorities at Risk project (1999); *Keesing's Record of World Events* (1955–99); Minahan (1996); SIPRI (1987–98); and Wallensteen and Sollenberg (1998).

10. Cultural diversity is operationalized as a dichotomous variable based on the native language and religion of the ethnic group, on one hand, and the language and religion of the country's majority, on the other. Where the ethnic group and country's majority speak languages that belong to the same linguistic phylum and linguistic group *and* they practice religions that belong to the same religious sect (for example, Sunni versus Shi'i Islam, Protestantism versus Roman Catholicism) they are classified as ethnically homogeneous dyads; otherwise, as diverse dyads.

11. The regime at the beginning of the period is operationalized by three dichotomous variables based on their Polity Scores (Marshall and Jaggers, 2000). The default category comprises those in-between cases, sometimes called "anocracies," with polity scores less than 6 and more than -6.

proportion of the country's total population,[12] (7) whether the ethnic group is an "immigrant group" with a remote (noncontiguous) territory, and (8) the country's gross domestic product per capita (natural logarithm).[13]

How much did power-sharing institutions increase the likelihood of ethnonational crises and violence? The answer is "substantially so," at least doubling the probabilities of crisis and violence in every instance. Consider, for example, the otherwise average ethnic group that was not a cultural minority and lacked an experience of separate statehood immediately prior to incorporation into the current state. As table 5 shows,[14] the likelihood of an ethnonational crisis was 17.2 percentage points higher (23.5 percent versus 6.3 percent) and the likelihood of violence in these crises was 5.5 percentage points higher (8.2 percent versus 2.7 percent) for the ethnic group that had political autonomy within the state than for an otherwise similar ethnic group that was incorporated without autonomy within a unitary state. Next consider the cultural minority that had no prior statehood. The probability of an ethnonational crisis was 31.3 percentage points higher and the likelihood of violence was 14.4 percentage points higher for the autonomous group than for the otherwise similar cultural minority within a unitary state. That is, autonomy raised the probability of an ethnonational crisis at least once during a five-year period involving a cultural minority that had no prior statehood and was otherwise typical from about one-in-six odds (17.1 percent) to almost even odds (48.4 percent). Autonomy increased the likelihood of violence for such groups from one-in-twelve odds (8.3 percent) to somewhere between one-in-five and one-in-four odds (22.7 percent). Finally consider cultural minorities with the experience of prior statehood. The likelihood of a crisis was 35.5 percentage points higher and the likelihood of violence was 22.0 percentage points higher for the autonomous group than the otherwise similar cultural minority within a unitary state.

12. The proportion of the majority or titular group of a country is set to zero in the numerator, but not in the denominator.

13. These data are measured in US dollars at 1990 prices and are taken from United Nations (1993–97).

14. That is, the regime and immigrant group variables are set to zero and other variables are set to their mean values as the individual power sharing, cultural, and prior statehood variables vary in the indicated way. The estimates of probabilities in the text and in tables 5 and 6 are derived with the Clarify Procedure developed by King, Tomz, and Wittenberg (2000).

Table 5

Probabilities and Logit Estimates—Ethnonational Crises and Violence

	Ethnonationalist crisis (probability)	Use of violence (probability)
Ethnic group (not a cultural minority) without prior statehood, *but*		
with first-order autonomy, *or*	23.5	8.2
in a unitary state	6.3	2.7
Cultural minority without prior statehood, *but*		
with first-order autonomy, *or*	48.4	22.7
in a unitary state	17.1	8.3
Cultural minority with prior statehood, *and*		
with first-order autonomy, *or*	73.0	38.5
in a unitary state	37.5	16.5

	Logit equations			
	Coefficient	(z)	Coefficient	(z)
First-order autonomy	1.512***	(13.23)	1.154***	(8.35)
Second-order autonomy	−0.535**	(−3.00)	−1.112***	(−4.31)
Disfranchisement	1.217***	(10.59)	1.127***	(8.50)
Cultural minority	1.125***	(13.53)	1.195***	(11.21)
Prior statehood	1.061***	(7.01)	0.762***	(4.51)
Democracy at beginning of period	0.040	(0.39)	0.537***	(4.18)
Autocracy at beginning of period	−0.466***	(−5.04)	−0.229	(−1.92)
Turmoil at beginning of period	0.323*	(1.98)	0.747***	(4.04)
Proportion of population	4.471***	(9.00)	3.297***	(5.55)
Immigrant group	−3.142***	(−10.42)	−2.807***	(−7.18)
GDP per capita (*ln*)	1.217***	(4.46)	−1.134***	(−3.29)
Constant	−3.719***	(−17.41)	−2.949***	(−11.17)
	n = 8074		n = 8074	
	χ^2 = 1029.83		χ^2 = 631.14	
	Pseudo − R^2 = 0.163		Pseudo − R^2 = 0.140	

Legend: Significance: *** at .001 level; ** at .01 level; * at .05 level.

Moreover, power-sharing institutions may magnify the effect of other factors that increase the likelihood of crises and violence. To verify these interactions will require further research, but table 6 suggests that these interaction effects may be substantial. There is greater likelihood of an ethnonational crisis involving cultural minorities than other ethnic groups. Yet, it is more prominent in the presence of cultural autonomy (+24.9 percentage points) than in a unitary state (+10.8 percentage points). Similarly, there is greater likelihood of a crisis when the cultural minority also has a recent, preincorporation history of separate statehood. Again, this is more prominent under power sharing (+49.5 percentage points) than in a unitary state (+31.2 percentage points). The results suggest that in this last instance autonomy turns roughly one-in-three odds (31.2 percent) of a crisis into almost three-in-four odds (73.0 percent).

Table 6

Probabilities and Changes in Probabilities of Ethnonational Crises
Due to Cultural Diversity, Prior Statehood, and Power Sharing[*]

	In unitary state	With autonomy
Cultural minority with no prior statehood	17.1	48.4
Not cultural minority	6.3	23.5
Cultural minority with prior statehood	37.5	73.0

* Probabilities from table 5.

Are These Lessons Still Relevant to the Postcommunist World?

Yet another body of evidence suggests that the consequences of power sharing that were observed during the transition from communism have continuing relevance. This comes from the Balkans in the postcommunist era—the recent experiments with power sharing after civil conflicts in ethnically divided societies. These experiments are of recent origin and constantly evolving, so it would be imprudent to predict their ultimate outcomes. Nonetheless, even in the first months of these experiments, many problems of power sharing found in the transition from communism became apparent once again—notably, the privileging of nationalistic appeals and the exclusion of moderate and cross-cutting interests from the political process, the polarization of preferences among the governments of the autonomous regions, and the proliferation of institutional weapons that permit these local leaders to resist the central government.

First, the leaders of the separate communities empowered by power sharing used this autonomy and power to create monopolistic political machines within their respective regions. In Bosnia, international assistance funneled through the new power-sharing institutions enabled nationalist elites at entity and local levels to tighten their grip on communities. Leaders of the Serb, Croat, and Bosniac microstates were given the power to maintain separate armies, police forces, and judiciaries (Malik, 2000) and, by 1999, fully 93.7 percent of the police officers and 97.6 percent of the judges and prosecutors in the Republika Srpska were Serbs (ICG, 2002a: 4; 2002b). They created separate administrations, including separate police forces, not only in the ethnically distinct regions, but also in mixed areas (Okuizumi, 2002: 731–32). In their respective cantons and even in such multiethnic districts as Brcko, Bosniacs, Croats, and Serbs maintained "three separate administrations, health care and education systems, pension systems, payment bureaus, and police forces" (Lyon, 2000: 112; ICG, 2002c: 6). Even in the still shorter life of the peace accords in Macedonia (known as the Ohrid Agreement), these problems associated with power sharing also began to emerge. The International Crisis Group (2002d: i, 3) warned that under the accords

> ...instead of attenuating ethnic differences through shared government, Macedonia's ruling parties have functioned as corrupt coalitions, dividing the turf among and within ministries and even on the ground for separate exploitation. The division of "turf" functions as a rehearsal for division of territory as politicians cynically present themselves as defenders of the national interest while in fact conspiring with the other side for personal or party enrichment.

Second, these leaders championed extreme nationalistic appeals and silenced those within their communities who would challenge their rule from moderate platforms. In Bosnia, local ethnic elites discouraged moderation and opposition from within their communities. They intimidated voters to deter them from supporting opposition parties—particularly those making cross-ethnic appeals. As a consequence, in the local elections in 1997, nationalist parties garnered 90 percent of the vote and fully 96 percent in the Republika Srpska (Pugh and Cobble, 2001: 30, 34). Roberto Belloni (2001: 173) noted that "by fostering community isolation, mobilization, and a general feeling of insecurity, ethnic elites legitimize each other and maintain a tight grip on their constituencies." Ironically, the power-sharing institutions created a hothouse that kept alive and fostered Croat and Serb extremism within Bosnia at the very time radical nationalists lost power in neighboring Serbia and Croatia (Chandler, 2001: 114). Also in Macedonia, as the International Crisis Group (2002d: i, 3) noted, power sharing accelerated this polarization of positions: the Ohrid Agreement "invites outright collusion between ethnic leaders to heighten tensions and plays a substantial role in making the country ripe for conflict."

223

Third, as in other power-sharing systems, the empowered ethnic elites used their institutional weapons to weaken the common state (Malik, 2000: 313). Andrea Kathryn Talentino (2002: 34) observed that at the central level in Bosnia and Herzegovina, "there is a structure of government but little interest in making it work, not least of all because those who control the entities prefer running them as fiefdoms rather than as subordinate units of a national whole" (see also Malik, 2000). Ironically, in order to make the power-sharing institutions appear to work, the High Representative had to intervene with imposed solutions that papered over the lack of agreement and with methods that were the antithesis of power sharing and representative democracy. In short, the recent experience in the Balkans suggests that even in a postcommunist world, power sharing is seldom a viable mechanism for preserving the peace and shoring up democracy in a state which lacks a nation.

Conclusions and Implications

The gradual expansion of the democratic peace with each wave of democratization has depended on the deeper tectonic movement toward a global regime of nation-states. Since 1815, there have been four phases in the creation of new nation-states—the classic period from the Congress of Vienna to the Congress of Berlin, the first quarter of the twentieth century, the three decades that followed World War II, and the decade that straddled the end of the Cold War. That is, the revolutions of 1989 represent the third time in one century that the modern international system has been rocked by a reconfiguration of many states because nations claimed a right to self-rule. Despite the dangers of each shift and the bloody excess to which nationalism can give rise, this world of nation-states may well be the most secure foundation for democracy and peace.

The experience of the postcommunist transitions calls for a dialogue about the role of nations in the modern state system. Specifically, the transition from communism suggests that we should reintroduce the third element in the Kantian-Wilsonian tripartite formula that saw democracy and peace advancing along with national self-determination. In particular, we need to examine more carefully the national or demographic conditions under which democracy is likely to flourish. This requires fuller development of an undertheorized area as well as fuller empirical evidence. This calls for closer examination of the role of the usual institutional remedies to the common ills of democracy when confronted with a potentially catastrophic malady such as the absence of national unity. Only under the most favorable conditions are these usual institutional answers likely to help substantially. Mill apparently was right when he argued that there are limits to what can be accomplished through constitutional engineering. In these cases, the issue of national self-determination cannot be avoided by artful constitutional design.

References

Alesina, Alberto and Enrico Spolaore (1997) "On the Number and Size of Nations." *Quarterly Journal of Economics* 112 (November): 1027–56.

Alesina, Alberto, Enrico Spolaore and Romain Wacziarg (1997) "Economic Integration and Political Disintegration." NBER Working Paper Series No. 6163. Cambridge: National Bureau of Economic Research.

Alesina, Alberto, Reza Baqir and William Easterly (1999) "Public Goods and Ethnic Divisions." *Quarterly Journal of Economics* 114 (November): 1243–84.

Barany, Zoltan (1998) "Ethnic Mobilization and the State: The Roma in Eastern Europe." *Ethnic and Racial Studies* 21 (March): 308–27.

Barkan, Joel (1998) "Rethinking the Applicability of Proportional Representation for Africa." In Timothy D. Sisk and Andrew Reynolds (eds.) *Elections and Conflict Management in Africa*. Washington, D.C.: United States Institute of Peace Press, 57–70.

Barrington, Lowell (1995) "The Domestic and International Consequences of Citizenship in the Soviet Successor States." *Europe-Asia Studies* 47 (May): 731–63.

Bebler, Anton (1993) "Yugoslavia's Variety of Communist Federation and Its Demise." *Communist and Post-Communist Studies* 26 (March): 72–86.

Belloni, Roberto (2001) "Civil Society and Peacebuilding in Bosnia and Herzegovina." *Journal of Peace Research* 38 (March): 163–80.

Bremmer, Ian and Cory Welt (1995) "Kazakhstan's Quandry." *Journal of Democracy* 6 (July): 139–54.

Breslauer, George W. and Catherine Dale (1997) "Boris Yel'tsin and the Invention of a Russian Nation-State." *Post-Soviet Affairs* 13: 303–32.

Bromlei, Iu. V. (1988) *Narody mira: istoriko-etnograficheskii spravochnik*. Moscow: Sovetskaia entsiklopediia.

Brubaker, Rogers (1996) *Nationalism Reframed: Nationhood and the National Question in the New Europe*. Cambridge: Cambridge University Press.

Bunce, Valerie (1999) *Subversive Institutions: The Design and the Destruction of Socialism and the State*. Cambridge: Cambridge University Press.

Butora, Martin and Zora Butorova (1993) "Slovakia: The Identity Challenges of the Newly Born State." *Social Research* 60 (Winter): 705–36.

Chandler, David (2001) "Bosnia: The Democracy Paradox." *Current History* 100 (March): 114–19.

Chapman, David (1999) *Can Civil Wars Be Avoided? Electoral and Constitutional Options for Ethnically Divided Countries.* London: Institute for Social Inventions.

Claude, Inis L. (1964) *Swords Into Plowshares: The Problems and Progress of International Organization,* 3rd ed. New York: Random House.

Cobban, Alfred (1951) *National Self-Determination.* Chicago: University of Chicago Press.

Cronon, E. David (ed.) (1965) *The Political Thought of Woodrow Wilson.* Indianapolis: Bobbs-Merrill Company.

Dahl, Robert (1971) *Polyarchy: Participation and Opposition.* New Haven: Yale University Press.

Denitch, Bogdan (1990) *Limits and Possibilities: The Crises of Yugoslav Socialism and State-Socialist Systems.* Minneapolis: University of Minnesota Press.

Doyle, Michael W. (1986) "Liberalism and World Politics." *American Political Science Review* 80 (December): 1151–69.

Draper, Stark (1997) "The Conceptualization of an Albanian Nation." *Ethnic and Racial Studies* 20 (January): 123–44.

The Europa World Yearbook (1990–2000) London: Europa Publications.

Facts on File (1955–1999) New York: Facts on File.

Freedom House (1990–2002) *Freedom in the World: Political Rights and Civil Liberties,* annual volumes. New York: Freedom House. Scores available online at www.freedomhouse.org/ratings/index.htm.

Friedman, David (1977) "A Theory of the Size and Shape of Nations." *Journal of Political Economy* 85 (February): 59–77.

Furnivall, J.S. (1944) *Netherlands India: A Study of Plural Economy.* New York: Macmillan Company.

Goldman, R. (1985) "Consociational Authoritarian Politics and the 1974 Yugoslav Constitution: A Preliminary Note." *East European Quarterly* 19 (June): 241–49.

Gurr, Ted Robert (1999) *Minorities at Risk Project* [website]. College Park: University of Maryland. Available online at www.bsos.umd.edu/cidcm/mar.

Harris, Peter and Ben Reilly (eds.) (1998) *Democracy and Deep-Rooted Conflict: Options for Negotiators.* Stockholm: International Institute for Democracy and Electoral Assistance.

Hill, Ronald J. (1993) "Managing Ethnic Conflict." *Journal of Communist Studies* 9 (March), 57–73.

Hislope, Robert (1997) "Intra-Ethnic Conflict in Croatia and Serbia: Flanking and the Consequences for Democracy." *East European Quarterly* 30 (January): 471–94.

Horowitz, Donald L. (1985) *Ethnic Groups in Conflict.* Berkeley: University of California Press.

Huntington, Samuel P. (1991) *The Third Wave: Democratization in the Late Twentieth Century.* Norman: University of Oklahoma Press.

International Crisis Group (ICG)(2002a) "Implementing Equality: The 'Constituent Peoples' Decision in Bosnia & Herzegovina." ICG Balkans Report No. 128. Sarajevo/Brussels, April 16.

ICG (2002b) "Policing the Police in Bosnia: A Further Reform Agenda." ICG Balkans Report No. 130. Sarajevo/Brussels, May 10.

ICG (2002c) "Bosnia's Alliance for (Smallish) Change." ICG Balkans Report No. 132. Sarajevo/Brussels, August 2.

ICG (2002d) "Macedonia's Public Secret: How Corruption Drags the Country Down." ICG Balkans Report No. 133. Skopje/Brussels, August 14.

International Institute for Democracy and Electoral Assistance (1998) *Voter Turnout from 1945 to 1997: A Global Report on Political Participation.* Stockholm: IDEA.

Jennings, Ivor (1958) *The Approach to Self-Government.* Cambridge: Cambridge University Press.

Kaiser, Robert and Jeff Chinn (1995) "Russian-Kazakh Relations in Kazakhstan." *Post-Soviet Geography* 36 (May): 257–73.

Keesing's Record of World Events [earlier *Keesing's Contemporary Archive*] *(1955–1999)* Cambridge: Cartermill Publishing.

King, Gary, Michael Tomz and Jason Wittenberg (2000) "Making the Most of Statistical Analyses: Improving Interpretation and Presentation." *American Journal of Political Science* 44 (April): 341–55.

Kolsto, Pal and Boris Tsilevich (1997) "Patterns of Nation Building and Political Integration in a Bifurcated Postcommunist State: Ethnic Aspects of Parliamentary Elections in Latvia." *East European Politics and Societies* 11 (Spring): 366–91.

Lapidoth, Ruth (1996) *Autonomy: Flexible Solutions to Ethnic Conflicts.* Washington, D.C.: United States Institute of Peace Press.

Leff, Carol Skalnik (1999) "Democratization and Disintegration in Multinational States: The Breakup of the Communism Federations." *World Politics* 51 (January): 205–35.

Liebich, Andre (1996) "Getting Better, Getting Worse." *Dissent* 43 (Summer 1996): 84–89.

Lijphart, Arend (1977) *Democracy in Plural Societies: A Comparative Exploration.* New Haven: Yale University Press.

—— (1984) *Democracies.* New Haven: Yale University Press.

—— (1995) "Multiethnic Democracy." In Seymour Martin Lipset (ed.) *The Encyclopedia of Democracy,* volume 3. Washington, D.C.: Congressional Quarterly, 853–65.

——— (1999) *Patterns of Democracy.* New Haven: Yale University Press.

Linz, Juan J. and Alfred Stepan (1996) *Problems of Democratic Transition and Consolidation: Southern Europe, South America, and Post-Communist Europe.* Baltimore: The Johns Hopkins University Press.

Lustick, Ian (1979) "Stability in Deeply Divided Societies: Consociationalism versus Control." *World Politics* 31 (April): 325–44.

Lyon, James M.B. (2000) "Will Bosnia Survive Dayton?" *Current History* 99 (March): 110–16.

Malik, John (2000) "The Dayton Agreement and Elections in Bosnia: Entrenching Ethnic Cleansing Through Democracy." *Stanford Journal of International Law* 36 (Summer): 303–55.

Marshall, Monty and Keith Jaggers (2000) "Polity IV: Political Regime Characteristics and Transitions, 1800–1999." *Dataset User's Manual.* Available online at www.bsos.umd.edu/cidcm/polity/p4manual.pdf.

Mill, John Stuart (1962) *Considerations on Representative Government.* Chicago: Henry Regnery.

Miller, David (1996) "The Nation State: A Modest Defense." In Chris Brown (ed.) *Political Restructuring in Europe: Ethical Perspectives.* London: Routledge.

Minahan, James (1996) *Nations Without States: A Historical Dictionary of Contemporary National Movements.* Westport: Greenwood Press.

Nordlinger, Eric A. (1972) "Conflict Regulation in Divided Societies." Occasional Papers in International Affairs No. 29. Cambridge: Harvard University, Center for International Affairs.

Okuizumi, Kaoru (2002) "Peacebuilding Mission: Lessons from the UN Mission in Bosnia and Herzegovina." *Human Rights Quarterly* 24 (August): 721–35.

Park, Andrus (1994) "Ethnicity and Independence: The Case of Estonia in Comparative Perspective." *Europe-Asia Studies* 46 (January): 68–87.

Przeworski, Adam, Michael Alvarez, Jose Antonio Cheibub and Fernando Limongi (1996) "What Makes Democracies Endure?" *Journal of Democracy* 7 (January): 39–55.

Pugh, Michael and Margaret Cobble (2001) "Non-Nationalist Voting in Bosnia Municipal Elections: Implications for Democracy and Peacebuilding." *Journal of Peace Research* 39 (January): 27–47.

Rabushka, Alvin and Kenneth A. Shepsle (1972) *Politics in Plural Societies: A Theory of Democratic Instability.* Columbus: Charles E. Merrill Publishing Company.

Ray, James Lee (1997) "The Democratic Path to Peace." *Journal of Democracy* 8 (April): 49–64.

Reilly, Ben and Andrew Reynolds (1999) *Electoral Systems and Conflict in Divided Societies.* Washington, DC: National Academy Press.

Reynolds, Andrew (1998) "Elections in Southern Africa: The Case for Proportionality, A Rebuttal." In Timothy D. Sisk and Andrew Reynolds (eds.) *Elections and Conflict Management in Africa*. Washington, D.C.: United States Institute of Peace Press, 71–80.

Roeder, Philip G. (1998) "Liberalization and Ethnic Entrepreneurs in the Soviet Successor States." In Beverly Crawford and Ronnie D. Lipschutz (eds.) *The Myth of "Ethnic Conflict": Politics, Economics, and "Cultural" Change*. Berkeley: University of California, International and Area Studies, 78–107.

—— (1991) "Soviet Federalism and Ethnic Mobilization." *World Politics* 43 (January): 196–232.

—— (2001) "The Rejection of Authoritarianism." In Richard D. Anderson, Jr., M. Steven Fish, Stephen E. Hanson and Philip G. Roeder *Postcommunism and the Theory of Democracy*. Princeton: Princeton University Press, 11–53.

—— (2003) "Clash of Civilizations and Escalation of Domestic Ethnopolitical Conflicts." *Comparative Political Studies* 36 (June).

Russett, Bruce M. (1993) *Grasping the Democratic Peace: Principles for a Post-Cold-War World*. Princeton: Princeton University Press.

Rustow, Dankwart A. (1967) *A World of Nations: Problems of Political Modernization*. Washington, D.C.: The Brookings Institutions.

Schermerhorn, Richard (1970) *Comparative Ethnic Relations*. New York: Random House.

Selznick, Philip (1960) *The Organizational Weapon: A Study of Bolshevik Strategy and Tactics*. Glencoe: The Free Press of Glencoe.

Stockholm International Peace Research Institute (1987–1998) *SIPRI Yearbook: World Armaments and Disarmament*, annual editions. New York: Oxford University Press.

Sisk, Timothy D. (1996) *Power Sharing and International Mediation in Ethnic Conflicts*. Washington, D.C.: United States Institute of Peace Press.

Smith, Michael G. (1965) *The Plural Society in the British West Indies*. Berkeley: University of California Press.

Suny, Ronald G. (1993) *The Revenge of the Past: Nationalism, Revolution, and the Collapse of the Soviet Union*. Stanford: Stanford University Press.

Talentino, Andrea Kathryn (2002) "Intervention as Nation-Building: Illusion or Possibility?" *Security Dialogue* 33 (March): 27–43.

Tilly, Charles (1975) "Reflections on the History of European State-Making." In Charles Tilly (ed.) *The Formation of National States in Europe*. Princeton: Princeton University Press, 3–83.

Tolz, Vera (1998) "Conflicting 'Homeland Myths' and Nation-State Building in Postcommunist Russia." *Slavic Review* 57 (Summer): 267–94.

United Nations (1993-1997) Department of Economic and Social Information and Policy Analysis, Statistical Division. *Statistical Yearbook,* annual editions. New York: United Nations.

Vachudova, Milada Anna and Tim Snyder (1997) "Are Transitions Transitory? Two Types of Political Change in Eastern Europe Since 1989." *East European Politics and Societies* 11 (Winter): 1-35.

Van den Berghe, Pierre L. (1981) *The Ethnic Phenomenon.* New York: Elsevier North Holland.

Varady, Tibor (1997) "Minorities, Majorities, Law, and Ethnicity: Reflections of the Yugoslav Case." *Human Rights Quarterly* 19 (February): 9-54.

Verba, Sidney (1971) "Sequences and Development." In Leonard Binder (ed.) *Crises and Sequences in Political Development.* Princeton: Princeton University Press.

Verdery, Katherine (1996) "Nationalism, Postsocialism, and Space in Eastern Europe." *Social Research* 63 (Spring): 77-95.

Wallensteen, Peter and Margareta Sollenberg (1998) "Armed Conflict and Regional Conflict Complexes, 1989-97." *Journal of Peace Research* 35 (July): 621-34.

Weber, Max (1958) *From Max Weber: Essays in Sociology.* New York: Oxford University Press.

Wittman, Donald (1991) "Nations and States: Mergers and Acquisitions; Dissolutions and Divorce." *American Economic Review* 81 (May): 126-29.

Wolchik, Sharon L. (1994) "The Politics of Ethnicity in Postcommunist Czechoslovakia." *East European Politics and Societies* 8 (Winter): 153-88.

Power Sharing as Ethnic Representation in Postconflict Societies: The Cases of Bosnia, Macedonia, and Kosovo

Florian Bieber

Managing deeply divided societies has become a concern for policy makers around the world in recent years. The experience of Bosnia and Kosovo demonstrated that facilitating the creation of a sustainable polity is no easier than ending a war. Because the preservation or restoration of ethnic diversity was one of the main aims of international intervention and due to the reluctance of most countries to recognize new states, especially if not based on preexisting administrative boundaries, the creation of institutions which recognize and manage diversity was the only policy option available to designers of postconflict institutions in the Balkans.[1]

All three primary means for maintaining diversity—territorial autonomy, cultural autonomy, and power sharing—can form part of a postconflict institutional arrangement. This chapter is concerned with power sharing for two reasons. First, aspects of power sharing feature in the three main peace agreements in the former Yugoslavia, namely in Bosnia and Herzegovina, Kosovo, and Macedonia, while territorial autonomy is only substantially developed in the Bosnian case. In both Kosovo and Macedonia, territorial devolution based on ethnicity has been implicitly or explicitly excluded.[2] Second, power sharing has a profound impact on the governance of the respective countries or regions. By emphasizing the need for ethnic co–decision making, such institutional arrangements signal a departure from classic nation-states where the dominance of one ethnic group, at least in the state's central institutions, is of crucial importance. Nevertheless, the concept of ethnic cogovernance equally excludes a civic polity where ethnic belonging is of secondary importance.

Research for this paper was supported by the International Policy Fellowship program. Parts of this chapter draw on Florian Bieber (2004) "Power sharing after Yugoslavia." In Sid Noel (ed.), From Power-Sharing to Democracy: Post-Conflict Institutions in Ethnically Divided Societies. *Kingston & Montreal: McGill–Queens University Press.*

1. On the dichotomy of recognizing and denying diversity, see McGarry and O'Leary (1993: 1–40). For southeastern Europe specifically, see Todosijevic (2001: 77–93).

2. Thus, the Framework Agreement for Macedonia explicitly states: "There are no territorial solutions to ethnic issues." Art. 1.2, Framework Agreement, August 13, 2001. While falling short of outright territorial autonomy, strengthening local self-government has been a key aspect of the Macedonia arrangement.

Constrained by the need to incorporate politicized ethnicity in a polity's institutional arrangement, while also recognizing some of the inherent challenges of institutionalizing ethnicity, this chapter falls in two parts. The first half examines the two core institutional mechanisms of power sharing related to group representation: parliamentary representation and grand coalitions. It will be argued that there is a need to look beyond power sharing, in other words, to conceive of a means to reduce the dominance of ethnic identity in politics. Thus, in the second part, the possibility to shift—or at least supplement—power sharing and political representation with strengthened minority rights will be examined. This section will also discuss the possibility of conceiving of institutional design in multiethnic societies as a process that might allow for an eventual deethnification of some spheres of the political decision-making process.

Power sharing in deeply divided societies can encompass a range of different measures to accommodate ethnic (or other) diversity. It would be flawed to conceptualize power sharing as a rigid catalog of institutions and legal protection that must be fulfilled to qualify as power sharing. Already, the different means of power sharing advocated by experts point to the absence of an agreed set of instruments (Sisk, 1996: 34–45). The institutional realities in divided societies around the world display an even greater variety of institutions. For the purposes of this chapter, and based on the institutional reality in the three cases under consideration here, the chapter will mostly rely on Arend Lijphart's (Lijphart, 1977: 25) definition of consociational arrangements, which describes a more narrow type of power sharing.[3] He attributes four main criteria to consociational arrangements:

- A grand coalition;
- Proportional representation of all relevant groups in parliament (and the public administration);
- Veto rights;
- A high degree of autonomy.

Here, we shall only be concerned with the representation of groups in government and parliament. Political representation is based less on the theoretical considerations of power sharing per se but rather on emerging international standards of minority rights[4] and international intervention in war-torn societies. What will emerge from the discussion of the varying mechanisms in use in the cases under examination

---

3. On the relationship between power sharing and consociationalism, see Bogaards (2000: 395–423).
4. See Art. 15, Framework Convention for the Protection of National Minorities, Strasbourg, February 1, 1995; Henrard (2000: 271–76).

here—Bosnia, Macedonia, and Kosovo—is that, while there is a variety of instruments to ensure representation, most tools are unlikely to lead to long-term stabilization of the societies, unless they include more secure minority rights and mechanisms for the evolution of postconflict institutions.

Parliamentary Representation

Parliaments are the legislative organ and—of particular importance in divided societies—the principle body of representation for communities. A parliament allows groups and individuals to formulate concerns, shape the political agenda, and supervise the executive's work. In order to ascertain parliament's role in power-sharing arrangements, one needs to take into consideration the way in which the diversity in the given society is represented and the power the parliament and the different communities hold within the society.

Generally, representation of groups in the parliament is determined through common features of electoral systems, most importantly the system by which elections are held, votes counted, and the existence and level of thresholds. These instruments are not group-specific but can boost or diminish parliament's degree of representativeness. As will be discussed, most cases under consideration here employ additional special mechanisms for group representation, such as reserved seats.[5]

When examining election processes, the two crucial considerations are who and what should be represented. The choice of election procedures can have a profound impact on who will represented in parliament and what strength these different groups will have. A general assumption of power-sharing systems is that parliaments should strive to be generally representative of all groups, not excluding some communities or grossly overrepresenting others. In case of smaller minorities, even a degree of overrepresentation or positive discrimination might be desirable. The question of what should be represented is considerably more difficult to manage, and the subtle influence of electoral systems is often hard to assess. Here one has to consider whether the electoral process aims to represent the groups as groups or whether the electoral process should conduce cooperation and aims for the the electoral success of either moderate (candidates and parties not primarily campaigning on the basis of ethnic identity) or cross-communal forces.[6]

---

5. Adopted from Myntti (2001: 15–27).
6. This choice describes on the primary differences in the divergent approaches of Arend Ljiphart and Donald Horowitz to power sharing systems.

Electoral systems offer the greatest variety of tools in determining who is elected. The conventional dichotomy of majoritarian and proportional electoral systems does not indicate the variety of subsystems available. Generally, a form of proportional representation has the advantage that most major groups can expect to gain representation in the parliament, while majoritarian systems tend to favor the strongest party, candidate, or—in deeply divided societies—ethnic groups in the respective electoral district (Reilly and Reynolds, 1999).

All three cases under study here have adopted a variation of proportional representation for the election of their parliaments. This marks a shift from the early 1990s, when most countries in the region employed either a mixed electoral system or outright majoritarian electoral systems. Presidential elections are held in a first-past-the-post system in two cases (at the central [state] level in Bosnia and Herzegovina and in the Serbian entity, the Republika Srpska) or in a two round run-off (Macedonia). The only experiment with alternative voting, which seeks to pool voters to yield electoral success of moderate candidates with a cross-ethnic appeal, in the Republika Srpska in the presidential election in 2000, failed due to the largely homogenous electorate (Bieber, 2002b). As a result, the president of the Republika Srpska (along with, since 2002, two vice presidents from the two smaller communities, in other words, Bosniac and Croat) and the three members of the Bosnian presidency primarily represent their respective ethnic group rather than having a cross-ethnic appeal. Only in Macedonia has some significant cross-ethnic voting taken place in presidential elections.[7]

Thresholds are another important tool for engineering the electoral process. Most Western democracies rely on electoral thresholds to prevent a fragmentation of parliamentary representation into numerous small parties. As thresholds might exclude smaller minorities, they can be either lowered for all parties participating in elections, or, alternatively, minority parties can be exempt from the threshold or face a lower threshold. In the electoral systems of Bosnia, Kosovo, and Macedonia, the thresholds are low or nonexistent, allowing a large number of parties to enter parliament. In Bosnia and Macedonia, the threshold is 3 percent, whereas in Kosovo there is no threshold. While low thresholds prevent the existence of a hurdle for some communities, smaller groups can be excluded even by these low thresholds. This is because party systems in the former Yugoslavia, with the partial exception of Montenegro, mostly follow ethnic divisions, and majority parties offer only little incentive for minorities to vote for them. And since there is often more than one party for each ethnic group, these parties can split the vote of their respective ethnic community, with the

7. This has been, however, mostly viewed in the light of possible electoral fraud surrounding the election of current president Boris Trajkovski. See Mehmeti (1999).

result that no party clears the threshold. Nevertheless, in Macedonia, for example, some minority parties have succeeded in entering parliament as part of coalitions with majority parties. This can, however, make smaller communities dependent on the state majority or other larger groups.

There are certain special mechanisms for group representation that do guarantee community representation. Peter Harris and Ben Reilly note two main types of "explicit recognition of communal groups" that can be found in the region under consideration here: communal electoral rolls and reserved seats. Separate communal electoral rolls place the emphasis on the electorate rather than the elected official. Different communities possess different electoral rolls and vote for their respective candidates. With the exception of Croatia, this system is generally not in use in southeastern Europe, or Europe in general, because of the highly problematic practice of recording ethnicity in voting records. More common is the system of reserved seats where a certain number of seats are set aside for minority representatives. Without using specific electoral rolls, this system of representation is based on the assumption that groups will vote for representatives of their respective community. This has led to wide-spread abuse in some countries, such as Bosnia and Hungary, where individuals who do not really represent the interests of the group have been elected. In a number of cases, the minorities can also compete in the elections for the remainder of the regular seats and gain additional representation. Generally, this tool is in use for smaller minorities when other mechanisms are less likely to ensure adequate representation through conventional means of electoral systems.[8]

Reserved seats are in place in all but one case—Macedonia. In Kosovo, ten seats are reserved for Serbs, and an additional ten are reserved for other minorities (four for the Roma, three for Bosniacs, two for Turks, and one for the Gorani). Seats are allocated to the parties of the respective communities according to their share in the elections. Since these seats are in addition to seats gained as part of the overall proportional-representation system, the Serb community was able to gain 12 additional seats in the 2001 elections, while three other minority parties gained one additional seat each. In Bosnia, the reserved seats primarily apply to the three constituent peoples (Bosniacs, Serbs, and Croats), with additional seats set aside at some levels for "others" (ethnic groups other than the three constituent peoples, including smaller minorities, such as Roma, and citizens not running as members of the three dominant nations). In the Bosnian state (central) parliament and the parliament of the Federation of Bosnia and Herzegovina (the Bosniac-Croat entity), the upper chamber, known as the House of Peoples, provides equal representation

8. On these issues, see also the European Commission for Democracy through Law (Venice Commission) (1999).

for all three communities. The Federation parliament further provides additional representation for the "others." The Republika Srpska's upper house, which is elected by parliament, has a similar function. Additionally the lower chambers of all three parliaments have mechanisms to guarantee group inclusion. Both entity parliaments are required to have at least four members from each of the three communities. The state parliament has a formula according to which two-thirds of its members must be from the Federation and one third from the Republika Srpska. Due to the geographically concentration of communities in Bosnia, this translates into some degree of ensured inclusion of all three groups. In Kosovo's legislature, the House of Representatives of the Federation, the president and vice presidents of the Republika Srpska, and the National Assembly of the Republika Srpska, candidates must declare their ethnicity to benefit from the reserved seats. The ballots in Bosnia, however, do not indicate the candidate's ethnicity.[9] Reserved seats are also in use in neighboring Montenegro, exclusively for the Albanian community.

While leaving less room for manipulation than other electoral measures and offering predictable results, reserved seats are a blunt tool with considerable disadvantages. First, this method frequently contains an element of positive discrimination (as in Kosovo), which easily attracts the majority's resentment. While it might increase representation, it does not necessarily promote participation or cooperation. Second, reserved seats might complicate the electoral process when having to consider other factors, such as the geographic distribution of mandates.[10] The ensuing complexity could reduce voter confidence in the electoral process. Third, the system encourages voters to vote for candidates of their own ethnicity, rather than voting for members of other groups.

Participation in Government

No power-sharing arrangement would be complete without broad group representation at the government level.[11] Since they are usually formed among like-

9. Both in Kosovo and in Bosnia, however, the ethnicity of most candidates can be identified by their names. In Bosnia, Serbian parties generally use Cyrillic script on the ballot papers, while Bosniac and Croatian parties use Latin script.

10. In the House of Peoples of the Federation, deputies must, be on a whole, equally represented while also being representative for the cantons in which they are elected. In the aftermath of the 2002 elections, this has resulted in the situation where an insufficient number of Serbs were elected to the cantonal assembly to fill the required number of seats in the House of Peoples. *Oslobodjenje*, January 15. www.oslobodjenje.com.ba.

11. Lijphart (1977: 25–31) considers it to be the most important element of consociationalism.

minded parties on a joint electoral platform, governments require cooperation. While representation can be legislated through the means discussed above, legislating cooperation at the government level is considerably more challenging.

A legal framework can achieve representation of all groups in government through three tools. The first option assigns a numerical or proportional formula according to which the different groups must be included in the government. The second option is to require that each ministry has deputy ministers from the various ethnic groups to ensure that every ministry is run—or at least contains some degree of oversight—by all groups. Finally, a range of procedural rules can avoid the concentration of power within one community. Such mechanisms include a rotating primeministership or presidency (as in Switzerland).

There are legal requirements for representation of different communities in the institutions at the state- and entity-level in Bosnia, as well as in Kosovo. Whereas this has been an aspect of Bosnian state-level governance since its inception, the entities were only recently required to include nondominant communities in their governments. In the Federation, Serb participation has been minimal, and, in the Republika Srpska, the first Bosniac minister joined the government only in 2001.

In the two Bosnian entities and in Kosovo, a set number of ministries must be run by members of the nondominant groups. At the state-level in Bosnia and in the Federation, deputy ministers representing the ethnic group other than the minister are appointed as well.[12] A similar mechanism is employed for the presidency. At the state-level, a three-member presidency (with one member from each of the constituent peoples) rotates in regular intervals, whereas, in the two entities, the two vice presidents must be from an ethnic group other than that of the president. Macedonia has no formal requirements for a grand coalition. Nevertheless, since the first freely elected government following the 1990 elections, parties representing the Albanian community have been included in the government. Here, similar to Bosnia, it is the general practice to include a deputy minister from an ethnic group other than that of the minister.

In addition to the danger of making the government emulate the same dynamics as in the parliament, additional difficulties can arise from the above arrangements. The deputy ministers can often be powerless, without real influence over the workings of the ministries. Without a defined division of tasks, deputy ministers run the risk of being only window dressing. Intragovernmental dynamics can also lead to an ethnification of ministries. In this situation, ministries cater to the needs and demands of the minister's ethnic community and also compete with the other

12. Until 2002, there were two deputy ministers for every minister. With the formation of a new government in 2003, now only one deputy minister from the other constituent nation is nominated.

ministries.[13] In other cases, such as in Montenegro at the level of the joint Serbian-Montenegrian state, minority ministers have been appointed to the ministries tasked with minority affairs, a practice which primarily has symbolic importance, rather than reflecting actual participation in decision making.[14]

A key difference between Macedonia, on the one hand, and Kosovo and Bosnia, on the other, is the nature of government coalition building, which can be partly related to the difference between the informal tradition of grand coalitions versus the formal requirements of such. In Macedonia, there have been preelection coalitions or at least partnerships between Macedonian and Albanians parties. Thus a change of the governing majority party also brought a new minority party to power. As a result, in addition to an ample degree of interethnic electoral campaigning and competition, there has also been campaigning between the parties of each community. Yet, in Kosovo, the Serb minority and Albanian majority parties have not cooperated in either pre- or postelection coalitions. Although there has been only one election, it seems likely that this pattern will continue in the medium-term. In this case, the participation of minorities in the government simply fulfills a legal requirement rather than being part of the political process of coalition building. Bosnia has had only one experience with a broad cross-party coalition representing more than one ethnic group. However, this coalition, known as the Alliance for Change, only came about after the elections in 2000 and involved heavy-handed intervention from international actors (Cvijanovic, 2001). The ten-member coalition disintegrated in less than two years, and its member parties subsequently lost the elections in October 2002.

In the case of Bosnia, the key challenge has been that, for most of the postwar period, each community (with the partial exception of Bosniacs) has given overwhelming support to just one national party. Thus, coalition building was hampered by the difficulty of the lack of choice. Cross-cutting issue-oriented coalitions are not possible, and intragroup competition is considerably lower than in Macedonia.

The willingness to pursue joint decision making and inclusion, however, requires that the major parties participating in government formation consent to include the other communities. Legislated representation otherwise runs the risk of being mere compliance with the law. Grand coalitions are particularly problematic when each group is represented by only one dominant party, resulting in limited variations for coalitions. Furthermore, in postconflict societies, the parties which will participate in a government frequently were at war during the conflict, making cooperation par-

---

13. This has been the case, for example, in the election campaign in Macedonia between the Ministry of Justice and the Ministry of Interior (RFE/RL *Newsline*, August 8).

14. There is the additional danger that these ministers primarily cater to their minority, rather than to all communities.

ticularly difficult. The emphasis on elite cooperation in theories of consociationalism is put to the test with the executives in postconflict states in the former Yugoslavia.[15]

Looking Beyond Power Sharing:
Group Rights and Escaping the Ethnic Question

As the overview of the different mechanisms of representation in power-sharing in Macedonia, Kosovo, and Bosnia highlight, these institutions alone are insufficient in transforming the respective polities into stable political systems that are not dominated by ethnic identities. While power-sharing systems can be improved and fine-tuned, additional mechanisms, including institutional ones, must be conceptualized to render the given societies stable. There is little doubt that, in deeply divided societies, some of which have a self-determination dispute at their core (Kosovo and Bosnia), majoritarian democracy and other conventional approaches to democratic institutions are insufficient. While accepting the need for power-sharing institutions, there are two policies which can mitigate some of the negative aspects of power sharing—the ethnification of institutions and inefficient decision making. This chapter will first argue that a stronger emphasis on group rights, rather than group protection, can help shift some aspects now firmly entrenched in the sphere of political decision making to less contested rights. Second, power-sharing systems must be conceived of as being more flexible and process oriented, eventually leading to a diminishing of ethnic identity, rather than static and unchangeable.

Group Rights and Power Sharing

As outlined above, approaches toward group inclusion generally concentrate either on *representation* or *cooperation*.[16] In debates about minority rights, the emphasis has been put on representation, as exemplified by the first article of the Lund Recommendations on the Effective Participation of Minorities in Public Life:

> Effective participation of national minorities in public life is an
> essential component of a peaceful and democratic society. Experience
> in Europe and elsewhere has shown that, in order to promote such

---

15. Lijphart (1977: 99–103) considers grand coalitions to be the most important element of consociationalism. See also Bogaards (1988: 33).

16. This divide is usually associated with Lijphart and Horowitz. For a short overview of the two alternative approaches, see Sisk (1996: 34–45).

participation, governments often need to establish *specific arrangements* [emphasis added] for national minorities. These Recommendations aim to facilitate the inclusion of minorities within the State and enable minorities to maintain their own identity and characteristics, thereby promoting the good governance and integrity of the State.[17]

The Lund Recommendations of 1999, drafted by international experts for the High Commissioner on National Minorities, is the first comprehensive list of mechanisms aimed at achieving minority inclusion in public institutions.[18] While referring to international human-rights protection mechanisms, the recommendations move well beyond international legal standards and, instead, draw from the rich experience of ensuring minority representation in numerous European countries. This experience argues that political participation constitutes an important aspect of minority-rights protection.

Instead of being understood as simply self-standing rights, political participation should be conceived of as an *instrument* of minority-rights protection. Recent experience in the former Yugoslavia, as will be reviewed in broad strokes, suggests that minority rights without minority participation in public institutions and the institutional framework of the protection of these rights has been largely ineffective. At the same time, political participation of minorities alone, without a comprehensive framework of minority-rights protection, as again will be explored on the basis of the former Yugoslavia, is equally inadequate for securing the rights of minorities. In fact, there has been a danger that, in the former Yugoslavia, political representation has received excessive importance over substantive minority rights.

The argument that minorities' rights cannot be protected without the participation of minorities in public life and in the mechanisms of protection is a straightforward point. First, the protective mechanisms run the risk of being irrelevant for the minority community, in other words, they might focus on the protection of educational rights, whereas social rights might be of more fundamental importance. This has been a common challenge with adequate protection of Roma communities across Eastern Europe. Second, enforcement has been a critical difficulty with minority-rights protection in the region.[19] Laws have often been

---

17. Foundation on Interethnic Relations (1999) *The Lund Recommendations on the Effective Participation of National Minorities in Public Life*, Art. 1.1.

18. The Framework Convention for the Protection of National Minorities contains only a vague commitment in Art. 15 to ensure the minorities' participation in public life.

19. Already the minority treaties, concluded with some countries after World War One, largely failed to improve the life of minorities due to the absence of enforcement and implementation.

drafted to satisfy international demands and criteria for accession to international organizations. However, states have been reluctant to implement these laws. This was the case particularly in Tudjman's Croatia and Milosevic's Yugoslavia. The reality for minorities was poor, despite the ideal minority-rights instruments that existed pro forma in the law (Varady, 1997). Admittedly, neither of the two were democracies during the 1990s, thus the lack of implementation of legal and democratic standards was not just limited to minorities. At the same time, similar difficulties, albeit less pronounced, can be found in the democracies of the region (OSI/EU Accession Monitoring Program, 2002). Enforcement through representation in state institutions and some autonomous minority institutions, such as exist in Hungary, are thus crucial for the protection of minority rights.

The case of Bosnia and Herzegovina and Macedonia exemplify, however, that political representation alone cannot suffice in protecting the interests of the different ethnic groups or in stabilizing these two countries. Nondominant groups[20] have enjoyed broad political representation in parliaments and governments. Both in Macedonia since the early 1990s and in Bosnia since the end of the war, coalition governments incorporated representatives of the different groups. While Macedonia did not possess specific tools for ensuring representation of Albanians in parliament or government, Albanian parties were never excluded from the political process. In Bosnia, equitable representation in parliament and government is constitutionally regulated at the state level and in the Bosniac-Croat Federation. In the Republika Srpska, however, the two nondominant groups, Croats and Bosniacs, were not represented in governments before the constitutional changes adopted in 2002 required this, although they did sit in the entity's parliament before the amendments. This degree of representation did not, however, provide sufficient safeguards for the protection of the nondominant groups. In Macedonia, the absence of adequate representation of Albanians in the state administration, especially in the police force, and the limited ability to use Albanian in the public administration, as well as other minority-rights related issues, furthered broad support among the Albanian population for the armed conflict during the spring and summer of 2001. In Bosnia,

---

20. In Bosnia, the term minorities is reserved for communities other than the three constituent peoples (Bosniacs, Serbs, and Croats). Thus, here the term nondominant groups refers to any of the three constituent people where they are not in a dominant position. Serbs in the Federation and Bosniacs and Croats in the Republika Srpska would qualify. Furthermore, Croats in Sarajevo or Bosniacs in Western Herzegovina would equally qualify. Key is the relationship to the respective layer of governance. Due to the dispersion of power among multiple layers, one individual can be non-dominant in his/her interaction with one layer, but not with another. In Macedonia, the term minority is more clear-cut, but no less continuous. Thus, the use of nondominant people primarily refers to the Albanian community, which has aspirations beyond the mere safeguard of minority rights.

nondominant groups fail to enjoy adequate rights in terms of employment and schooling and frequently faced discrimination in local administrations. This has been a key factor in delaying the so-called minority returns—refugees or internally displaced persons returning to their prewar residence in areas where they now constitute a nondominant group.

In both cases, the argument could be made that the inadequacies of minority protection derive from insufficient political representation. There is little doubt that there has been inadequate political representation of nondominant groups in both cases—Albanian parties tend take less seats in the Macedonian parliament than their share of the population would suggest. Likewise Croat and Bosniac parties were not included in governments or the administration of the Republika Srpska before 2002.[21] Nevertheless, a number of observations suggest that enhanced political representation is not the solution to facilitate the protection of the rights of nondominant groups.

First, political representation is largely unconcerned with cooperation between the different communities' representatives in the various political institutions and also less inclined to decree a share in the decision-making process. The reason for this is obvious. While it is easy to find legal instruments to ensure representation, neither cooperation nor co-decision making is easily legislated. In a number of cases, representation, even at the government level, does not translate into participation in the decision-making process. In fact, representation can lead to pluralistic window dressing with the dominant nation controlling the political process.

Second, in a system without firm legal safeguards for minority rights, these rights must be constantly negotiated by the representatives of the respective community. As ethnic issues often easily mobilize the electorate and might even have additional institutional safeguards (such as veto rights), parties have an interest in extending the sphere of ethnic issues. This leads to an ethnification of the political process, extending well beyond the narrow community interests.

Third, protecting the communities through political representation is likely to benefit larger communities with adequate representation and disadvantage smaller groups, who, either due their size or their weaker political mobilization, are less able to pursue their demands. Thus, minorities other than the three constituent nations in Bosnia and minorities other than Albanians in Macedonia have been largely excluded from negotiations of the protection of rights.

21. In 2001, for the first time a member of the Bosniac community became a minister in the Republika Srpska.

Fourth, representation of the nondominant group does not always equal representation of the entire group. Just as within majorities, minority communities often support largely different political options. Rights for the Croat minority in the Republika Srpska will be perceived to be largely different whether the Croatian deputy is from the multiethnic Social Democratic Party or the nationalist Croatian Democratic Community. As minority representation inherently will be less numerous than that of the majority, the entire diversity of the nondominant community will not be be represented. It could be argued that minority-rights protection can also protect the community from some its own political leaders.

Just as instruments protecting human rights and the rule of law are also necessary also in functioning democracies, minority rights cannot be short-circuited by political representation. Minorities can only be included in their state through representation and measures safeguarding of the rights of the group. Political representation without the protection of minority rights is likely to result in instability and arbitrariness such as is the case in a state governed by elections but missing legal safeguards preventing abuse by the state.

Escaping the Ethnic Question:
Toward a Process Oriented Conception of Power Sharing

It has often been argued that power-sharing systems run the risk of being excessively rigid. Also, some claim that due to their cumbersome decision-making procedures, these systems are less likely to adapt to changes over time compared to other forms of democracy (Schneckener, 2002). This is a serious concern, as many divided societies are in the developing world, where states must adapt to various types of transition, as is certainly the case in the countries discussed here. More significantly, power-sharing systems enshrine interethnic relations that are driven by highly volatile group identities, which can change significantly over time. Scholarship on power sharing often assumes the perennial nature of national identities and their interrelationships (Lijphart, 1991). While identity changes do not occur overnight, there can be little doubt that they change over the years. Such a development might be primarily qualitative, with different aspects of national identity gaining strength and others weakening (Schneckener, 2002: 485). For example, the protection of separate Croat and Serb languages was a crucial aspect of national identity in the first half of the 1990s, but it has become substantially less significant in recent years. Quantitative changes occur as well. While the degree of the increase of nationalism in the former Yugoslavia during the late 1980s is much contested, there is little dispute over the increase in national self-identification. Similarly, the importance of national identity in relation to other political identities has decreased in many other regions.

As power-sharing arrangements in the cases under consideration here were designed to end a violent conflict, they were all conceived at the height of interethnic confrontation. Thus, these arrangements give more prominence to a particular type of ethnic relations than might eventually develop in the postconflict society. For example, in Bosnia, Dayton's detailed requirements regarding the national identity of public officials means that ethnicity matters in institutions—even if this might no longer be the case in society at large.

Power-sharing systems can be conceptualized both as permanent unchangeable arrangements and as process oriented. For example, despite the clearly defined procedure for constitutional change contained in Art. X of Bosnia's constitution (Annex 4), the Dayton arrangement has been largely viewed as immutable. On the other hand, by its very nature as a framework, the Macedonian Framework Agreement implies a process of legal development rather than the conclusive settlement of all issues relating to interethnic relations. This is affirmed by one of its guiding principles as stated in Art. 1.4:

> A modern democratic state in its natural course of development and maturation must continually ensure that its Constitution fully meets the needs of all its citizens and comports with the highest international standards, which themselves continue to evolve.

In another consociational experiment, since 1943, Lebanon's constitutions have contained a commitment to the provisional character of confessionalism, which is the legally required practice of distributing political and administrative posts according to religion. Article 95 of the Constitution reads: "During the *transitional phase,* the confessional groups are to be represented in a just and equitable fashion in the formation of the cabinet" [empasis added]. The constitutional amendments of 1990, which contributed to the end of the war, reaffirmed and specified this commitment. The first transitory period lasted from the passing of the constitution in 1943 to the Tai'f Accords in 1990. The second transition has lasted already for well over a decade, and still no steps have been taken to changes the practice of confessionalism. In fact, Lebanon is often given as an example of the inflexibility of power-sharing arrangements (Sisk, 1996: 58). The situation in Lebanon suggests that a mere constitutional commitment to abandon or reduce power sharing is insufficient. Without detailed procedural provisions specifying how such a practice might be changed, it is unlikely to take place, due to (1) the vested interests of office holders, and (2) the need to first agree on the terms for negotiations on the process of changing the arrangement, which is essentially based on intergroup negotiations.

Postconflict power-sharing arrangements must have an inbuilt process allowing reform and change. More importantly, the power-sharing system must be conceptualized as such, rather than as a definite and conclusive arrangement that cannot be reconsidered. The case of the constitutional commissions in both Bosnian entities provide interesting example on how such a process could be institutionalized. The two bodies, appointed by the Office of the High Representative, contained members from the three constituent people and the "others" and were charged with drafting constitutional amendments required by a decision of the Bosnian constitutional court which aimed to safeguard the protection of the groups in the respective entities (Bieber, 2002a: 205–18; Perry, 2002). The commissions were eventually unsuccessful since the High Representative ultimately imposed the amendments, which differed from the proposals of the commissions. Nonetheless these commissions constitute the first attempt at managing constitutional change in special bodies charged with safeguarding group interests. As such, these commissions can be a model for a permanent system of negotiating change in power-sharing systems. Additional means could also include provisions in power-sharing systems that require review within a set period of time.

Whatever the tools used, a crucial consideration for postconflict power-sharing systems, as outlined above, must be their flexibility and ability to evolve over time to reflect (and encourage) changing interethnic relations.

Conclusion

Power sharing remains the most promising tool in managing deeply divided societies. As this chapter has sought to demonstrate, there is a great degree of variation in how such systems can be structured. Often, small institutional choices can have a significant impact on the performance of power-sharing systems. The comparison of the different cases in the former Yugoslavia should not suggest that there is one blueprint that will work equally well across different countries. Instead, the comparative analysis of different mechanisms demonstrates that a comprehensive evaluation of power sharing is in urgent need. Some tools in use, such as the combination of ethnic and territorial requirements in the Bosnian presidency, are clearly inadequate. Others, such as restrictive veto rights for minorities in Macedonia, might offer a way forward in rendering power sharing more successful.

As highlighted in the second half of this chapter, the improvement of power-sharing arrangements should not be the only factor considered. Strengthening group rights to match (and moderate) group representation will be of great importance to render power-sharing arrangements successful. Additionally, the systems must possess inbuilt mechanisms for change. Here one has to be careful to avoid letting high-profile constitutional debates disrupt negotiations in other spheres but rather ensure that there is a constant low-key process in place, which monitors and adjusts the existing arrangement.

Both approaches, strengthening group rights and establishing a process for change, seek to address a fundamental concern of divided societies after civil strife: fear. The immutabiity of power-sharing systems often results from the fear of the participants or the exploited fear of the constituent communities (Lake and Rothschild, 1997: 97–131). The very safeguards that are intended to reduce fear actually facilitate the rigidity of the system, itself a considerable source of concern. Although no legal standards can provide definitive protection against authorities or highly mobilized groups with no will for moderation, they do provide security in an environment where a minimum intergroup consensus exists. An institutionalized process of change has a two-fold function. First, it allows for regulated debate on the most contentious issues in the given polity—especially when a self-determination dispute is at the heart of the power-sharing system—seeking moderation through continuous contact between the communities. Second, it aims at changing the concept of interethnic institutional arrangements. Once any given constitution or institution is no longer perceived as a definite arrangement, compromise appears more possible.

Reducing fear in a postconflict environment is not an easy task and one that cannot be tackled by institutional arrangements themselves. Nevertheless, some of the approaches outlined above are more likely to be more conducive to cooperation and a long-term reduction of fear than others.

References

Bieber, Florian (2002a) "Bosnia-Herzegovina: Developments Towards a More Integrated State?" *Journal of Muslim Minority Affairs* 22(1) April: 205–18.

—— (2002b) "Regulating Elections in Post-War Bosnia: Success and Failure of Electoral Engineering in Divided Societies." Paper presented at the Workshop "Electoral Laws in Post-War Societies," Beirut, September 27–28.

Bogaards, Matthijs (1998) "The Favourable Factors for Consocational Democracy." *European Journal of Political Research* 33.

—— (2000) "The Uneasy Relationship Between Empirical and Normative Types of Consociational Theory." *Journal of Theoretical Politics* 12(4).

Cvijanovic, Zeljko (2001) "The Last Year of the Dayton Accords." Alterntivna Informativna Mreza [Alternative Information Network] AIM, June 6. www.aimpress.org.

European Commission for Democracy through Law (Venice Commission) (1999) "Electoral Law and National Minorities." Strasbourg, January 12. CDL-MIN (99) 1 rev. 2.

Henrard, Kristin (2000) *Devising an Adequate System of Minority Protection.* The Hague: Martinus Nijhoff Publishers.

Lake, David and Donald Rothchild (1977) "Containing Fear: The Origins and Management of Ethnic Conflict." In Michael E. Brown et al. (eds.) *Nationalism and Ethnic Conflict.* Cambridge: MIT Press.

Lebanese Constitution, 1990.

Lijphart, Arend (1977) *Democracy in Plural Societies. A Comparative Exploration.* New Haven: Yale University Press.

—— (1991) "The Power-Sharing Approach." In Joseph V. Montville (ed.) *Conflict and Peacemaking in Multiethnic Societies.* New York: Lexington.

Macedonian Framework Agreement, August 13, 2001.

McGarry, John and Brendan O'Leary (1993) "Introduction: The Macro-Political Regulation of Ethnic Conflict." In John McGarry and Brendan O'Leary (eds.) *The Politics of Ethnic Conflict Regulation: Case Studies of Protracted Ethnic Conflict.* London: Routledge.

Mehmeti, Ibrahim (1999) "Presidential Elections and Interethnic Relations in Macedonia." Alterntivna Informativna Mreza [Alternative Information Network] AIM. December 2. www.aimpress.org.

Myntti, Kristian (2001) *A Commentary to the Lund Recommendations on the Effective Participation of National Minorities in Public Life.* Åbo: Institute for Human Rights, Åbo Akademi University.

OSI/EU Accession Monitoring Program (2002) *Monitoring the EU Accession Process: Minority Protection* vol. 1. Budapest.

Perry, Valery (2002) "Constitutional Reform and the 'Spirit' of Bosnia and Herzegovina." European Centre of Minority Issues Brief No. 7, February.

Reilly, Ben and Andrew Reynolds (1999) *Electoral Systems and Conflict in Divided Societies.* Papers on International Conflict Resultion No. 1. Washington, D.C.: National Academy Press.

Schneckener, Ulrich (2002) *Auswege aus dem Bürgerkrieg.* Frankfurt: Suhrkamp, 321–33.

Sisk, Timothy D. (1996) *Power Sharing and International Mediation in Ethnic Conflicts.* Washington: USIP.

Todosijevic, Bojan (2001) "Macro-Political Means of Ethnic Conflict Management in Southeast Europe. A Critical Examination." *Southeast European Politics* 2 (2) October.

Varady, Tibor (1997) "Minorities, Majorities, Law, and Ethnicity: Reflections of the Yugoslav Case." *Human Rights Quarterly* 19.

Electoral Systems and the Management of Ethnic Conflict in the Balkans

Matthijs Bogaards

Introduction

The third wave of democratization has been accompanied by a resurgent faith in the crafting of democracies. An entire literature has developed around the issues of democracy promotion, constitutionalism, and electoral reform (for a recent collection, see Reynolds, 2002). Underlying the often fervent discussions about democratic design is the belief that institutions matter and that institutional choices can have profound effects on the prospects for new democracies. Traditionally, the choice of electoral system has been seen as a trade-off between representativeness and governability. Representativeness is associated with the electoral system of proportional representation in multimember electoral districts, while governability is associated with the electoral system of plurality majorities in single-member districts (Powell, 2000). The idea is that plurality systems result in a two-party system and single-party governments whereas proportional representation brings with it a multiparty (that is, more than two) system and coalition governments.

The *International Handbook for Electoral Design* tells governments: "When designing an electoral system, it is best to start with a list of criteria which sum up what you want to achieve, what you want to avoid and, in a broad sense, what you want your parliament and government to look like" (Reynolds and Reilly, 1997: 9). It lists eight criteria for design, but, for most purposes, these can be conflated into a single question: What kind of party system do you want? This question is of primary importance in heterogeneous societies, in which people differ from each other in language, religion, color of skin, or other socialcultural and ascriptive attributes. The way in which subnational cleavages are politically organized, or not, has important implications for ethnic-conflict management and democratic consolidation (see Lijphart, 1977, 1985; Horowitz, 1991, 1994).

As Dahl (1971: 223) noted: "The party system ... is not a natural, spontaneous or inevitable mirroring of social cleavages. It is dependent to some degree on electoral arrangements. And these can be deliberately manipulated in order to maximize or minimize fragmentation."[1] In fact, electoral-system design can be used for a wide range of purposes, including ethnic-conflict management. Sartori (1968: 273) famously called electoral systems the "most specific manipulative instruments of politics." This chapter explores how electoral arrangements can and have been used in the Balkans to shape the political organization of ethnic cleavages in the emerging party systems and how these choices have contributed to or detracted from achieving social peace and democratic consolidation. In the process, the chapter will propose corrections to two prevailing conceptions about electoral engineering for conflict management. First, the current preoccupation with electoral systems should not obscure that, in a heterogeneous society, the choice of electoral system follows from the choice of party-system function, that is, the desired role of the party system as an intermediary between social and political cleavages. Second, the longstanding juxtaposition of plurality elections or first-past-the-post (FPTP) and proportional representation (PR) loses much of its relevance when sociocultural groups are geographically concentrated, as is the case in the Balkans. Rather, the menu of choice is between electoral systems that promote aggregation of sociocultural divisions and those that facilitate the political translation of ethnic differences.

Party-System Functions

Modern politics is party politics, and modern democracy is party democracy. In Sartori's (1976: ix) words, "Parties are the central intermediate and intermediary structure between society and government." Looking at the way parties connect society and government, three party-system functions can be distinguished. The party system can *aggregate* social cleavages, *translate* social cleavages into political cleavages, or *block* the politicization of social cleavages. The three party-system functions correspond with the three models of party system that are still at the basis of most party-system typologies: the one-party state, a two-party system, and a multiparty system. There is a strong if imperfect correlation between the relevant number of parties, relevant to the formation of government (Sartori, 1976) and the dominant function of the party system. The one-party state maximizes blocking; the two-party system is thought to be best in achieving aggregation; the multiparty system is most suited to translation.

1. Zielinski (2002) has rediscovered this fact and without referring to the crucial role of electoral institutions points at the importance of the early stages of party-system formation.

Table 1

Party-System Models

Type of party system	One-party	Two-party	Multi-party
Number of relevant parties	one	two	more than two
Party system function	blocking	aggregation	translation

The avowed function of the one-party state is to block the political translation of sociocultural cleavages through political parties. Ethnicity, religion, language, and culture are considered such highly divisive issues that their politicization must be prevented. The one-party state keeps social differences out of electoral politics, at least nominally. Any electoral competition will be between individuals. The most powerful apologetics of the single party used to claim that nation building and integration of population groups could only be achieved through the "one-party, no cleavage state" (Bienen, 1971).

The classic British or Westminster two-party system has the avowed function of aggregating cleavages. The case for the two-party system is based on its aggregative potential. Because there are only two parties, by necessity, they must aggregate a diversity of interests, resulting in heterogeneous parties. As Almond and Powell (1966: 102) pointed out, "some party systems aggregate interests much more effectively than others. The number of parties is a factor of importance. Two-party systems which are responsible to a broad electorate are usually forced toward aggregative policies."

Proponents of proportionality, the multiparty system, and parliamentary government, such as Lijphart (1977, 1999), reason that, since the political organization of social differences is an intrinsic part of democracy and since these differences cannot be reconciled at the mass level, this translation through so-called segmental parties should be as precise as possible so that social differences can be accommodated at the elite level. The political-cleavage structure should be an exact copy of the social-cleavage structure. The translation function is not merely appreciated because of its instrumental role in making elite accommodation possible, it is also seen as a goal in itself.

Although the different party-system functions correspond closely to the number of relevant parties and concomitant party-system models, function cannot be reduced to number nor can the number of relevant parties be derived from function. As will be shown below, the blocking function is optimized in the one-party state but not restricted to this regime type. Although the two-party system in general optimizes aggregation, it can also reflect major divisions, as in the case of a bipolar society. Consociational democracy combines a translation of some cleavages with an aggregation of others. The neo-Marxist critique of consociational democracy in the Netherlands, for instance, holds that the politicization of religion obscured class cleavages and hindered their political organization (Kieve, 1981). Because political elites were suspected of doing this on purpose, one could even detect a blocking function.

Choosing a Party System (Function)

The literature on electoral-systems design and electoral choice for divided societies is strongly centered on means rather than ends, on the question of "how" rather than "what for." This single-minded emphasis on the independent variable of the electoral system has come at the expense of attention to the party system as the dependent variable. The argument developed in this chapter is that the choice of electoral system is only of second order importance. The first thing to clarify when designing or redesigning the representative institutions of a modern democracy, especially in a heterogeneous society, should be: How does one see the role of the party system as an intermediary between society and government? Should the party system block the politicization of ethnicity and religion by restricting political competition to ideological and socioeconomic issues? Should it aggregate sociocultural divisions in broad-based multiethnic or explicitly nonethnic parties? Or rather, should it translate social cleavages into political fault lines through ethnic parties? In case none of these pure functions is deemed desirable, should a mix of party-system functions be pursued, and, if so, what should the balance be? In other words, choosing a party-system function comes first. The choice of electoral system follows logically from the choice of party-system function. How party-system function relates to electoral-system features is shown in table 2. Electoral systems are listed roughly on the basis of their expected effectiveness, with the electoral system most likely to achieve the designated party-system function at the top of each cell.

The blocking function can be achieved through a one-party state, the denial of voting rights to minorities, party bans and plurality and majority elections (double ballot) in single-member districts in case of a dispersed minority. In a democracy, the first two options are clearly not sustainable. Several Western democracies have legislation prohibiting antidemocratic parties, notably Germany, but none ban subnational parties (Gordon, 1987; Avnon, 1995). Dispersed minorities will find it exceedingly difficult to win seats under plurality elections in single-member districts, effectively having their representation blocked. Sartori (1994) recommends the double ballot because it offers voters the possibility of revealing their true preferences in the first round with a more strategic choice in the second round, after parties have bargained for cross-party support. In France, the double ballot has contributed to the exclusion of extremist parties from parliament. Little is known about how two-round majority elections perform in heterogeneous societies, although it would seem to disadvantage dispersed minorities, especially when they cannot agree alliances with other parties.

Table 2

The Function of Party Systems and the Choice of Electoral System

Party-system function	Appropriate electoral system
Blocking	• One-party state • Denial of voting rights to minorities • Party bans • Majority elections (double ballot) in single-member districts (in case of dispersed minorities) • Plurality elections (in case of dispersed minorities)
Aggregation	• Alternative vote (AV) • Single transferable vote (STV) • Distribution requirement • Cross-ethnic list voting • Multi-ethnic list voting
Translation	• Communal rolls • Reserved seats for minorities • List proportional representation (PR) • Minority parties exempted from electoral threshold • Plurality and majority elections in single-member districts (in case of concentrated minorities)

Aggregation can be achieved through a range of electoral systems. The choice of electoral system depends on three factors: the number and relative size of social groups, their geographical distribution or concentration, and the existing party system. The classic idea of a moderate two-party system with broad-based parties that converge toward the center, stimulated by plurality elections in single-member districts, only applies to homogeneous societies. In heterogeneous societies with communal voting, plurality elections will not produce aggregation. Five electoral systems will: preferential voting in the form of the alternative vote or the single transferable vote, cross-ethnic and multiethnic list voting, and vote distribution requirements.

The alternative vote (AV) is a preferential majority voting system with strong incentives for vote pooling given the right circumstances. Vote pooling occurs in a heterogeneous society when political leaders seek support outside their own group to win elections, and voters exchange votes across group boundaries. AV asks voters to rank the candidates. If a candidate receives an absolute majority of first preferences, he or she is elected; if not, the weakest candidate is eliminated, and the ballots with that candidate as first preference are redistributed according to the second preferences. This process continues until one of the candidates has gathered a majority of the votes and wins the seat. When no party in a district can count on an outright majority, AV necessitates electoral cooperation between the parties, and "to obtain votes across ethnic and racial lines by agreements with other parties to trade second or third or fourth preferences, reciprocal moderation on ethnic or racial issues is required" (Horowitz, 1991: 177). Not all parties follow this strategy. Alongside vote pooling parties, flank parties will arise. These are "ethnically based parties surrounding a multi-ethnic coalition and typically espousing ethnically more extreme positions than the coalition, with its mixed support, is able to do" (ibid: 167). Ethnic voters will tend to cast their first preference for one of these flank parties that appeal to their primary identities but may give their lower preferences to more moderate and inclusive candidates, perhaps even from other sociocultural groups.

AV is not widely practiced. Australia uses AV in elections for the most important chamber of parliament. Papua New Guinea, a highly diverse society, recently reintroduced AV. Reilly (2001: 94) presents a favorable review of the preindependence experience with AV in Papua New Guinea, especially when compared to the performance of the first-past-the-post system in use since independence, concluding that "it would be hard to find a clearer example of the importance of political institutions in general, or the case for centripetal strategies of institutional design in particular."

AV only leads to vote pooling under two conditions: a multiparty system and heterogeneous electoral districts. The fewer are the parties or candidates that contest the elections, the greater the likelihood of a party winning on the basis of its own support group and the less the need to reach out to other groups. According to Reilly (2001), three parties or groups would be the minimum number necessary for vote pooling to occur, implying that AV is less likely to work in bipolar societies. The second precondition for a vote pooling effect of AV is heterogeneous electoral districts, where heterogeneity stands for the absence of an ethnic majority. In the case of a limited number of groups who are geographically concentrated, it may be difficult to draw heterogeneous districts. This is the situation in the Balkans. The precondition of heterogeneous electoral districts without a majority group able to secure a majority on first preferences shows the importance of group demographics and political geography for the working of the electoral system. To a certain extent, the preconditions are contradictory. As a majoritarian electoral system, AV has a relatively high disproportionality. It is well known that the number of political parties is inversely related to the electoral system's degree of proportionality (Sartori, 1968; Lijphart, 1994).

The single transferable vote (STV), practiced in Ireland, Malta, and Australia, supports a measure of interethnic vote pooling or aggregation. STV is a proportional electoral system practiced in small multimember districts with typically between three and eight seats. Voters are required to number the candidates in order of preference. To be elected, a candidate must win a quota and the larger the number of seats, the lower the quota. This logic is common to all proportional electoral systems. Typical for STV is its preferential voting scheme and the transfer of votes. Superfluous votes for candidates who have already won a seat and the votes for the lowest ranked candidates are redistributed until all seats are filled. Under STV, a candidate needs a lower percentage of the vote to be elected than under AV. This reduces the need for candidates to reach out and broaden their appeal. STV is a proportional electoral system and gives only weak incentives for moderation. STV failed to produce moderation in Northern Ireland in the 1970s but was more successful in the 1998 elections (Reilly, 2001). STV was used for the first post-Soviet parliamentary elections in Estonia in 1990, but there is little evidence of interethnic voting (ibid). In 1992, Estonia changed to list PR. Because STV works with multimember districts, it is somewhat easier to draw the necessary heterogeneous districts than with AV, practiced in single-member districts. Although preferential voting schemes are sometimes criticized for being difficult, the only real difficulty in STV is the counting of the votes, which is done by electoral officials. The actual casting of the vote is only complicated by the need to rank candidates, which admittedly requires the voter to know more candidates that just the favorite.

Two more unusual electoral systems that promote aggregation are a distribution requirement and what could be called cross-ethnic list voting. In Nigeria and Kenya, the successful presidential candidate not only has to win an overall majority or plurality respectively, he/she also has to draw a minimum percentage of votes from a minimum number of regions (see Horowitz, 1991).[2] The obvious problem with this requirement, which has been suggested for presidential elections in Bosnia (see International Crisis Group, 1999), is the possibility of inconclusive elections. A final method of promoting cross-ethnic voting is the proposal of the International Crisis Group (1999) to place Bosnia's parties on three ethnic lists, give each voter three votes, and have them cast a vote for a party on each ethnic list. The expectation is that voters will vote for a nationalist party on their own ethnic list but prefer a moderate party on the other two lists. Combined with proportional representation, this should result in a stronger presence of moderate parties in parliament. The paradox of this system is that it places parties on ethnic lists as a means to overcome ethnic voting.

---

2. Applied to party registration, a distribution requirement for signatures or membership can easily turn into an instrument of blocking. This is what happened in Russia (Flores Juberías, 2000).

An easier solution is to require each party to field multiethnic lists, as happens in Lebanon.

The party-system function of translation can be ensured through the adoption of reserved seats and communal rolls. Both procedures are contested as they rely on the predetermination of sociocultural groups and the identification of candidates and/or voters as belonging to designated groups. This implies that separate voter registers must be maintained or candidates need to declare the ethnic group they are standing for. More commonly and less controversially, translation is best served by list proportional representation although it can also be achieved with plurality elections in case of geographically concentrated minorities. PR facilitates the political organization of small social groups that do not have to be geographically concentrated to have a chance of parliamentary representation. The number of relevant parties can be reduced through the adoption of an electoral threshold. Lest the threshold inadvertently bar ethnic minority parties, they can be exempted from it. In certain circumstances, overrepresentation of a minority can be recommended (Lijphart, 1986).

If blocking simply aims to keep ethnicity out of politics, and aggregation reconciles conflicting interests and values within parties, a party system based on the faithful translation of ethnic cleavages into political cleavages does little to accommodate them. The problems are simply projected onto the state's decision-making bodies, where additional arrangements are required in the form of power sharing. Horowitz (1991: 171) warns that "... the mere need to form a coalition will not produce compromise." Post-Dayton Bosnia provides a graphic illustration of this shortcoming, despite the elaborate power-sharing arrangements (Bose, 2002).

In sum, it is possible to categorize electoral systems on the basis of the party-system functions they promote. However, the function of an electoral system can never be assessed independent of the social and institutional context in which it is applied. How a particular electoral system functions in a divided society crucially depends on context. This is well illustrated by the fact that plurality elections can result in blocking or translation depending on the size and geographical distribution of social groups.

Electoral Choices in the Balkans

After having elaborated the framework of party-system function and electoral-system design, it is now possible to examine the experiences in the Balkans. Cases covered include Albania, Bulgaria, Romania, Kosovo, and four of the six former Yugoslav republics—Bosnia and Herzegovina, Croatia, Macedonia, and Slovenia. The analysis aims to establish what type of function constitutional and electoral engineers envisioned for the party system, what electoral institutions were put into place, and how these have helped to manage ethnic conflict. Table 3 gives an overview of contemporary party-system functions and electoral systems in the region. To simplify representation and keep the analysis focused on the main issues, no details of electoral reforms are given (for a useful overview, see Shvetsova, 1999).

Table 3
Party-System Function and Electoral-System Design in the Balkans

Party-system function	Electoral system	Political system
Blocking	Party bans	Albania Bosnia and Herzegovina (1990) Bulgaria
Aggregation	AV	Republic Srpska's presidential elections in 2000
Translation	Reserved minority seats	Croatia Kosovo Romania Slovenia
	Double ballot/PR	Macedonia
	List PR	Federation of Bosnia and Herzegovina Kosovo Macedonia Republic Srpska Romania Slovenia

Three countries have pursued blocking through party bans: Bosnia and Herzegovina, Bulgaria, and Albania. It is surely a cruel irony that the first parliament in the region to ban political organization on the basis of nationality (ethnicity) was the Bosnian parliament in the electoral law of March 1990. The Constitutional Court declared this provision unconstitutional and removed it from the law under which the 1990 elections were later conducted (Burg and Shoup, 1999: 46). Bulgaria prohibits parties on a subnational basis. The last all-communist parliament passed a law on political parties in 1990 containing a provision banning "political parties formed on an ethnic basis" (Ganev, forthcoming). However, this did not prevent the Sofia District Court from registering the Turkish-based Movement for Rights and Freedoms (MRF). In the elections later that year, the MRF proceeded to win 6 percent of the votes and 23 of parliament's 400 seats. It is claimed that 90 percent of the MRF's members and voters are ethnic Turks (Ilchev, 2000: 252). Article 11 of the new constitution of 1991 stipulates that "there shall be no political parties organized on ethnic, racial or religious lines, nor parties which advocate the violent seizure of state power." The next article specifies that "citizen associations, including trade unions, shall not pursue any political objectives, nor shall they engage in political activity which belongs in the domain of political parties." An attempt to seek registration as the Party of Rights and Freedoms failed. The Central Electoral Commission rejected the application, and the Supreme Court upheld this decision. The organization then sought registration under its old name, claiming its 1990 registration was still valid. The Central Electoral Commission accepted this by a 13–12 vote, only to have this decision appealed before the Constitutional Court by the Bulgarian Socialist Party. The Constitutional Court finally ruled in favor of the MRF by the narrowest of margins in a complex and nuanced judgment that placed the ban on ethnic parties in the context of other constitutional principles, prominently that of democratic pluralism, concluding that the MRF did not threaten the constitutional order (see Ganev; Smilov, 2002). The MRF has since played a pivotal role in Bulgarian politics, often being a necessary partner in the coalition governments that rule the country, including the current government of former king Simeon II. In 2000, the Constitutional Court did ban OMO Ilinden-PIRIN, a tiny Macedonian party that collected 2,000 votes in local elections in 1999. The party was judged unconstitutional on the basis of Article 44.2, which contains a prohibition of parties whose activity is "directed against the sovereignty, the territorial integrity of the country, and the unity of the nation" (Smilov, 2002).

Albania banned "parties based on religious, ethnic or regional bases" in the Law on Political Parties of July 1992. Because the electoral law stipulated that only political parties, coalitions of parties, or individuals would have the right to field electoral candidates, the failure to register religious, ethnic, or regional parties would lead to their exclusion from political competition. While this measure was initially proposed to veto the old satellite organizations of the Worker's Party, it directly affected Omonia, a Greek minority group from the south that had obtained five seats in the 1990 elections. Omonia had been able to participate in the elections as a movement but was forced to transform itself into a political party on the basis of the electoral law. However, according to the law on political parties, it was not eligible for registration because it had an ethnic and regional basis. "Faced with domestic and international pressure—the latter coming mainly from the Greek government," Flores Juberías (2000: 38) reports, "the Ministry of Justice ultimately accepted the registration of a Party for Defense of Human Rights, which was simply Omonia broadened slightly to admit some ethnic Albanians into its ranks under a name that, like the Movement for Rights and Freedom (MRF) in Bulgaria, couched the party's ethnic appeal in a universal idiom." The party still exists and won three seats in the 2001 elections, although its position remains difficult (Pettifer, 2000).

In Bulgaria and Albania, the combination of a party monopoly on nomination, and a simultaneous, if formally independent, prohibition of subnational parties threatened to undo the cultural minority party. These measures were a deliberate and purposeful attempt by the main political parties to exclude by law an established ethnopolitical force from political competition and representation. In both cases, the measures were directed at an organization that had already demonstrated its popularity and electoral support in free and competitive elections by winning representation in the national parliament. Significantly, in both cases, minority parties were ultimately accepted as human-rights parties. In Bulgaria, the ban on ethnic and religious parties was not officially stricken. In Albania the draft of the new constitution included a prohibition of political parties with a religious or ethnic basis, but the clause was dropped for the 1998 constitution. This happened after protest from international organizations (see Venice Commission, 1995). In general, international organizations are highly critical of any attempt at restricting the freedom of association, especially of minority parties, and only allow for a ban on political parties that promote or engage in violence (Venice Commission, 2000; OSCE, 2001).[3]

It is significant that aggregation is largely absent as a party-system function in the Balkans. STV and AV have not been used for parliamentary elections. AV has been used in the Republic Srpska in the presidential election of 2000. Observers agree it had no impact on ethnic accommodation (Reilly, 2001; Bieber, 2002), while one commentator even suggests AV helped consolidate the Serb electorate behind the victorious extremist party (Bose, 2002: 232). Clearly, AV will not result in cross-ethnic vote pooling in largely monoethnic elections. For the same reason, there is little point in having Bosniacs, Croats, and Serbs elect their own representative on Bosnia's tripartite state presidency using AV, as was proposed by the Office of the High Representative in 1999 (Reilly, 2001).

As can be seen in table 3, translation is by far the most popular party-system function in the Balkans.[4] The prevalence of PR or a mixed system with a PR component in heterogeneous societies is itself an indicator that the electoral system aims at a party system mirroring sociocultural cleavages. Because of the geographical concentration of minorities in the region, it does not matter greatly whether PR,

3. Other means of blocking are also ruled out as evidenced by the international reaction against the denial of voting rights to Russian minorities in Estonia and Latvia (Benoît-Rohmer and Hardeman, 1994).
4. For Bosnia and Herzegovina, only the direct elections to the parliaments of the constituent units are included.

FPTP, or the double ballot are used, either by themselves, or in combination (for an overview of mixed electoral systems, see Kostadinova, 2002). For example, due to their geographical concentration, Albanian minority parties in Macedonia were able to win seats in majoritarian single-member districts as well as on the PR list.[5] The translation function is buttressed by the use of reserved seats for minorities in Romania, Croatia, Slovenia, and Kosovo.[6] Reserved seats for minorities guarantee that designated sociocultural differences find political translation.

Of particular interest is the article in Croatia's electoral law, adopted in 1992, which explicitly introduced the notion of ethic proportionality. Article 10.1 specified that ethnic minorities with a share of the population of 8 percent or more are entitled "to be represented in the Parliament proportionally to their respective participation in the overall population" (Flores Juberías, 2000: 46). This principle was conceived mainly to satisfy the Serbian minority, estimated at around 11.5 percent of the population, translating into 13 seats. In order to fulfill this goal, article 26.1 of the electoral law ordered that if the stipulated share of the legislature was not achieved through the usual procedures, that is, by having ethnic Serbs elected on party lists, the "number of the representatives of the House of Representatives shall increase up to the number which is needed for the required representation to be attained, and the members of a certain community or a minority, who have been put up on the state list, but have not been elected, shall be considered as elected representatives in the order corresponding to the proportional success of each individual list in the elections" (Flores Juberías, 2000: 47). If, after this procedure, the preordered number of representatives was not elected, by-elections would be called in special electoral units. Since no deputies of Serbian origin were elected directly to parliament in 1992, the relevant parts of the electoral law were immediately activated. In addition to five independent Serbian candidates who had belonged to the former communist party, eight Serbian partisan candidates from three different parties obtained seats. Three of them belonged to the Serbian People's Party, which failed to meet the 3 percent threshold, but then saw the Constitutional Court rule that this threshold did not apply to it as an ethnic Serb party (Zakosek, 2000).[7]

5. In 1990 and 1994, Macedonia used the double ballot; in 1998, a combination of majoritarian elections and PR was introduced; while in 2002 all seats were elected with PR.
6. Hungarian parties are still debating how the constitutional requirement for minority representation in the national parliament should be organized (PER, 2001).
7. Ethnic minority parties are also exempted from passing the electoral threshold in Poland and Lithuania, allowing German and Polish parties into their respective parliaments.

This extraordinary procedure testifies to the belief, although perhaps more of the international community than the Croat regime itself, in the desirability of ethnic proportionality in parliament and a commitment to ensure that translation is achieved even if regular party competition fails to do so. The record of Serb parties up to that point justified a party ban more than special provisions. The main party of the Serb minority, the extreme nationalist Serb Democratic Party, withdrew from parliament after elections in 1990, and proclaimed secession of the territories under its control (Jovic, 1996). In any case, in the context of the Croatian Democratic Union's strong hold on parliament and the presidency, minority participation was little more than token.

The electoral law employed for the elections in 1995 reduced the special Serbian minority representation from 13 to 3 deputies, elected with special ethnic lists in one national district. The justification for this cut was the Serb exodus caused by the fall of the separatist republic in the Krajina, reducing the Serb share of the population to under the 8 percent entitling it legally to parliamentary representation. The four seats reserved for other minorities were maintained (Nohlen and Kasapovic, 1996). Slovenia stands out because its Hungarian and Italian minorities have a constitutional right to parliamentary representation. Moreover, minority voters in Slovenia have two votes: one for their minority representative in parliament and one to elect a representative through the general electoral system. This constitutes a deviation from the principle of one person, one vote but may be interpreted as reflecting a desire to provide minority representation while simultaneously integrating minorities into the political system at large through participation in the general elections for parliament. In Kosovo, voters have only one vote, but minority parties can win double seats, violating the principle that votes should have equal weight. Apart from competing for representation in the 100-seat legislature, self-declared ethnic parties can win additional seats in the competition for the ten seats set apart for the Serb community and another ten seats for other communities (Roma, 4; Bosniacs, 3; Turks, 2; and Gorani, 1).

In Romania, there was no official national attempt at outmaneuvering the political organizations of the national minority, despite the vociferous presence of extreme-right and nationalistic Romanian political forces. Already in the first elections, the Hungarian Democratic Union of Romanians won a solid 7 percent of the seats. Not only did Romania not try to ban ethnic minority political organizations, as in Albania and Bulgaria, the electoral law even provided for the parliamentary representation of minorities which were so tiny that their candidates were unlikely to win a seat even under PR. Romania has the most extensive provisions in the region for electing national minorities, and their number in parliament has risen to 19 after the 2000 elections (Deets, 2002).

Conclusion

Against the background of several postcommunist states destroyed by ethnic conflict, "scholars and politicians must find ways to accommodate ethnic interests so that democracy can proceed" (Hesli, 1997: 213). How have electoral systems contributed to ethnic-conflict management in the Balkans? Clearly, blocking the politicization of ethnic cleavages through a ban on ethnic, religious, and regional parties has not worked. Bosnia and Herzegovina repealed the clause, and Albania and Bulgaria desisted from enforcing the party bans that threatened to exclude their main national minorities from political participation and representation. This is undoubtedly for the better. The exclusion of the Turkish minority party in Bulgaria could have led to serious ethnic conflict with international ramifications. From the start, most countries in the region have opted for translation as the dominant party-system function. This resulted in the adoption of PR, either by itself or as part of mixed electoral systems, often reinforced with provisions for special minority representation. Due to the geographical concentration of minorities in the region, the choice between PR, plurality elections in single-member districts, and the majoritarian double ballot loses much of its relevance for the determination of party-system function. All three are likely to result in translation whether they are used by themselves or combined in a mixed electoral system. The real difference is between electoral systems that promote aggregation and those that facilitate translation. Apart from one rather pointless experiment with AV in the Republic Srpska's presidential election in 2000, there has been no attempt at aggregation in the Balkans. This leaves three questions to be answered. Why is translation as the dominant party-system function so popular? What have been the consequences of this choice of party-system function for ethnic-conflict management? And, if aggregation is deemed desirable, how can it be achieved?

The answer to the first question, regarding the popularity of the translation function and ethnic proportionality, has both a domestic and international component. A domestic motive is that translation allows ethnic political entrepreneurs to mobilize a predictable segment of the electorate. Translation through PR has also been promoted by the international community (Krastev, 2002). As a consequence, ethnic groups have been turned into legitimate participants in the political process. In Albania, Bulgaria, and Romania, this has been enough to avoid serious ethnic conflict. The pivotal role of minority parties in coalition governments in Bulgaria and Romania has also contributed to this outcome.

Comparative research on the relationship between electoral system, inclusiveness, and ethnic conflict is inconclusive. Using data from the Minorities at Risk project, Cohen (1997: 628) concludes that "proportional institutions are more effective than majoritarian institutions as democratic instruments of ethnic-conflict management."

Ishiyama (2000, 2001) finds that, in postcommunist politics, the degree of minority representation is inversely related to indicators of ethnic political protest and positively related to satisfaction with democracy. However, based on a much broader set of cases, Norris (2002: 233) reports that the "claim that PR party-list systems are directly associated with higher levels of political support among ethnic minorities is not confirmed by this study." In Bosnia and Kosovo, parties faithfully translate ethnic cleavages into political cleavages. This has done little to bring about social peace. In both political systems, elaborate power-sharing arrangements are in place (Bieber, 2002, 2003). For some time, Macedonia seemed to have secured a modicum of ethnic peace through coalition governments representing both the Macedonian majority and the Albanian minority (Szajkowski, 2000) before the war in Kosovo threatened to spill over. Macedonia only escaped civil war thanks to intensive foreign intermediation.

The experience in postconflict societies seems to indicate that an ethnically representative party system needs to be accompanied by extensive power-sharing arrangements. This is in line with consociational theory, which holds that consociational democracy is the only form of democracy likely to succeed in divided societies. Segmental parties representing specific sociocultural groups are the reason for and building blocks of consociational democracy although proportionality is only one of the four features. The other three consociational characteristics are a grand coalition, segmental autonomy, and a mutual veto (Lijphart, 1977). Divided societies need the entire package. In their overview of electoral systems and conflict in divided societies, Reilly and Reynolds (1999: 30) refer to the experience of list PR in post-Dayton Bosnia as a good example of how proportionality alone will not encourage accommodation. On the contrary, it serves to entrench ethnic divisions (Scholdan, 2000; Flores Juberías, 2000; Snyder, 2000; Bose, 2002).

In contrast, a party system based on aggregation is inherently moderating with an inbuilt tendency to depoliticize ethnic differences. It helps, of course, if other institutions, like federalism, reinforce such tendencies, but electoral-system design by itself can already provide important incentives toward aggregation and the emergence of cross-cutting cleavages. If Dayton and Rambouillet the peace agreement in Kosovo), resulted in a "patchwork that essentially perpetuates existing cleavages" and a "dynamic system is needed" (Bieber, 2001: 118), then aggregation becomes more attractive as the dominant party-system function. Reilly (1999: 120) concurs, concluding that "consociationalism may be a very good strategy for deeply divided societies in transition, but less appropriate for such societies attempting to promote democratic consolidation." Proponents of aggregation promoting electoral systems acknowledge that "systems which require a degree of bargaining and cross-ethnic voting may be less realistic in extremely divided societies ... than in cases where there is a degree of fluidity to ethnic identities" (Reilly and Reynolds, 1999: 53), and Bose (2002) expresses concern about the feasibility of integrative strategies in a fragile political system like that of Bosnia. Fortunately, it may not be necessary to choose between translation and aggregation. STV is a proportional electoral system that stimulates aggregation and facilitates translation.[8] Because it is practiced in relatively small constituencies, it also allows for a minimum of constituency representation. Provided heterogeneous electoral districts can be created, STV appears to offer an attractive combination of features that explains its increasing popularity among students of democracy in divided societies (see Reynolds, 1999; Reilly, 2001). As existing parties do not directly stand to lose by a change from list PR or a mixed electoral system to STV, electoral reform would appear feasible. If power-sharing arrangements are present, these should probably be maintained. Adoption of STV would signify a modest step in the pursuit of aggregation as a desirable party-system function for ethnically divided societies in the region.

References

Almond, Gabriel and Bingham G. Powell, Jr. (1966) *Comparative Politics: A Developmental Approach.* Boston: Little Brown.

Avnon, Dan (1995) "Parties Laws in Democratic Systems of Government." *The Journal of Legislative Studies* 1(2): 283–300.

Benoît-Rohmer, Florence and Hilde Hardeman (1994) "The Representation of Minorities in the Parliaments of Central and Eastern Europe." *International Journal on Group Rights* 2: 91–111.

Bieber, Florian (2001) "The Challenge of Democracy in Divided Societies: Lessons from Bosnia—Challenges for Kosovo." In Dzemal Sokolovic and Florian Bieber (eds.) *Reconstructing Multiethnic Societies: The Case of Bosnia-Herzegovina.* Aldershot: Ashgate, 109–21.

—— (2002) *Regulating Elections in Post-War Bosnia: Success and Failure of Electoral Engineering in Divided Societies.* Paper presented at the workshop on Electoral Laws in Post-War Societies, Beirut, September 27–28.

—— (2003) "Power Sharing as Ethnic Representation in Postconflict Societies: The Cases of Bosnia, Macedonia, and Kosovo," this volume.

Bienen, Henry (1971) "One-Party Systems in Africa." In Samuel Huntington and Clement H. Moore (eds.) *Authoritarian Politics in Modern Society: The Dynamics of Established One-Party Systems.* New York: Basic Books, 99–127.

8. For Bosnia, Emerson (2001) proposes a Quota Borda System to achieve the same goal.

Bose, Sumantra (2002) *Bosnia after Dayton: Nationalist Partition and International Intervention*. London: Hurst & Company.

Burg, Steven L. and Paul S. Shoup (1999) *The War in Bosnia-Herzegovina: Ethnic Conflict and International Intervention*. Armonk: M.E. Sharpe.

Cohen, Frank S. (1997) "Proportional Versus Majoritarian Ethnic Conflict Management in Democracies." *Comparative Political Studies* 30(5): 607–30.

Dahl, Robert A. (1971) *Polyarchy: Participation and Opposition*. New Haven: Yale University Press.

Deets, Stephen (2002) "Reconsidering East European Minority Policy: Liberal Theory and European Norms." *East European Politics and Society* 16(1): 30–53.

Emerson, Peter (2001) "How a Quota Borda System of Elections May Facilitate Reconciliation." In Dzemal Sokolovic and Florian Bieber (eds.) *Reconstructing Multiethnic Societies: The Case of Bosnia-Herzegovina*. Aldershot: Ashgate, 147–56.

Flores Juberías, Carlos (2000) "Post-Communist Electoral Systems and National Minorities: A Dilemma in Five Paradigms." In Jonathan P. Stein (ed.) *The Politics of National Minority Participation in Post-Communist Europe: State-Building, Democracy, and Ethnic Mobilization*. Armonk: M.E. Sharpe, 31–64.

Ganev, Venelin I. (forthcoming) "History, Politics and the Constitution: Ethnic Conflict and Constitutional Adjudication in Postcommunist Bulgaria." *Slavic Review.*

Gordon, Dan (1987) "Limits on Extremist Parties: A Comparison of Israeli Jurisprudence with that of the United States and West Germany." *Hastings International and Comparative Law Review* 10: 347–400.

Hesli, Vicki L. (1997) "Political Institutions and Democratic Governance in Divided Societies." In Robert D. Grey (ed.) *Democratic Theory and Post-Communist Change*. Upper Saddle River: Prentice Hall, 190–216.

Horowitz, Donald (1991) *A Democratic South Africa? Constitutional Engineering in a Divided Society*. Berkeley: University of California Press.

—— (1994) "Democracy in Divided Societies." In Larry Diamond and Marc F. Plattner (eds.) *Nationalism, Ethnic Conflict, and Democracy*. Baltimore: The Johns Hopkins University Press, 35–55.

Ilchev, Ivan (2000) "Emigration and the Politics of Identity: The Turkish Minority in Bulgaria." In Jonathan P. Stein (ed.) *The Politics of National Minority Participation in Post-Communist Europe: State-Building, Democracy, and Ethnic Mobilization*. Armonk: M.E. Sharpe, 237–68.

International Crisis Group (1999) *Breaking the Mold: Electoral Reform in Bosnia and Herzegovina*. Sarajevo.

Ishiyama, John (2000) "Institutions and Ethnopolitical Conflict in Post-Communist Politics." *Nationalism & Ethnic Politics* 6(3): 51–67.

Ishiyama, John (2001) "Ethnopolitical Parties and Democratic Consolidation in Post-Communist Eastern Europe." *Nationalism & Ethnic Politics* 7(3): 25–45.

Jovic, Dejan (1996) "Party System Developments from a Parliamentary Perspective in Croatia." In Attila Ágh and Gabriella Ilonszki (eds.) *Parliaments and Organized Interests: The Second Steps.* Budapest: Hungarian Centre for Democracy Studies, 395–413.

Kieve, Ronald A. (1981) "Pillars of Sand: A Marxist Critique of Consociational Democracy in the Netherlands." *Comparative Politics* 13(3): 313–37.

Kostadinova, Tatiana (2002) "Do Mixed Electoral Systems Matter? A Cross-National Analysis of Their Effects in Eastern Europe." *Electoral Studies* 21(1): 23–34.

Krastev, Ivan (2002) "The Balkans: Democracy Without Choice." *Journal of Democracy* 13(3): 39–53.

Lijphart, Arend (1977) *Democracy in Plural Societies: A Comparative Exploration.* New Haven: Yale University Press.

—— (1985) *Power-Sharing in South Africa.* Berkeley: Institute of International Studies.

—— (1986) "Proportionality by Non-PR Methods: Ethnic Representation in Belgium, Cyprus, Lebanon, New Zealand, West Germany, and Zimbabwe." In Bernard Grofman and Arend Lijphart (eds.) *Electoral Laws and Their Political Consequences.* New York: Agathon Press, 113–23.

—— (1994) *Electoral Systems and Party Systems: A Study of Twenty-Seven Democracies, 1945-1990.* Oxford: Oxford University Press.

—— (1999) *Patterns of Democracy: Government Forms and Performance in Thirty-Six Countries.* New Haven: Yale University Press.

Nohlen, Dieter and Mirjana Kasapovic (1996) *Wahlsysteme und Systemwechsel in Osteuropa: Genese, Auswirkungen und Reform Politischer Institutionen.* Opladen: Leske + Budrich.

Norris, Pippa (2002) "Ballots not Bullets: Testing Consociational Theories of Ethnic Conflict, Electoral Systems, and Democratization." In Andrew Reynolds (ed.) *The Architecture of Democracy: Constitutional Design, Conflict Management, and Democracy.* Oxford: Oxford University Press, 206–47.

OSCE (2001) *Guidelines to Assist National Minority Participation in the Electoral Process.* Warsaw: ODIHR.

Pettifer, James (2000) "The Greek Minority in Albania: Ethnic Politics in a Pre-National State." In Jonathan P. Stein (ed.) *The Politics of National Minority Participation in Post-Communist Europe: State-Building, Democracy, and Ethnic Mobilization.* Armonk: M.E. Sharpe, 167–88.

Powell, G. Bingham, Jr. (2000) *Elections as Instruments of Democracy: Majoritarian and Proportional Visions.* New Haven: Yale University Press.

Project on Ethnic Relations (2001) *Parliamentary Representation of Minorities in Hungary: Legal and Political Issues*. Budapest.

Reilly, Ben (1999) "Electoral Systems for Post-Conflict Societies: Lessons for Bosnia and Herzegovina," in European Commission for Democracy Through Law, *New Trends in Electoral Laws in a Pan-European Context*. Strasbourg: Council of Europe Publishing, 115–26.

—— (2001) *Democracy in Divided Societies: Electoral Engineering for Conflict Management*. Cambridge: Cambridge University Press.

Reilly, Ben and Andrew Reynolds (1999) *Electoral Systems and Conflict in Divided Societies*. Washington: National Academy Press.

Reynolds, Andrew (1999) *Electoral Systems and Democratization in Southern Africa*. Oxford: Oxford University Press.

—— (ed.) (2002) *The Architecture of Democracy: Constitutional Design, Conflict Management, and Democracy*. Oxford: Oxford University Press.

Reynolds, Andrew and Ben Reilly (1997) *The International IDEA Handbook of Electoral System Design*. Stockholm: Institute for Democracy and Electoral Assistance.

Sartori, Giovanni (1968) "Political Development and Political Engineering" in John D. Montgomery and Alfred O. Hirschmann (eds.) *Public Policy* 17. Cambridge: Harvard University Press, 261–98.

—— (1976) *Parties and Party Systems: A Framework for Analysis*. Cambridge: Cambridge University Press.

—— (1994) *Comparative Constitutional Engineering: An Inquiry into Structures, Incentives and Outcomes*. New York: New York University Press.

Scholdan, Bettina (2000) "Democratisation and Electoral Engineering in Post-Ethnic Conflict Societies." *Javnost* 7(1): 25–40.

Smilov, Daniel (2002) *Judicial Discretion in Constitutional Jurisprudence: The Experience of the Bulgarian Constitutional Court*. DPhil. thesis, Oxford University.

Snyder, Jack (2000) "Managing Ethnopolitics in Eastern Europe: An Assessment of Institutional Approaches." In Jonathan P. Stein (ed.) *The Politics of National Minority Participation in Post-Communist Europe: State-Building, Democracy, and Ethnic Mobilization*. Armonk: M.E. Sharpe, 269–85.

Shvetsova, Olga (1999) "A Survey of Post-Communist Electoral Institutions: 1990–1998." *Electoral Studies* 18(3): 397–409.

Szajkowski, Bogdan (2000) "Macedonia: An Unlikely Road to Democracy." In Geoffrey Pridham and Tom Gallagher (eds.) *Experimenting with Democracy: Regime Change in the Balkans*. London: Routledge, 249–72.

Venice Commission (1995) *Commentary on the Draft Albanian Constitution as Submitted for Popular Approval on 6 November 1994*. Strasbourg.

Venice Commission (2000) *Guidelines on Prohibition and Dissolution of Political Parties and Analogous Measures.* Strasbourg.

Zakosek, Nenad (2000) "Ethnic War and Disempowerment: The Serb Minority in Croatia." In Jonathan P. Stein (ed.) *The Politics of National Minority Participation in Post-Communist Europe: State-Building, Democracy, and Ethnic Mobilization.* Armonk: M.E. Sharpe, 213–36.

Zielinksi, Jakub (2002) "Translating Social Cleavages into Party Systems: The Significance of New Democracies." *World Politics* 54(2): 184–211.

Lessons Learned:
Nation- and State Building after Communism

Alina Mungiu-Pippidi and Ivan Krastev

There are two radical different perspectives used when assessing postcommunist Europe these days. On one hand, the region is seen as a huge economical and political success, with eight countries already members of the European Union, two (Romania and Bulgaria) well on their way in, and the rest queuing for some form of European status. This successful segment has rewarded liberal economists and transitologists, providing, in contrast with Latin America, accomplished transitions in barely a dozen years. On the other hand, as more than a half of the region in population terms is still far from enjoying a comfortable position, it can be read also as a disaster story, with ethnic conflicts, economic contractions the size of civil wars, even when civil wars are missing, and no perspective in sight. The difference between the two perspectives is largely a matter of the analyst's choice of seeing the glass half empty or half full. But in reality, on the ground, the border of enlarged Europe is about to separate the two halves mercilessly.

But one clear thread is visible in the postcommunist puzzle of success and failure. Only nation-states have succeeded so far in the European integration project. And the ethnic minorities of these countries have succeeded along with the majorities. These are the countries that have grown increasingly democratic and civic, while ethnic federations have broken up, and disputed states have ended as weak states, or even failed ones. This can be seen as merely stating the obvious—countries with fewer constraints did better, and ethnic heterogeneity was considered, as John Stuart Mill pointed out, as a constraint for democracy. But it is, of course, more complicated than that. The countries looked on as success stories—the Baltic republics, Slovakia, Bulgaria, and Romania—also faced problems related to ethnic heterogeneity during their transition. A share of the ubiquitous conflict measured by Philip Roeder in this volume did belong to the successful part of postcommunist Europe. In all fairness, this part of the region was better equipped to deal with the challenge. Local institutions were more fit or better chosen, national politicians and the international community made fewer mistakes, and external destabilizing factors were better controlled. The European integration of these countries was well served by a previous phase of nation building and state consolidation, necessary after decades of Soviet domination. It is the merit of both local political elites and the international community that these objectives were carried out while respecting the basic rights of ethnic minorities. While initial conditions of transformations, especially at the level of state building, vary greatly, some clear lessons do emerge out of a comparison between the successful and unsuccessful state-building projects in postcommunist Europe.

Lesson Number One:
Fair States are Strong States

Lesson number one of state building in postcommunist Europe seems therefore to be that political transitions need strong, preferably unitary states. Achieving those may need, as in the Baltic republics, *a period of intermediate or transitory institutions with the clear goal of producing such states*. At the other end of the continuum, in countries such as Moldova, the misunderstanding of this fact produced nearly failed states, unable to protect both majorities and minorities. These are the states that are incapable of mobilizing their citizens around a project on the scale of European integration. These states are often reduced to the passive role of producing large-scale emigration to the rest of Europe. While considerable repatriation has occurred in the Baltic states, in Albania, Moldova, and Ukraine, citizens are fleeing their failed states en masse. This is not the usual exodus of the poor toward rich countries but the tacit desertion of failed national projects. Western Europe's eastern border can barely stop this invasion, which consists of huge portions of the total workforce of these countries seeking labor elsewhere. Interpreting this quiet disaster simply as a lack of economic success would be a mistake. When a country's entire active workforce would leave if given the possibility, we are dealing with state failure, including the failure to produce a national identity and mobilization around a common national project. It is a cycle: failed states create hopeless societies, which become sponsors of state failure. In each country, political elites are responsible for managing state building, but there has also been considerable international assistance and intervention in constitutional matters. The international role has been important in some countries, for the better and worse. In sum, the question is how to *assist state consolidation and the enforcement of minority rights at the same time*, not only how to reorganize the state to ensure the protection of minority rights. As Florian Bieber correctly points out in this book, power sharing without rights enforcement is not helpful. Worse, it creates nonfunctional states. What are needed are states with strong implementation capacity. This is merely saying that power-sharing cannot work where there is no power to share.

Postcommunist Europe's success stories are the ones where the constitutional arrangements were classic. Nations were defined as civic nations, consisting of individuals, not communities, and equal rights and state support for cultural difference existed, including education in different languages and the use of minority languages in local government and courts where minorities constitute more than 15–20 percent of the local population. Representation of minorities through proportional electoral systems and reserved seats for smaller groups in national parliaments has also worked well. In Romania, Bulgaria, and Slovakia, the largest parties of ethnic minorities have become constant participants in government coalitions. Valerie Bunce and Philip Roeder make a strong argument, based on solid empirical evidence, that ethnofederalism is a poor institution for conflict prevention or containment. It aggravates ethnic tensions, fosters ethnic polarization, multiplies institutional weapons, and increases the likelihood of both ethnoconstitutional conflict and violence. They have less to say on ethnofederalism as a cease-fire strategy, but the Bosnian experiment is not encouraging.

The idea of ethnofederalism as an institution bringing justice to all parts of a society and diminishing conflict in the long run must be revisited. What worked in postcommunist Europe were formulas to make unitary states more inclusive and more accountable, through the adoption of international legal standards on minorities, (strong) external conditionality to ensure that these laws are implemented, and national cooperative politics. This is the package that has produced successful states and fair political societies. This does not rule out the case for federalism based on grounds other than ethnic concentration, but the fact remains that none of the postcommunist countries that had a successful democratic transition was a federal state. Institutional innovation should be discouraged when unnecessary, especially in a region where state consolidation cannot be taken for granted. Unitary states may also be preferable in a region where secession was prompted more by economic selfishness than by nationalism, as policies for development and cohesion need a national design, at least for a transitory period.

Theorists and human-rights activists alike agree that it is difficult for unitary states to be ethnically neutral. Ethnic neutrality should, however, be viewed in concrete terms, not absolute ones. States have an interest in preserving the majority language as the main language of communication. But this should not be viewed as ethnicism if the use of minority languages is also ensured. Constitutions are being modified daily to provide for the codification of official languages, leading to severe battles around these symbols of supremacy. It is more important to adopt and implement international legislation, giving those who speak a minority language equal opportunities with those who speak the majority one. The focus should be on practice, not symbols. Consolidated states are not possible if their structure is continuously challenged. Modification of operation—not structure—is necessary to ensure minorities' rights.

Lesson Number Two:
Policies Must Target External Sponsors of Conflicts

The second lesson tells us that no constitution, adoption of international legislation, and existence of a national elite committed to interethnic cooperation can produce an environment of interethnic cooperation if external sponsorship of the conflict continues. In this respect, it is perhaps useful to acknowledge that the failure of Bosnia, Macedonia, Moldova, and Georgia is not entirely the doing of these countries. The success of international assistance for these countries was severely limited by the failure to address their core problem: sponsorship of the conflict by diasporas and neighboring countries. Russia did not arm the Russian minorities in the Baltic states, but it did allow the arming of them in Moldova and Georgia. The former are now EU members; the latter are bordering state failure. No constitutional arrangement, regardless of how equitable, can prevent ethnic conflict if external sponsorship continues, rebels infiltrate borders, arms are brought in, and signals are sent by powerful neighbors to their kin in the disputed states that they should not let the matter rest. At the end of the day, this is merely saying that if the titular successor state (Russia or Serbia) decides to sabotage a minor successor state, it will always succeed. The international community frequently errs—by political correctness or hypocrisy or both—by treating such conflicts in isolation from the broad context which produced them, ignoring the powerful external factor while assuming that the parties needing mediation are the small state and its internal challengers, which are treated as a majority and minority ethnic group.

This formula is not entirely unfounded (it may still work in Macedonia, hopefully), but as a dominant paradigm, it is a recipe for disaster if there is no clear assurance that external sponsorship will cease. Macedonia originally started on the same path as Romania and Bulgaria, including an Albanian party in the government, and granting rights for Albanians, albeit slowly. It remains to be seen if the solutions designed after the overhauling of this model by fighters from across the border with a more radical agenda are sustainable.

Minorities supported by their kin states triggered two world wars in Eastern Europe. The time has come to acknowledge that a deal must be reached with the mother-state or the diaspora before even addressing the domestic conflict. This worked in Eastern Europe's biggest success story: the Hungarian minorities living outside Hungary. By the mid-1990s, intelligent intermediation (and conditionality) produced bilateral treaties between Hungary and it neighbors, in which Hungary freely acknowledged the borders of 1919 for the first time. This acknowledgement practically cleared the neighboring countries hosting Hungarian minorities of nationalism as a political force. In the next years, ethnic Hungarian parties in these countries became more and more influential, establishing themselves as important political partners in governments. This was a pure political solution. In other less fortunate cases, there is still a need for borders to be policed, arranging that troops leave (such as in former Soviet Union, where units of the Red Army stayed behind in successor states, lending a hand to ethnic entrepreneurs), and actively discouraging cross-border nationalist politics. It is a burdensome and relentless task for ethnic peace brokers, but, unless the external factors are addressed, any constitutional engineering is a loss of time, money, and what is more important, hope.

Lesson Number Three:
The Dramatic Need for Accountable Government

As the chapter on grassroots nationalism illustrates, nationalism and ethnic intolerance are prompted by the perceived and/or real failure of politics to address citizens' concerns and needs. As elites are often unable to deliver in the short- or medium-term, they are tempted to employ a political discourse based on appeals to "fairness." But these appeals tend less to help those than be turned against the better off or the different. Mobilization against someone is easier; it does not require an immediate delivery of goods. And it succeeds because frustration with politics and politicians is very high in postcommunist Europe. Strangely, frustration is equally high in both the success and failure stories in the region. But in the successful countries, protest votes seem to produce parties and politicians who eventually align with mainstream politics. In ethnically divided underdeveloped countries, protest votes create rebel leaders, nationalist presidents, and radical challengers.

Frustration with politics is natural in postcommunist societies. The communist legacy consists of institutions that are entirely deprived of built-in accountability systems. Reforms cannot immediately dismantle the hierarchical, top-down bureaucratic structure of administrations or law-enforcement agencies, which see the citizen as a solicitant rather than a customer, and the minority citizen almost as a culprit. Elections produce more politicians, already seen as parasites, and more talk. Policies and resources to increase horizontal accountability are desperately missing. A careful reader of survey data from the region cannot but grasp that while overall distrust in national representatives has endured throughout the region, trust in directly elected executives, such as mayors, has increased wherever decentralization policies have endowed local governments with the real means to run their communities. Decentralization works. To make it more popular with central governments, it should be sold in a package with the acceptance of the unitary state. Nationalist elites fear both decentralization and ethnofederalism. If ethnofederalism weakens the common polity through ethnic polarization, unitary centralized government also can weaken it through centralization and lack of accountability. For a unitary state to function properly, it must be decentralized to endow locally elected leaders with the means to satisfy their voters.

This is the best strategy to contain political discontent. It is also the best policy for minorities as it creates smaller units, which are more ethnically homogenous and therefore politically cohesive, with more power to solve their accountability problem. The more a community has a say in how its schools, police, and municipal services function, the less often ethnic entrepreneurs will find followers to challenge the central government and seek radical solutions. The existence of medium-size units of local government also means that more cooperation is needed among these units to pursue development strategies. This development policy should not be confused with the European regional development policy, which assumes far larger units. In fact, by European standards, the three Baltic republics combined are about the size of an average region. A sound approach assumes a policy of local, not regional development, of small-scale local executive bodies and councils, rather than regional parliaments, endowed with broad legislative powers. Accountability must first work in these smaller units to spill over to larger ones. In national or regional elections, voters lose representatives on the party list, and accountability decreases.

Where smaller communities are also split along ethnic lines, and some institutions need to be shared, there is clear need for ensuring that groups are represented proportionally in the public sector. Postcommunist societies understand proportionality and affirmative action, which have roots in the former communist policy toward minorities, better than they understand autonomy or self-government, which often results in dividing something among groups, which can foster trouble. Current policies should build on what was fair in the communist attempt to solve multiethnicity rather than import completely new institutions.

While proportional systems work reasonably well to accommodate ethnic minorities and foster cooperation among parties, there is growing discontent against party lists, seen throughout Eastern Europe as a means to prevent voters from voting out the representatives who failed them. Parliaments and representative bodies in general are the most unpopular among all the institutions of the new democracies. This is another argument to empower directly elected mayors rather than create additional regional parliaments. But when summing up the advantages and disadvantages, proportional systems with party lists seem to be a lesser evil than any other systems tried in the area. Electoral thresholds for parties and coalitions can create a party system with fewer parties. There is no evidence that electoral volatility is due to the electoral system rather than to the poor qualification of political elites and public disappointment with the degradation of living standards. From the systems not tried yet, Bogaards recommends the single transferable vote (STV) as an alternative to the party list. The introduction of STV is, however, unlikely to render parties more accountable in a real way. This system would require informed citizens, of which there are not many. It may work, however, in addressing the public perception of the lack of accountability. Responsibility would be transferred to the voter, enabled to choose among candidates. The media, often extremely critical toward parliamentarians, should applaud this possible change, which would contribute to legitimizing the system. Since, however, the main problem of East European parties remains their deficit of organization and discipline, this reform is not likely to foster their development. But the situation is different with ethnic parties, which need to mobilize their communities fully to get elected. Because of this, they have their own systems of choosing the most representative candidates. Either a minority has the choice of more than one party, which is often the case, or the ethnic party has some system to select among candidates (such as primaries, in Romania). Reforms of organically developed selection procedures for candidates should be avoided or attempted with great caution. In severely divided societies, a better solution is to ask candidates or parties to also gather a majority of votes from the second ethnic group, even if this does not translate into seats, but rather as a sort of transethnic threshold. When tried elsewhere, this system led to the creation of a larger, stronger political center and the need for interethnic alliances.

Lesson Number Four:
Cease-Fire Arrangements Pave the Way to Separation, not Reconciliation

Following the communist idea that the state is strong enough to both remold social structure and human behavior, influencing social structure by the state has now become an unreachable desiderate in many weak states in unsuccessful transition countries. This is why institutional revolutions should be viewed with some reservation. Where the development was organic—in unitary states—proportional systems and external conditionality have helped make ethnic bargaining a permanent component of the political process. Gains in such countries may seem minor compared to what Albanians in Macedonia won in one rebellion, but, unlike in Macedonia, the gains are completely accepted by the society and therefore sustainable. Organic development resulting from the process of political bargaining is superior to any institutional innovation.

But not all countries were lucky enough to experience organic development. As Valerie Bunce argues, federations in which republics have their own armies are almost certain to be subverted by their own structures in times of political disruption. As borders never manage to ensure ethnic homogeneity, the result is conflict. Successor states are then deserted by their minorities, who then attempt to secede. At this point, the international community steps in and must broker an arrangement with the collective actors to stop the fighting. Even if the fighting was initially among entrepreneurs only, peace brokering must deal with the main collective actors, transgressing the concept of individual rights. Individuals are forced into camps by the logic of war and postwar, and it is very difficult to appeal to those. This happened everywhere in the former Yugoslavia. But outcomes are very much influenced by the means by which the conflict was resolved and the institutions used for the immediate postconflict situation. Where the conflict exit was through two different states, as in the cases of Croatia and Yugoslavia, return of refugees and work on the border became the main tasks. After a war, borders usually remain where the balance of equilibrium that led to the ceasefire caught the two parties. Refugees, as a general rule, do not return. Although nobody agrees audibly with population exchanges and the redrawing of borders, successful peace brokering takes advantage of these processes, first initiated during the war. The conflict in Kosovo was solved the same way the conflicts were resolved in Croatia and Slovenia—by the creation of a government structure completely separate from the initial country. This makes Kosovo's eventual confederation with Serbia nearly impossible. Institutions have their own logic, and the logic of Kosovo's government structures fosters independence, not confederalization.

The outcomes negotiated for Bosnia or Moldova could not be more different from the above. In Bosnia and Moldova, rebels won, and some equilibrium was reached, although with great difficulty, leaving the former rebels armed and with a serious advantage. As the international community respects borders even when it cannot enforce them, but also does not want to encourage ethnic rebellion, rebels were not allowed to form a state of their own or to join the state they had originally hoped to join (and which sponsored the conflict). Instead, they were pushed into sharing the state with the titular people, often with little or no justice done for the crimes of war. In their small states or dominions, these rebels were successful at state building, as Charles King shows in this book, often more so than their competitors. Without international recognition, but with help from the mother countries, they have managed to control their polities, keep their economies afloat, and keep the central government hostage. This was also aided by their experiences with smuggling and the gun trade and the transformation of their rebel troops into effective security and domestic terror troops. They have little or no incentive to make power sharing work. Time works for them, consolidating ethnic distance.

Granting international recognition to rebels is, of course, a recipe for producing more rebels. But we must also acknowledge that borders were arbitrarily drawn without consulting all interested parties and better ones could be brokered.

Postcommunist Europe is a case apart. Its ethnic traumas were prompted by the most rapid and massive political change ever. But the pace of transformation has slowed down. The state formations now in existence are unlikely to go away, and the prominent role of the postconflict actors makes them even more difficult to change. Cease-fire institutions of this type, when each titular group has a share of the state, as well as of an army, can only pave the way to partition, not reconciliation. A partition of the state also has its supporters, but there is no evidence to prove whether it can work (Sambanis, 2000). If an external force does not step in to disarm former rebels and dissolve their entities, partition will become more of a reality as the entities become more consolidated. Path number two—confederalization—seems to have no exit except by path number one—separation.

The Balkans present a specific problem complicating the matter. The area known as the Western Balkans is relatively small. The region was a common space of socialization during the communist era (except Albania, but even in the last years of the communist regime, it had some connections with Yugoslav Kosovo) and remains a region, despite the fact that it has broken into many units. This means that the smart, case-by-case approach is unlikely to work here. Elites copy one another, and the publics know very well what deals their neighbors get. A solution for Kosovo's statehood problem, for instance, cannot be conceived if Kosovo is a separate country. As the UNDP survey analyzed in this book shows, the inhabitants of Kosovo do not want to reunite with Albania, but they do believe that the territories inhabited by Albanians in Macedonia should belong to Kosovo. Besides solutions for countries and borders designed by communist tyrants, we should conceive that solutions for peoples are sometimes needed.

Conclusions: Incentives, Conditions, and the Role of Europe

What is the ideal combination of sticks and carrots, given the benefit of hindsight? Conditionality worked to create fair states and peaceful environments in the postcommunist world when three circumstances were fulfilled:

a) The international community had a unified will concerning the final solution of a conflict and the strategy to reach it. The many blunders committed by the West in the management of the Balkans were due to the different approaches from the various international actors—the US, EU, NATO, OSCE, and so forth. The current transatlantic rift is bad news, as parties in conflict quickly learn how to use divisions among the West to their advantage.

b) The carrot was at least as large as the stick, and both were available for use. The improvement in the treatment of minorities in the Baltic states, Central Europe, and the Balkans was achieved due to strong conditionality, made possible by the perspective of European integration. Even so, sanctions by the Council of Europe, threats by NATO, and even the bombing campaign in the former Yugoslavia were needed. Transitions with a European perspective proved clearly safer than transitions without.

c) A critical mass of moderates was reached on the ground from each and every party in conflict before the conflict's resolution. This was empowered by international assistance or intervention. This mass did not exist everywhere and from the very beginning of the transition, but it has started to emerge after years of well-targeted foreign assistance, which empowered NGOs, political parties, liberal media, and other moderate actors. This worked better in Central Europe, the Baltics, and the Balkans, all areas where the West had more leverage, as opposed to CIS, where it had little leverage or none at all. In any event, while elections or an audience may still reward nationalist politicians or the media, Western assistance does not need to do so. It should clearly adopt a normative stand and tie its support to promotion of tolerance and proven records of moderation.

Despite NATO's enlargement, Europe is left to represent the will of the international community at the end of the first tumultuous decade in postcommunist Europe. The great enlargement of 2003 leaves Europe bordered by a huge variety of state formations, from former empires to not yet countries, such as Kosovo, all with problems of state building and severe underdevelopment. On one hand, from Kaliningrad to Transnistria, legacies of the Cold War remain, related to Russia's ambiguous status as both a great power and a weak state. These issues fall in the region of outer Europe, despite pledges to increase special relations between Europe and Ukraine or Russia. On the other hand, there is southeastern Europe, where Serbia is no longer a threat, and which has already received Europe's promise of integration. But many challenges remain.

Transitions with a European perspective are clearly safer than transitions without. Wherever the accession to Europe seems a realistic prospect, and even where it is not yet so, European policies override ethnic and nationalist ones in the public sympathy and win the support of political elites from almost all political parties. Integration remains the major incentive for peace and development, but integration itself cannot solve many of the problems these countries face. Rolling enlargement, meaning a continuous enlargement to countries as they become ready, is a great idea, but it is not a policy. There are reasons why these countries have difficult transitions, why these states are weak, and why these societies are engulfed in conflict. Beyond the essential incentive of accession, policies are needed to address their problems and bring them to nearly successful transitions, in the same place the Central European countries were before starting accession. Enlargement as usual, meaning the adoption and internalization of EU legislation only, cannot supplant development and state-building policies. Worse, it can even hinder them if tried prematurely. If Europe is serious about enlarging to a wider Europe, its instruments to help the transformations succeed in these countries need revisiting. EU assistance must be far more flexible and problem oriented.

Solving conflicts and building states is a difficult job for Europe, and the European Commission acknowledges it, calling for more active involvement in solving the conflicts remaining in the Balkans and Transnistria (European Commission, 2003). Recently, the idea was pushed forward that EU peacekeepers should replace the Russian Fourteenth Army in the small rogue state of Transnistria. Even if European troops have only a symbolic presence there, the step ahead will be formidable: the previous peace plan brokered by OSCE suggested that the Fourteenth Army, after a decade of being in double employment—for Russia and the rebels—may turn into the peacekeeping force on the ground. If we could not make them leave, the argument runs, why not give them some honorable employment?[1] As Russia has veto rights in the OSCE, such solutions emerge naturally, suggesting clearly that Russia, not Europe, has the de facto power to decide which former Soviet Republic can join the cordon sanitaire of Western Europe and which will stay in Russia's.

After a hesitant decade, Europe has started to improve its record wherever it showed commitment in conflicts over internal or external borders, from Macedonia to Kaliningrad. The need for the European defense initiative lies here, on the eastern border. This area is in Europe and, for both integration and conflict management, needs a Europe which is strong, united, and capable of resolve in foreign affairs and security, as well as in promoting development. NATO enlargement helped and the European leadership should work through NATO or in close cooperation. From the 400 peacekeepers in Macedonia to a true European defense force able to employ any means necessary to implement the peace agreements, there is still some way to go; nevertheless, the initial steps have been made and Europe's recent decision to deploy its troops in Transdniestria is worth praise.

Nationalism was the big scare of the first decade, and its shadow still hangs over the Western Balkans, Russia, Moldova and the Caucasus. In time analysts and politicians both have come to acknowledge that weak states are also a danger. Public opinion analyses show that nationalism and ethnic intolerance are prompted by the failure of politics to address citizens' concerns and needs. Endless painful economic transitions may endanger consolidation of new democracies in the CIS. Cohesion policies

1. Vladimir Socor (2003) "The EU Can Secure Its Own Neighborhood." *Wall Street Journal Europe.* July 27.

are necessary in preventing a new wall cutting across the Balkans and between them and Central Europe, creating new lines of division within the region. But as Vladimir Gligorov shows in his chapter, pure economic rationalization cannot explain balkanization and Europeization. Development is not in itself the key to solve nation and state building problems. Rather, it is the other way around. Development is slow, even when it progresses steadily, and can have paradoxical effects. As Gerald Knaus shows in his chapter on Macedonia, more education opportunities for Albanians in the absence of economic opportunities means more competition for the already scarce jobs in the public sector. The much needed regional integration, as Gligorov shows, will only progress through Europeization, which makes it a slower, not faster, process. In fact, only two economic policies have direct impact on ethnic peace and cooperation. The first is to increase economic opportunity in the short run. The large number of young unemployed males is a recipe for creating movements of freedom fighters, which thrive on smuggling, racketeering, and symbolic politics. Providing these people with possibilities, in the new police or security forces or in temporary jobs in more prosperous countries is essential (this is another reason why temporary labor immigration should be controlled rather than discouraged). The second policy option (Collier, 2001, 2002) is on the same target, although from a different direction. It increases the costs of rebellion, making it unaffordable, rather than the good business it has been for the past decade. This entails blocking illegal trade, confiscating assets, and actively preventing the economic gains of rebellions. Such a policy could work in the Balkans. This is less true in the CIS, where Ukraine and Russia are not committed to starving the secessionists but often turn a blind eye or even help them.

A corollary of this policy means that rebels should not be welcomed into politics at any time, even if results of their rebellion were accepted at some point. If an area is granted full autonomy after an ethnic war, a new leadership, both civilian and clean, should run the entity, not the rebels who made the war. The International Criminal Tribunal in The Hague started on this path when it removed Vojislav Seselj from the Serbian domestic political scene, where this alleged war criminal was profiling himself as a successful presidential candidate. Policing elections in postconflict societies is not antidemocratic. Rather, it is the only way to allow democracy to grow from an electoral democracy to a substantive one.

There has been considerable revisionism in recent years regarding multinational European empires. Triggered by the well-grounded antipathy toward small would-be nation states, "Ruritanias" as Ernest Gellner called them, this new view espouses the idea that nondemocratic empires were better at managing multiethnicity than the present democratic multiethnic nation-states. This is like saying that there is less of a chance for crime in a prison than outside it. This attitude is misleading on two accounts. First, it blurs the main cause of today's ethnic problems, specifically, the demography created precisely by imperial ethnic engineering (communism included). This view also suggests that small nation-states cannot evolve from a predominantly ethnic nationalism to a predominantly civic one. But the Western example illustrates that this is possible. Before rewriting history to make it politically correct for ethnic groups, restating its essentials accurately for policy makers seems an urgent task. In the Balkans, for example, the "most important change that the Ottoman rule brought to South-East Europe was the large scale demographic transformation of the area, the consequences of which still determine the relationship of its people to each other. Forced settlements by the Ottomans, and after 1699 by the Habsburg in the region acquired as a result of the Peace of Karlowitz, added to the demographic changes brought about by the movement of the people" (Sugar, 1977: 287–288, 283). Likewise, Europe's new Schengen border owes much to Stalin, who redesigned it to accommodate the Soviet Union's security needs. Finished and unfinished wars and national revolutions have crafted borders more arbitrary than anywhere else in Europe, and enlargement has complicated matters instead of solving them. The borders of the new member states will soon be the borders of the new Europe, closed to the less lucky neighbors by the Schengen treaty. Ukrainians, Russians, Moldovans, and Macedonians now discover that they need visas to travel to their neighboring countries, where the language is often their own, and where they previously vacationed in the communist era. This feeds frustration: this is not Gorbachev's promised "common house of Europe," which helped spark the rebellions of 1989.

Not every new border spells disorder and tension. Despite the existence of ethnic entrepreneurs, the problem of the Hungarian minorities in Central Europe holds almost no threat of potential ethnic conflict due to common prospects of European membership for both Hungary and the neighboring countries where the Hungarian minorities reside. Bulgaria's Turkish minority, who immigrated to Turkey at the beginning of the last decade, is now returning to Bulgaria, as it seems likely that Bulgaria will join the EU before Turkey. Conflict borders can be rendered superfluous via a process of unification through enlargement. Wherever enlargement is still a distant prospect, there must be a policy to insure that the imposition of the Schengen border, a necessary facet of Europe's security policy, does not feed insecurity in the border states. Eastern Europe must remain as close as possible to the common travel space it was in the communist era. If not, resentment against Europe and those neighbors who impose visas will only grow. Criminals do not apply for visas; they have other ways of crossing borders. A policy which hurts law-abiding citizens, students, and the traders who promote ethnic cooperation would be a mistake.

If state weakness is prompted by the uncertainty of state boundaries and disputes concerning which groups and territories are in the state and which are not, the decision over these matters should be taken sooner rather than later. Flexible borders only work between clearly delimitated polities. Ambiguous states foster conflict; they do not contain it. This does not mean that postcommunist Europe must become an area where the final triumph is granted to nationalism and ethnic cleansing. Rather it means that in this area, we must acknowledge that identities and citizenship will always entail some tension. Granting a European perspective to citizenship and keeping identity as remote from politics as possible create the only sustainable approach.

References

Collier Paul (2001) *Economic Causes of Civil Conflict and Their Implications for Policy.* World Bank.

Collier, Paul and Nicholas Sambanis (eds.) (2002) Special Issue on "Understanding Civil War." *The Journal of Conflict Resolution* 46 (1).

Sambanis, Nicholas (2000) "Partition as a Solution to Ethnic War: An Empirical Critique of the Theoretical Literature." *World Politics* 52 (4): 437–83.

Sugar, Peter (1977) *Southeastern Europe under Ottoman Rule 1354–1804.* Seattle: University of Washington Press.

Commission of the European Communities (2003) *Wider Europe—Neighbourhood: A New Framework for Relations with our Eastern and Southern Neighbours.* Communication from the Commission to the Council and the European Parliament COM(2003) 104 final. Brussels. March 11.

Index

accountability, 140, 143, 271–275
affirmative action, 274 (see also positive discrimination)
alternative vote, 212, 253
autonomy, 179, 182, 188, 215, 219–222
  status 64, 151, 156
  of a republic, 153, 156, 164, 219–222
  of a district/area/region/territory, 163, 171, 183n, 188, 214, 219, 231, 280
  Autonomous regime/self-governance, 164, 219–222, 231, 274
  Autonomous administrators, 215n, 216
  of institutions, 241
  communal, 214
  cultural, 231
  financial, 140
  local, 131, 153, 156, 187–188
  segmental, 263

borders, 45–47, 50
  ethnic, 20, 50, 276
  internal, 13, 70
  problems of, 30, 272–273, 276–277, 279–281
  stable, 180, 183
  state, 50, 57, 64–65, 181–188, 276–277, 281

  threat to, 51–52, 57, 72, 79–80

cease-fire, 152–153, 156, 158, 271, 275–277
central government, 103, 118, 126, 131, 138–140, 147–151, 155–157, 160–172, 212–222, 273, 276
citizenship, 15, 20–21, 25, 65, 74, 156, 162–163, 187–189, 201, 207, 210–211, 282
cleavage, 15, 18–19, 215, 249–252, 256, 259, 262–263
cohabitation, 13, 26, 47, 65, 68–70
cohesion, 144, 271, 279
Commonwealth of Independent States (CIS), 7, 153, 162n, 169, 278–280
conditionality, 73, 271–272, 275, 277–278
confederalization, 276–277
conflict
  management, 14, 35, 141, 211, 213, 249–268, 279
  prevention, 35, 213, 271–272
  resolution, 14, 87, 144, 148, 156, 161, 202, 276, 278
consociational/consociationalism, 212, 215, 232, 236n, 239, 244, 252, 263
constitution, 16, 29, 52, 140–141, 143, 156, 164, 184, 189, 201, 204, 212–218, 224, 241, 244–249, 256–261, 270–273